CW00542053

STAGHUNTER

THE REMARKABLE STORY OF

Ernest Bawden

Paddy King-Fretts

"Those who attain to any excellence commonly spend life in some single pursuit, for excellence is not often gained upon easier terms."

Dr Samuel Johnson (1709-1784).

HALSGROVE

First published in Great Britain in 2005
Reprinted 2005

British Library Cataloguing-in-Publication Data
A CIP record for this title is available from the British Library

ISBN 1 84114 460 6

HALSGROVE
Halsgrove House
Lower Moor Way
Tiverton, Devon EX16 6SS
Tel: 01884 243242
Fax: 01884 243325
email: sales@halsgrove.com
website: www.halsgrove.com

Printed and bound in Great Britain by The Cromwell Press, Trowbridge

CONTENTS

	Foreword	5
	Introduction	7
	Acknowledgements	9
Chapter 1	The Hallmarks of Greatness	11
Chapter 2	Hawkridge, Exmoor and the Bawdens from Cornwall	19
Chapter 3	Ernest Comer Bawden	26
Chapter 4	From Boy to Man	37
Chapter 5	Soldier Brave	43
Chapter 6	Johnny Boer and the Veldt	48
Chapter 7	Home Again	59
Chapter 8	Hunting the Deer	68
Chapter 9	Servants of the Hunt	78
Chapter 10	Beginner's Luck!	89
Chapter 11	1918 and the New Partnership	97
Chapter 12	The Horn Tucked well into his Coat	105
Chapter 13	The Golden Years	121
Chapter 14	Sunset	144
	Epilogue	158
Annex A	The Bawden Family Tree	159
Annex B	Chronology of Ernest Bawden's life	161
Annex C	His Favourite Hunting Horn	162
Annex D	"The Day of all Days"	164
Annex E	Hunting Talk	166
Annex F	Exmoor Game Recipes	170
Annex G	Obituary	180
	Glossary	184
	Bibliography	187
	General Index	189

EXMOOR

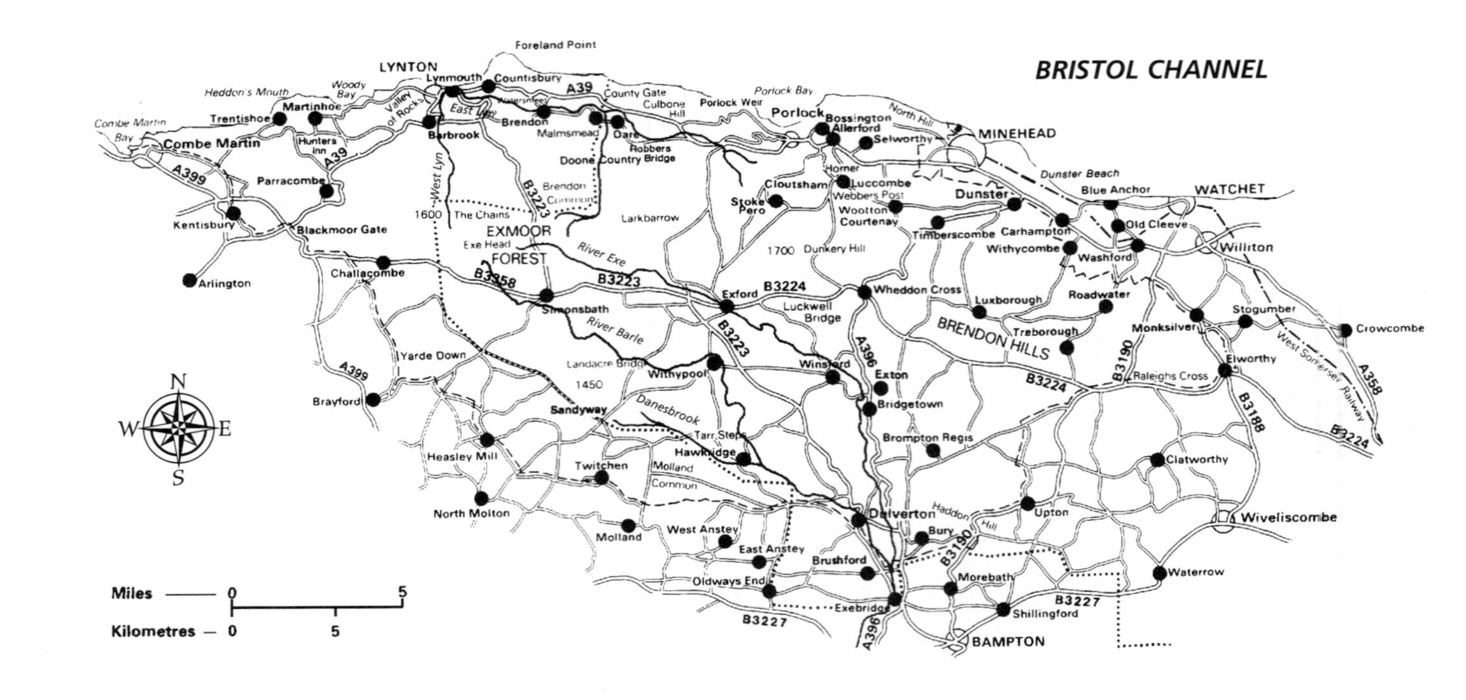

This map was prepared by the Exmoor National Park Authority from aerial survey photography, the copyright being held by the Authority.

E.N.P. Boundary – – – – – – – – – –

County Boundary ....

Approximate Height in feet above sea level — 1500 —

The Baroness Mallalieu Q.C.

Foreword

Staghunter is a remarkable book. It is more than just a biography of an exceptional man or even a study of Exmoor nearly 100 years ago when life was far harder than today. It also contains the explanation of why staghunting still remains so central to life on Exmoor and why its continuation is crucial to the survival of the herds of red deer. But this is a story of a genius and it deserves to be read by all who seek to learn the secret of excellence.

Ernest Bawden is accepted as being one of the greatest huntsmen of all time. Difficult, complicated, ruthless and with a notoriously short temper, he lived for his work for thirty three years with the Devon and Somerset Staghounds.

Crowds flocked to see him. Sportsmen from as far away as America came to hunt with him. He was truly a legend in his own lifetime and remains one long after his death.

Genius, of course, defies analysis. A skilled huntsman must understand the science of venery and be able to practise the art, but he also needs an intuition and the ability to perform magic. Ernest Bawden had all this and more.

In this meticulously researched book, Paddy King Fretts, himself brought up on Exmoor, has brought this extraordinary man and his times to life.

I commend this book not just to those who cherish our countryside heritage but also those who do not share the passion which hunting arouses and wish to understand further.

A. Mallalieu.

INTRODUCTION

It all began with a glass of wine in the garden one evening last summer. I was discussing with Bruce Heywood, a friend since boyhood and a great nephew of Ernest Bawden, what I might try next. I knew something of the great staghunter and when I was a boy I had known Bruce's father, Hector, a famous harbourer. Gradually, and I will never know quite how, the conversation seemed to drift towards the idea that I might like to attempt Ernest's biography.

Time was running out, for Ernest had given up the horn more than sixty-five years ago. Those who were left from those far-off days and who could remember him with any certainty were seventy-five at least and time stands still for no man. However, if I were to get on with it immediately, there were still enough people around who had tales to tell, in particular his close family and those who had hunted when he carried the horn.

I knew Exmoor well, having been brought up there as a boy, and had hunted with various packs of foxhounds and the Devon and Somerset Staghounds – my slot, awarded in 1953, still hangs proudly in the hall. Furthermore I had been a soldier for most of my adult life and might, therefore, be able to throw some light on Ernest's short but eventful military career. All in all it seemed a good idea and the more I thought about it the more curious I became about the man whose exploits captivated the hunting world for so long. I rang Bruce a few days later and he gave me the go ahead.

Ernest Bawden's life story is a remarkable tale about a remarkable yet complicated man, who rose to the very pinnacle of his profession and whose name sits comfortably among the greatest huntsmen of all time. How exactly he achieved what he did will never quite be understood for there was about him something of genius – those who followed him and his hounds simply shook their heads in wonder. I have unravelled as much of his character and 'modus operandi' as I believe possible and attempted to bring his exploits in the field to life. It has been a fascinating exercise; I hope you will be able to see why.

South Molton 2004

Acknowledgements

I have been extremely fortunate in the offers of help and the assistance that has come my way. Everyone to whom I have turned has willingly answered all my questions, after which they have either listened to or read my interpretation of what they had to say. Others have shown or lent me precious family documents and much treasured photographs with commendable faith. Their comments, criticism and advice have been invaluable.

I could not have begun to write objectively without the full support of Ernest's family, in particular his son, Percy, whose powers of recall at the age of ninety-five have been quite exceptional. He, like the rest of the family, knew that in order to be objective, I had to have every angle of the story. Ernest Bawden was not an easy man – and I am indebted to his honesty and frankness about the more difficult times. I would like to thank also his grandson, Gerald, as well as his great-nephews and nieces Ken, Alan, Gwen and Barbara Bawden, Jean Campbell, the Heywood family and many others. In addition, I would like to thank Dr Pamela Durrant and Mr Barry Pendry who went to such trouble in examining the complexities lying deep within Ernest's personality, together with the causes and effects of his difficult childhood.

And it has been the same with the hunting. Of particular note has been the help and advice given by Capt. E.R. "Dick" Lloyd. Dick, who first hunted as a young boy when Ernest was in his prime, is acknowledged throughout the hunting world as one of the greatest living experts on the ways of the wild red deer of Exmoor and the staghounds. He has held every position of authority with the Hunt bar Master and is currently President. The sum total of his knowledge is awesome and I cannot thank him enough for his time and patience. Bruce Heywood, himself a dedicated hunter, has also been a great source of advice and encouragement. Others whose opinions and experiences I have sought are the present huntsman Donald Summersgill and his predecessor Dennis Boyles. Then there was George Scoins (second or third horseman to Ernest), Lorna Stickley (daughter of Ralph Slocombe) and her daughter Susan, and Tony Sloley (son of Gilbert). Finally, I am grateful to Sir Jerry Wiggin for revealing so much about the life and times of his illustrious great-uncle. The Lock family of Hawkridge, in particular Tom and Edna, gave me a fascinating insight into what life must have been like in the village when Ernest was a boy.

I have been extremely fortunate in gaining access to private and hitherto unpublished diaries and letters. Ernest himself was a prodigious writer and kept a complete record of every day he had with hounds. These diaries form a unique record of staghunting between 1917 and 1937 and I have both referred to and quoted from them extensively. The late Rose Wallace was kind enough to allow me access to her late husband's diaries, also Mr Frank Pape who showed me letters from Ernest to his own father, Archie, together with his father's diaries. In addition, he lent me the diaries of Ernest's Commanding Officer in South Africa, Colonel Percy Browne, which threw fresh light upon the exploits of the Royal North Devon Hussars – and indeed Ernest himself. Mrs Sally Ferdinando lent me the unpublished essays of her Godmother, Eva Dunbar, the one-time hunting correspondent of the *Morning Post.* It was through these fascinating and authoritative papers that I was able to provide the reader with the hallmarks of greatness. Lord Patrick Beresford, Sir Alan Ramsay and Guy Thomas-Everard are among others who helped me.

Finally, and above all, I am eternally grateful to Victoria Heywood (Ernest Bawden's great-great-niece) for her patience and skill in getting my writing up to scratch. Far more than merely checking the spelling, punctuation and grammar, she trawled my best efforts sentence by sentence, advising me constantly as to where and how what I had written might be improved: the instances were legion and her advice accepted readily. To them all, I owe my gratitude.

Chapter 1

THE HALLMARKS OF GREATNESS

Ernest Bawden never slept in the afternoon. His eyes might close but his senses remained as vigilant as those of the deer he had hunted for so long. That day he sat alone by the door.

Suddenly he stiffened, mind and body instantly alert. Hounds were about. He knew for sure yet it was neither the sound of the horn nor hounds that told him; it was the magpies along the riverbank. He could tell at once that the deer had gone down the water, and he leapt from his seat. By the time he returned, the valley was filled with the sound of hound music; riders appeared along the skyline and he heard the horn.

What happened next is the very stuff of legend. Nothing and nobody save only very, very few can stop hounds when they are racing down their deer. None of the pack, now running hard below Hinam, knew Ernest Bawden for he had long since retired. Alfie Lenthall, the new man, was right up there with them and they were working well.

Ernest moistened his lips then blew just once, the plaintive note of his old horn floating across the deep Exmoor combe. In an instant there was silence: unaccountably the pack had responded and stopped in their tracks. Moments later they came up through the woods in answer to a horn they had never heard to find a man they had never known.

Why so? What was it that had passed across the fields and down through the woods to the twenty or so couple of hounds hell bent on closing with their quarry? Was it simply the sound of that distant horn that arrested them? Hardly, they knew nothing of it. Was it that they had suddenly lost the line? Never, not all forty of them at once. Was it something the huntsman had said or done to stop them? Impossible, he had been urging them on. What was it then that had lifted a running pack off the line?

We shall never know for sure but one thing is certain: those big doghounds of the Devon and Somerset Staghounds had felt the touch of genius. Something indefinable had coursed through them all, striking deep into their souls as it had done to their forefathers all those years before. In some mysterious way the magic of the master huntsman had reached out to them and they responded as though they were his .[1]

* *

To some extent, Ernest Bawden's magic, the qualities that made the legend are identifiable. Certain elements of his personality run through the man like strands of steel. In her series of short essays on the fifteen or so huntsmen she considered to be the greatest of the eighteenth and nineteenth centuries, Eva Dunbar, hunting correspondent to the *Morning Post* in 1930, leaves the reader in no doubt at all about what was required if those men were to be considered even modestly successful. In her preface she remarks that the extra something needed to elevate their status required a touch of genius. All those whose deeds she chronicled had this quality and she went on to identify three more – mental and physical toughness, patience and raw courage.

Take, for instance, Thomas Assheton-Smith of the famous Quorn. The year was about 1810. In spite of the heat that day, scent was good and hounds were running well. The huntsman was doing his level best to keep in touch when the pack came to a navigable canal called "The Fosdyke". There were two stone bridges over the obstacle, side by side but separated: one for carts, the other for riders and pedestrians. Each bridge was guarded by a high metal rail to prevent people from falling into the water.

Assheton-Smith rode along one of these bridges but found his way out blocked by a gate. Seeing the gate open at the end of the parallel bridge, he immediately put his horse at the rails and jumped across, and over the opposite rails, onto the other bridge – about as dangerous a leap as a horseman could make. Dunbar went on to wonder what our modern heroes of three-day events, at Badminton and elsewhere, would have made of such a test for horse and rider.

To the pop-fed youth of the present time, she wrote, brought up on a diet of sloppy sensationalism and ready-made amusements, it must seem strange that anyone could enjoy life with no luxuries and few simple pleasures. But these men of character enjoyed their lives and were happy and contented to a degree almost unknown in modern times when the sole criterion of success is the amassing of money. These and other such comments of hers were recorded by her privately way back in 1930, yet her essays have never been published.

And how those men thrived on hardship and challenge! Men such as John Mytton of the Shropshire and Shifnal who took bets at the dinner table that he could drive his tandem for a mile across country in the moonlight to the turnpike road. He did just that, negotiating in the process a fence, two hedges with ditches and a broad deep drain, galloping full tilt at the last with such vigour that the chaise whirled through space and landed on terra-firma with a yard to spare.

Then there was the unassuming Tom Hill of the Old Surrey who in 1829 was forced to accept a challenge from Charles Peak the local gamekeeper. Peak, a lusty young giant of twenty-six; taller, heavier and ten years younger than Hill, had publicly and repeatedly insulted the huntsman before questioning his courage. The younger man was still swaggering and cocksure as he arrived with his gaggle of admirers at the agreed rendezvous the following morning.

The two fought bare-knuckle for over half an hour in a disused sawpit. So terrific were their blows that they were described later by an onlooker as two horses kicking each other. At the end, Peak was carried out unconscious, his face battered almost beyond recognition, while the victor, once more his own temperate and mild-mannered self, left with barely a mark on his body. These and others became household names, held in awe by their fellows and praised to the heights by masters and peers.

Before even glancing at the subject of this biography or attempting to make comparisons, it is necessary to study Dunbar's critical appraisals and draw from them what it was that made a great huntsman. She chose the hunting countries of central and southern England but any corner of the land could have produced (and would have) men of similar calibre. She could have chosen the hills and fells of the north, the great packs of Ireland or those whose countries bestrode the Welsh Marches; it made no odds, for the same stirling qualities would have been demanded wherever she looked – qualities without which no huntsman could have made his name.

* *

The first and, without doubt, the most important quality of all is that to which Eva Dunbar refers early in her preface – this mystical affinity with hounds; a gift possessed by so few. She mentions it repeatedly. There was Jack Raven, huntsman of the Quorn for twenty-four years, about whom Nimrod, that unsurpassed commentator of hunting, remarked: "Every hound turned at the sound of his voice, without assistance from the whipper-in; and except in dense woodland, the horn was never used, even to bring in stragglers. Raven simply called them by name and they appeared as if by magic!" He was able to call them off the line where they would come to him and lie at his feet even while their kinsman hunted on until they, too, were stopped by his voice.

Then there was William Jones of Mr Billy Coke's hounds (1775–1820), regarded by the great Hugo Meynell (soon to be Jack Raven's master) as the best huntsman in England due principally to his powerful and melodious voice that exercised such control over the pack. Tom Firr, huntsman of the Quorn for twenty-seven years from 1872 to 1899 and George Sharpe who carried the horn for King George the Fourth were blessed with a similar touch.

Jack Musters, a man born to great wealth, had his own hounds in South Notts in the early 1800s after hunting the Pytchley and was as devoted to his hounds as they were to him. He never allowed the hunt-servants to use the thong, he himself having an almost uncanny knack of making his hounds obedient without punishing them or using any violent methods. Some of Eva Dunbar's heroes used their voice, some relied principally on the horn, others a combination of both. It matters not which, the secret was perfect harmony, a complete understanding between man and beast.

But it was not all one way; the hounds themselves had to be first class in order to produce the results and it was in the kennels that the very best of these men stood apart from the ordinary, proving their sound judgement in the selection and breeding of their packs. Indeed it is in the kennels that the quarry is really killed. In 1824 Nimrod visited the Belvoir when Tom Goosey was huntsman.

"I found them as I expected to find them, very clean in their skins; but I was particularly struck with the fine length of their frames. And the strongly marked and uniform character of the pack... I liked Goosey's manner with his hounds very much indeed. Their speed, that essential in their country, has ever been notorious, and is so now, but, by the good management of Goosey, by his patient discretion, as he tempered their speed with a faculty of hunting; and though they now fly, they fly not without scent. From all I heard – and I asked a good number of judges – the Belvoir kennel never stood anything like so high before; in short, it now stands rubric in the sporting world." It was no coincidence that, with his pack in such condition, Goosey was to achieve immortality.

Dunbar went on to single out Philip Payne of the Duke of Beaufort's from 1802–1826 and Will Goodall of the Belvoir from 1840–1850 as others who had the patience and ability to breed outstanding hounds, a science that was to reap rewards in the field many times over. There can be little doubt that to identify and to communicate intimately with hounds is of the very essence; it is the *sine qua non* of the huntsman. It is a sentiment endorsed strongly by Denis Boyles and Donald Summersgill, past and present huntsmen of the Devon and Somerset Staghounds, two men with more than sixty years experience between them.[2] Without this gift no man could hope to rise above mediocrity.

If men such as these were to keep in touch with their hounds then it was their horse and their ability as a horseman that enabled them to do so. Tom Firr of the Quorn was noted for his superb horsemanship. Always with his hounds, no matter how far they ran or over what difficult country, he never seemed in a hurry. Slight and wiry, with a thin foxy face and keen clear eyes that saw everything, he rode rather long in the stirrups and seemed almost part of his horse.[3]

Here, surely, is the next essential quality – horsemanship. The three-day eventer who clears fences that all but the boldest would avoid has but himself and his horse to consider. Impressed though the spectators may be, they should remember that the rider knows exactly where he is going and what comes next. He has walked the course and studied it carefully beforehand and both he and his mount remain secure in the knowledge that their progress will not be disrupted. Jockeys have a more difficult time by far for there are the other riders – and loose horses – around them, as it is with those in the hunting field. But what of the huntsman?

A pack of hounds running pell-mell – screaming – would close down on an Olympic sprinter in no time at all and they can keep up such a pace for field after field. When they come to an obstacle they throw themselves at it, scrambling through, wriggling under, swimming across or whatever in their efforts to keep going. Then on they go again, running like the very wind, letting nothing get in their way.

It is with these that the huntsman must keep in touch. More than that, he has to be right up with them not lagging fields behind, always ready to encourage them quietly and patiently when they check. Sometimes even, he or his whipper-in has to get ahead to stop them when danger approaches or when they have switched to fresh quarry.

How does he do it? How can a horseman keep up such pace across country, following each twist and turn of the pack, every one of which brings him sudden and unexpected challenges? How does he, at one and the same time, anticipate the movements of the fox, keep in close touch with his hounds, direct his whippers-in and remain in control of such a rapidly changing situation? His priorities are forever altering, his mind racing continually.

The answer is through a detailed and intimate knowledge of the country and by riding to the very limits of his and his mount's ability. Risks have to be taken, corners cut, little-known paths that twist through close cover taken at a gallop; continual contact with the pack being of the utmost importance.

John Mytton's nocturnal and alcohol-fuelled exploits apart, these men had to have nerves of steel. They had to be boldness itself – ruthless even – tackling any obstacle that stood between them and the shortest route to their hounds. And they had to do it, if necessary, hour after hour – certainly for three or more days a week and for six months on end.

And they *had* to succeed. One blank day would be forgiven but after two or three the field would become restless. Scores, hundreds even, would have come for a day's sport and would not appreciate standing around in the cold and wet while the huntsman floundered about. The muttering would begin. Someone would know somebody who could make a better job of it. Such failure with the horn is unthinkable – it is also unforgivable.

On 24 February 1800, when conditions were miserable, Jack Raven drew Billesdon Copse. The fox got away quickly and they ran to Enderby Gorse, a distance of 28 miles, in two hours fifteen minutes – a truly amazing feat considering the conditions. Only six out of the field of more than two hundred finished the run that day. Imagine the ground those few riders had to cover, but imagine also the skill and determination of the huntsman who had to ride further and faster than all of them to be up with his pack at the end.

On another bleak February day sixty-six years later, the Pytchley had their famous Waterloo run. John Anstruther Thomson was huntsman, all sixteen stones of him mounted on a magnificent animal – and it needed to be just that. Hounds found in Waterloo Gorse at two o'clock and ran eighteen miles over the finest Pytchley and Tailby countries in a shade under two hours when they checked for the first time. Thomson was one of the very few with them, both whips having been thrown somewhere along the way. He cast his hounds (with no one now left to turn them) and held them on the line for a further hour and a quarter until he was compelled to give up owing to failing scent and light.

Wonderful runs, and in the dead of winter too, but salute the huntsmen who had to be up there throughout. Anything less and the pack would have disappeared into the distance, vanished without sight or sound, and there would have been chaos and recrimination. Only horsemen – and horses – of the very highest order could have achieved that and it would have taken a quite exceptional man to hunt hounds as well.

* *

These men were hard and ruthless, of that there is no doubt, but they were also quiet and thoughtful when it mattered, patient and prepared to persevere. Drawing a covert is an art in itself, the success of the day ahead depending upon it. The field is held some way off and the whips have been placed out. There must be no movement, no chatter or laughter, just the huntsman on his own with his hounds.

Sometimes luck will be with him as the pack finds quickly but sometimes he has to try and try again, the whole time determining whether or not the fox is there after all. It might be sheeting down with rain, half a gale blowing and the hounds less than enthusiastic but *still* he has to go on….*and on* until he has found what he has been looking for.

But few runs are completed without a check, many are little more than stop and start affairs and it is here again that the huntsman's skill is tested so thoroughly. Unless he is up with the hounds he will have little idea of what has thrown them. It could be poor scent or stock crossing the line; it could have been water or the cunning of the fox. All these thoughts must cross his mind as he brings the pack together and lifts them on to what he believes to be the right line. If he is wrong he must try again pitting his wits against the situation, gently and quietly coaxing the pack – no shouting or rushing about, no use of the whip, simply patience and understanding. These men had it, every one of them.

There will be times when all seems lost and it is here that the huntsman needs self-discipline. Should he continue with just one more cast or should he lift the pack and draw afresh? Instinct will persuade him one way or the other but he has the field to consider. They have come for their sport and, while he might wish to set his heart on defeating his fox, they will want to get on. But he must never be intimidated by their impatience, especially those determined to thrust their way ahead.

These thrusters, and they are to be found in every hunting field, have to be kept under control and out of the huntsman's way. It is a task undertaken usually by the field master whose beady eye has identified the potential troublemakers and for whom a word of one tone or another is usually sufficient. But should they make the cardinal error of crossing the huntsman's path while he is about his business then it is within his gift to vent his wrath – and how some of them did. Eva Dunbar must have smiled to herself as she related how the likes of Hugo Meynell, the usually mild-mannered Tom Goosey and the fiery John Thomson reacted to such impudence.

Discipline has always been an essential ingredient of the successful huntsman – self-discipline, hound discipline and discipline in the field. He has more than enough distractions and problems to contend with and everything that can possibly be brought under control must be so. If nobody else will see to it then he will, for he knows well what will happen once order is lost.

⁂

These then were the qualities identified and portrayed by the pen of the *Morning Post's* Hunting Correspondent. They remain as pertinent today as ever they were and it is difficult to imagine a more stringent or demanding list to which a man must aspire. But these men possessed them all and in abundance; they must have done for they are qualities *essential* to success, without which they would never have been able to achieve what they did.

A figure is beginning to emerge of what the men must have looked like and how they would have behaved. It is as though there existed a degree of similarity between them all, a common thread that ran from one to the other. Yes, but they were all very different as well. Some were large men like the 6-foot 3 Thompson of the Atherstone and Pytchley, some portly even, though most were small and wiry. Some possessed explosive tempers, one Dunbar labelled cantankerous, while others, like Tom Firr, were placid.

A few were beautiful horsemen; others rode in an ungainly fashion. One, the short, fat Raven of the Quorn with his big, ugly head, was a horrible sight. A few were born to great wealth and privilege, such as John Mytton whose £18,000 a year private income in 1816 would be three quarters of a million today, but most were men of humble origin. A number drank (Goosey of the Belvoir could sink a bottle of brandy and more at a sitting) or gambled recklessly while others were content to abstain.

All seemed blessed with an unbelievably rugged constitution that took them through so many years in the saddle. A long apprenticeship was standard in those days where the average career as a whipper-in was ten years at least before promotion to the horn and it is easy to see why. All then carried the horn and the enormous responsibilities that went with the job, for year after year. Two of them, Hill and the ubiquitous Assheton-Smith hunted hounds for no less than *fifty* years, Jack Musters for forty-seven, Tom Sebright for thirty-nine, while Will Goodall of the Belvoir and Tom Goosey, though no less great, a mere seventeen and nineteen respectively.

There remains, however, one final quality highlighted by Dunbar but about which she refrained from passing comment – humility. Society in those days was structured rigidly; it took anyone, even the most odiously ambitious, generations to climb just one rung of the social ladder. Yet almost all of these men found themselves propelled by their own deeds into an extraordinary social position. Their very success elevated them far above their own surroundings and lowly background.

Suddenly, and with no warning, they found themselves somewhere between their family and friends and the great and good of the day, who came from a different way of life – a different world almost – but who were now happy enough to follow them, to shake them warmly by the hand and who would later sing their praises in the great country houses. It was a lonely position, but it was more than that.

They had unwittingly become celebrities wherever they went. Like it or not, they had become famous locally and nationally, the wealthy and the titled would travel hundreds of miles to ride with them. They were men whose exploits were talked about (embellished no doubt, much to their chagrin) and commented upon wherever country folk gathered.

It has never been easy to talk with crowds and walk with kings, less easy still for these men from whom the world demanded so much. But live with it they did and there is no mention of arrogance or presumption, neither is there of any who cracked under the pressure or who succumbed to 'stress', that wonderful catch-all modern disclaimer.

They were indeed remarkable, and set standards against which all others have been judged down the years. Men could never be trained to achieve and retain so much; it was in their blood, the natural gifts honed by years of apprenticeship. They were, and remain, a very special breed.

* *

On 3 March 1878 one such man was born. Ernest Comer Bawden, for that was his name, was the sixth of ten children. His parents, James and Harriet, farmed in the tiny village of Hawkridge high on the southern slopes of Exmoor. Those who gazed down at the new arrival on that early spring day could have had no idea of his destiny. Barely three years later the child was to ride out to hounds, perched high on the saddle in front of his father. Not only did they ride out but they galloped all the way and were in at the kill.

A staghunter had been born and this book is the story of his life.

Notes

1. The full story of this incident is told by Bruce Heywood, his great-nephew, at Annex C.
2. Interviewed by the author, Sept. 2003.
3. Described in more detail by Roy Heron in his biography, *Tom Firr of the Quorn*.

Chapter 2

Hawkridge, Exmoor and the Bawdens from Cornwall

There are no street lights in Hawkridge – no streets either for that matter – neither are there any speed limits or shopping precincts. There are no garages or traffic wardens, no litter, no graffiti and no vandalism. The little village is a haven of peace and orderliness. It is as though the maelstrom of modernity has somehow missed the place, sparing it from all that ratchets up so viciously the pace of life today and leaving it as it was all those years ago.

"The land hereabouts is not so lush as the countryside elsewhere, but it lies further from the traffic and is, therefore, twice-blessed." So wrote J.H.B.Peel in his *Portrait of Exmoor. "Whenever I come to Hawkridge, I see and hear an especially rich array of those things which Wordsworth heard and saw in Lakeland:*

...the earth
And common face of Nature spake to me
Rememberable things..."

The casual map-reader might be excused for failing to spot the few dots that represent the whereabouts of the village and, even then, there are only three approaches. One brings the traveller in from the high moors to the north while the second approaches by crossing the ancient stone bridge at Tarr Steps, but this route is impassable to motors. The only other way is so narrow that the hedges either side brush the vehicle while grass sometimes tickles the underneath. The road, made just wide enough for horse and cart, descends a 1 in 3 hill before it climbs up and out the valley the other side.

Hawkridge is gloriously and cleverly hidden from all but the most persistent and, for that, the inhabitants are mighty glad.

* *

Whenever it was that man first stood on the spot where these roads now meet, he must have glanced around approvingly. The site was perfect and he would have had no doubts about settling there. Although almost 1000 feet high on the south-eastern prow of the moor, it remained sheltered from the worst of the elements; the ground behind rising further in great folds, into which the farms and cottages of today snuggle for protection.

There were clear, cool springs bubbling out of the ground. The wooded hillside faced south and the earth, rich enough for cultivation, was warmed by the sun. Below the settlement, the Danesbrook ran swiftly through the woodland and hazel thickets before tumbling into the larger River Barle. And there was game in abundance – deer, both red and fallow, wild boar and hare – while salmon and trout filled the clear waters. The ancient, pre-Christian burial mounds that crest the high moorland hilltops give some clue as to the long history of the area.

The Romans made their way up the river valleys from the Legion's headquarters in Exeter, building camps along the edge of the moor to protect them from the savages who lived above and beyond. Later there were the Danes, then the Saxons and after them came the Normans; each era adding its own particular marks to the development of the countryside, their monarchs taking what they wanted for themselves. An extract from a chronicle of this time sums it up exactly so:

"A bad man was the king…
He was sunk in greed and utterly given up to avarice.
He set apart a vast deer preserve and imposed laws concerning it.
Whoever slew a hart or hind was to be blinded.
He forbade the killing of boars even as the killing of harts,
For he loved the stags as dearly as though he had been their father.
Hares, also, he decreed should go unmolested.
The rich complained and the poor lamented,
But he was indifferent to his people's hatred,
And those who wished to keep their lands and goods and his favour
Had to submit entirely to his will." [1]

By the time of Henry and his Plantagenets the villages around the moor were well-established, many, like Hawkridge, bearing signs of Norman architecture. The roads, bounded by tall hedges so typical of West Somerset and North Devon, were set deep into the ground between the high banks, the land around cleared of cover and cultivated. But behind and above the cluster of farmsteads and houses the land was wild and untamed, used only for summer grazing while the lower pastures were rested, a situation that remained until the time of King John. He decided to take the moorland for himself, using the land as one of his official hunting grounds – Exmoor had become a Royal Forest.

The stoic, independent folk of Devon and Somerset felt robbed of their livelihood and were outraged. They had struggled hard to make a living here and use of their moorland was essential for survival, providing sustenance for their flocks and herds. They had their own rules and regulations as to who was allowed to graze what, and the numbers that were involved; it was an orderly business, part of the annual cycle. This sudden high-handedness and arrogance – theft of their livelihood by a monarch they neither knew nor cared about – would destroy this delicate balance of life.

They stood up to the decision. Just how they demonstrated their defiance is not recorded but it must have taken steady nerves in the days when such insurrection was likely to be met with the sword and branding iron. However, they prevailed, forcing the King by the terms of the Magna Carta to reverse his decision and promise them disafforestation.[2]

Years later, after many perambulations, the boundaries of the forest were redrawn with the villages of Hawkridge, Exford, Withypool and Winsford omitted. Even now the inhabitants were still not satisfied, demanding, in addition, exemption from the harsh Forest Law where death or mutilation was the penalty for killing deer or other wild creatures. All they wanted was to be left in peace to farm the land, graze the uplands and hunt the countryside.

But that was too much; of all these wild creatures the noble red deer stag was the beast that caught the eye, firing the imagination of monarch and peasant alike. Exmoor remained a Royal Forest, the control of which was entrusted to the Keeper or Warden under whom the verderers dispensed justice.[3] An uneasy peace prevailed, lasting until the end of the seventeenth century, the locals forever suspicious and hostile to those who rode roughshod over what they considered to be theirs by right.

The Civil War did not much affect Exmoor but once Cromwell had disposed of the monarchy the Parliamentarians surveyed the ancient Crown lands again, this time deciding to sell off the hunting forests. In 1635, Exmoor was purchased by a Mr James Boevey from London, a man as remarkable as he was unpleasant to all those who crossed his path, in particular those who claimed rights to the moor for livelihood or pleasure.[4] Not content with raising the rents on his new acquisition to extortionate levels, he set about making spurious claims on the surrounding commons, causing frustration and disquiet among all those who, once more, had settled down to an orderly and peaceful way of life.

For years the battles raged in and out of the law courts. Boevey, seemingly impervious to pleads or threats, alienated the inhabitants of every parish that surrounded his domain including the villagers of Hawkridge – and it is easy to imagine how they felt at such irrational behaviour. Even when Exmoor reverted automatically to the monarchy at the Restoration in 1660, Boevey was not finished. He remained defiant to the end, having been clever enough to buy out certain Crown leases, fighting both the law and his neighbours for a further thirty years until 1696 when his death put an end to the whole dreadful saga.

He was indeed an extraordinary man, reviled in many ways, yet one of vision whose legacy to Exmoor was building his impressive home deep in the ancient forest where the shepherds' and hunters' tracks crossed the moorland. Simonsbath House, as it is now called, is at the geographical, as well as spiritual, heart of modern Exmoor.

The last two decades of the seventeenth century proved to be turbulent years for the country. King Charles had an apoplectic fit, died, and was succeeded by his brother James; an act which tempted the Duke of Monmouth to sail for England and claim the monarchy. He landed in Lyme Bay and from there marched on Taunton but his ambitions were short lived.

He was defeated by the King who immediately unleashed Judge Jefferies, a servant of the Crown not known for his compassion. Jefferies toured the Westcountry, ruthlessly setting about his task. More than three hundred of Monmouth's followers were condemned to death and a further thousand ordered to be sold into slavery during his notorious "Bloody Assizes". Soon after, William of Orange landed; an altogether different problem for James, who took to his heels and fled to Ireland.

War broke out with France while, at home, there was more trouble. This time it was in the Highlands where the new uprising was crushed vigorously. Amidst it all a bright comet, first reported prior to the battle of Hastings, reappeared and was identified by the astronomer Halley. A shower of toads rained down on Acle in Norfolk and, if that was not enough, the last wild boar was killed.

Beneath these great events, and subsequent to their outcome, there was much movement among the population. The New World was attracting émigrés in their thousands, many setting out from Westcountry ports such as Plymouth and Brixham, Bristol and Falmouth. Internally, also – due to restlessness, fear or new opportunities – people were on the move; sometimes as whole communities but often alone or in families.

* *

In about 1750, one such family, for generations miners in Cornwall, decided to move on to pastures new. They did not go far – travelling only from Bodmin to the southern slopes of Exmoor, where they found a countryside not dissimilar to their own Cornish heathlands.

However, they were not destitute like so many that were forced to seek a new life, in fact, they appeared to be comfortably off and well able to look after themselves. But they were hard working and determined to succeed: the fear of failure must have been a great incentive after any such move. Opportunities there must have been, for they settled near the village of Hawkridge and began by farming a small plot of their own land before taking on the tenancy of a well-developed farm.

A Mr John Bawden had arrived,[5] bringing with him his family and all their worldly goods. For them it was to be a fresh start, one far removed from the horrors of the Cornish tin mines they left behind. It was hard for they were among strangers and had to prove themselves to the community among whom they had come to live, but they persevered – son succeeding father as is the way on farms: the hard-won skills passing down the generations. In 1832, the youngest of them at the time, another John, married Mary Milton, a local girl from neighbouring Withypool, the newlyweds taking over the tenancy of Cloggs Farm, a homestead barely a mile to the north west of Hawkridge.

Life was not easy; yet again the world beyond Exmoor seemed to have gone mad and for years the country had been in turmoil. By now the industrial revolution was in full swing but, in Middle England where the weavers and cloth makers were fearful that new machinery would force them into redundancy, serious rioting broke out amongst all this new prosperity. King George III had indeed gone mad, and was declared insane. It was the age of the waltz and quadrille, and Britannia ruled the waves.

In London the Tory Prime Minister, Spencer Perceval, was assassinated in the lobby of the House of Commons. His successor, Lord Liverpool, introduced the first Corn Laws which, while protecting the price of British crops, put the price of a loaf of bread way beyond many; an act which only added to the distress of the poor. Further afield, Lord Elgin relieved the Greeks of their treasured marble frieze. Napoleon retreated from Moscow while, from the south, Wellington marched on France.

It was in 1815, just as the dust of war on the continent was clearing, that the recently appointed Crown Commissioners for Woods, Forests and Land looked at Exmoor yet again. This time, and after much deliberation, they decided to sell the place for good rather than conduct the tortuous process of seeking new tenancies.[6] An auction was arranged in South Molton and a short time later the ancient King's Allotment of more than 10,000 acres was sold to a Mr John Knight from Worcestershire for a sum of £50,000 (several millions of pounds at today's values).[4] In the spring of 1819, Exmoor ceased to exist as a Royal Forest – this time for ever.

Knight, an ironmaster from the Midlands and a man of enormous wealth and energy, had his plans. He bought as much land as he could from his neighbours, adding it all to his estate before encircling the whole with a 30 mile long stone and earth wall 6 feet high and 6 feet wide. Inside this he broke the land, built roads and laid out farms: more than a dozen totalling over seven thousand acres between them.

Unlike his notorious predecessor, Knight worked with, rather than against, his neighbours and the locals. When he moved into Boevey's old house at Simonsbath, he and his son Frederic built cottages for his workers, then the village school and finally the church, thus establishing the Parish of Exmoor.

Where they failed was in their search for minerals, which they were certain lay under his land in rich abundance. While a sad and costly blow to the enterprise, it was a blessing to Exmoor, sparing it the scars, the slagheaps and industrial development that have ruined so much of the English countryside.

Exmoor was changing, and changing forever, a fact not missed by those whose homes and lives were bound up with this environment. But the villages and hamlets just down from the moor were changing too. Housing and agricultural methods were improving, schools were being built and markets developed. Roads were becoming surfaced and railway engineers began to nose their way slowly around the edges of the moor.

The rural communities worked hard but they enjoyed life also, the annual cycle of routine and drudgery broken from time to time by fairs, carnivals and feast days. Even so the communities remained isolated, barely knowing each other although no more than a few miles apart. Only once a year would the young men and maidens of Hawkridge walk across the moor to join those living in Withypool or Exford for a day of dancing and jollity. Then it would be their turn to entertain the neighbours, but that was all. For the most part the villagers had to find their own amusement, and this they found in the hunt.

Hunting, once for food but now for sport, was in their blood. It was the social gathering of the calendar when tools were laid aside and every available animal pressed into service. Those who could not find a mount followed on foot; those who could not manage that came to watch, to meet friends and exchange the gossip and news with those they had not seen for weeks or months.

By now local hunts on and around Exmoor were well-established. Parson Jack Russell was making his name (and his little dog), the North Devon Staghounds and several packs of foxhounds were running well. It was the same everywhere: many miles away, George Sharpe was hunting hounds for King George IV, Tom Goosey the Belvoir and Jack Musters the South Notts. Not far from them the desperate horsemanship and hair-raising exploits of Tom Assheton-Smith kept field and fox alike on their toes. It was the dawn of a golden age in country sport.

But then tragedy struck. The staghounds that had been hunting the moors for more than a hundred years were sold. Unbelievable as it may sound, a Mr Stucley Lucas of Baronsdown who had succeeded Lord Fortescue as Master in 1818, sold the pack to a German nobleman and that was that.[7] The herd of deer, so carefully nurtured by the hunt, was savaged by gun and snare; the poacher resuming his work of destruction, now unchecked by landowners and hunting folk alike. Numbers were decimated and the herd would have gone for good were it not for a few who strove hard to keep some form of hunting going and thus control what was left of the deer.

A new pack emerged briefly. Now known as the Devon and Somerset Staghounds, it struggled on for a few years before collapsing through lack of funds sometime in the early 1840s. It seemed as though both the ancient sport and quarry were doomed until a remarkable man – Mr Mordaunt Fenwick Bisset – undertook to revive the glories of the royal sport and so save the wild red deer of Exmoor from extinction. In the summer of 1855, the colours of the Devon and Somerset Staghounds were raised once more and hunting began again.

John Bawden of Cloggs had by this time retired. Now approaching his sixtieth year, he handed the farm on to his son, James, the eldest of his five children. James worked alone for a while, then on 27 December 1865 he married Harriet Comer, daughter of a wealthy lime merchant and farmer from Simonsbath,[8] originally employed by Frederic Knight on his Exmoor estate. It was an Exmoor marriage through and through, one of the very first in the village at the church of St Luke's in the Parish of Exmoor.

Harriet, a strong willed and well-educated woman, must have found life at Hawkridge comparatively easy after the wild solitude of Simonsbath. In 1867 their firstborn, John, arrived, followed three years later by his brother, James. Cloggs was too small for three generations of the rapidly expanding family so James and Harriet moved to East Hollowcombe, a large, well-appointed farm set in the village itself and barely 200 yards from the church of St Giles. Three more children arrived in 1871, '73 and '77. Then, on 3 March 1878, they were blessed with their sixth – Ernest. Four more were to follow – the last, Archie, in July 1887.

It was a big family by any standards, the more so as none were lost at childbirth, rather every one of them surviving to adulthood, marrying and producing families of their own. The Bawdens of Hawkridge had by now arrived in numbers and today the name is one of the best known on southern Exmoor, almost every village and hamlet boasting at least one Bawden family.

Notes

1. Extracts from a Norman Chonicler. *Yesterday's Exmoor.* H. Eardley-Wilmot.
2. *A Little History of Exmoor.* Hope L. Bourne.
3. *Portrait of Exmoor.* J.H.B. Peel.
4. *The Heritage of Exmoor.* Roger A. Burton.
5. Bawden/Heywood family lineage.
6. *The Reclamation of Exmoor Forest.* Orwin, Sellick and Bonham-Carter.
7. *The Devon and Somerset Staghounds 1907–1936.* E.T. MacDermot.
8. Simonsbath Census, 1861. County Record Office, Taunton.

Chapter 3

ERNEST COMER BAWDEN

Sometimes life in the middle of a large family can be problematical. To the outsider – an only child, perhaps – a situation in which there are always others with whom one can laugh and play, share secrets and confidences, might seem enviable – but not always. For those whose siblings at either end of the long line are out of touch through age or temperament, life can be tough: survival takes on an importance all of its own.

Everything has to be fought for, while attempts to gain recognition or the attention of parents are constantly frustrated. It is bad enough in a loving and harmonious atmosphere but when there is jealousy or violence, or when cliques are formed and favourites preferred, then it can be devilish. Ernest Bawden's early life was like this – a miserable and lonely affair.[1]

* *

When James and Harriet left Cloggs to set up on their own at East Hollowcombe, they were comfortably off, not rich yet well removed from the poverty line. The farmhouse and buildings they had taken were substantial, the home farm boasting more than 250 acres, together with its share of moorland grazing.

His father and grandfather had long since earned their reputation amongst the farming community and the Bawdens were well-respected and accepted as true Exmoor farmers. The roof over their heads was sound, the larder full and the children clothed and shod. The school and church were but a short distance away, and they had taken on four servants all of whom lived in the main house.[2]

Perhaps it was all too easy, but the man of the house soon earned for himself a reputation far removed from that won by his forbears. Whatever his ability as a farmer (and Hollowcombe was a well-run farm) Jim Bawden was possessed of a wild streak which only too often got the better of him. He drank heavily, usually with cronies at The Lamb in Dulverton where the landlord knew him well.

Watching his customer carefully and timing things nicely at the end of the evening, he would help him to the door then settle him aboard his patient and long-suffering pony that had been tied to the rail outside. A slap on the rump would see them away into the night, the animal picking his way carefully along the riverside tracks, his master somehow remaining in the saddle.

As he drank, so Jim Bawden's eyes roved. He was a handsome man, took life as it came and was not averse to being led astray. The ladies knew it; they had an eye for him also, and there were those who obliged, although word of his carousing soon reached Hollowcombe and the indomitable Harriet. He was a gambler, too, unable to resist chancing his luck with horses and cards. But, above all, it was hunting that took his fancy – carousing and philandering mere bagatelle in comparison. Whenever and however he was able, Jim Bawden rode to the staghounds; a wild and daredevil horseman who cared for nothing once hounds were about. Hunting, rather than family, farm or high jinks was his life.

Fred Goss, the famous harbourer, recalled an incident when Jim, then a young man, was ploughing his father's land at Cloggs when he heard the horn. Unharnessing the plough horse, he jumped aboard and rode it bare back, passing through thirteen parishes before he and the other survivors found themselves at the kill. Upton, King's Brompton, Withiel, Treborough, Luxborough, Exton, Winsford, Exford, Withypool, Hawkridge, East Anstey, Dulverton and Brushford to be precise. Only six of them finished that day: Jim Bawden resplendent in his ploughman's clothes and with no more than a hemp halter for a bridle![3]

Mercifully, the autocratic Harriet, who was made of sterner stuff, took it upon herself to raise the family as she saw best. She would have known her husband's ways but stood by him loyally, no doubt taking a jaundiced view of what she saw and heard but taking a deep breath as well. Agitated confrontations were commonplace – two such disparate characters would have seen to that – yet the marriage prevailed.

Jim, for all his failings, was a lovable man, weak in so many ways yet well-liked and a great man to follow in the hunting field. What he needed was guidance and forgiveness: Harriet provided that in abundance although there must have been times when her undivided attention tested his nerve. According to her grandson it was she who ruled the family – and her man as well – and dominated them with a rod of iron, dispensing justice to the younger ones through her eldest son, John, by this time her firm favourite.

It must have been difficult for the youngsters to identify with authority in such a household. When lucid and around the home, the father would have re-established his position to a degree but it was only a matter of time before he was off on one of his escapades again. Then the much feared John, eleven years older than Ernest and a fighting man, one who ruled with his fists and the cane, would be summoned to keep order.

At this stage in his life John appears to have been something of an unsavoury character – violent and cruel to anyone who stood in his path such as the gypsies at Molland fair. A drunken dispute had broken out between John Bawden and a group of travelling horse dealers. As usual it turned to violence, culminating in a battle royal close to the railway line where John's nose was flattened by the heavy bone handle of a hunting crop. Shaking the blood from his face and the stars from his head, the young Bawden knocked his adversary unconscious then picked him up and threw him over the fence and on to the railway track where he lay prostrate by the rails. A forbidding character, his very presence at Hollowcombe brought a sense of fear and dread to the younger ones.

James, the second son, affable and genial like his father, was not a strong character, he too eventually succumbing to the bottle and cards. But he was a kindly soul and it was he who taught Ernest about the wild. As soon as the younger boy was old enough, the two would go off for hours together. It was James, or 'young-Jim', who taught Ernest to shoot; how to swing with the run of the quarry and how to stalk and draw a bead quietly before shooting straight. Moving targets such as rabbits were anybody's prize but it was the longer range, static targets that became Ernest's domain.

He became an expert marksman, later winning prizes in the Yeomanry and, later still, fame in the Boer War. James would have taken him to watch deer and they would have gone birds' nesting together. They would have tickled for trout in the streams and gaffed salmon in the Barle, shamelessly poaching whatever they could find.

Frederick, number three, had little effect on the younger children but the fourth son, Francis, (or 'Frank' as he was known) and Ernest never got on when they were young. They were constantly at loggerheads with the older boy usually coming out on top. It was inevitable that in such a large family there would be intense rivalries somewhere along the line and the two boys, both determined characters, were best kept apart. Much later, when Ernest was working at the hunt kennels, the hatchet was buried and the two became close.[4] But not so at Hollowcombe Farm and it was here, as a child, that Ernest needed all the support he could find.

Next in line and immediately above Ernest came a sister, Harriet, or 'Jessie' as she was known. There were only two sisters in all, one either side of him. Here at last, or so it seemed, there was someone with whom he could feel safe and find some affinity. By now the little boy must have been longing for the affection and companionship that was missing from his life, and it is easy to imagine him trying to gain Jessie's attention. She, however, would have none of it. It appears that she was a hard, unfeeling girl, interested only in her elder brothers and the excitement they brought into the house. James apart (and he was eight years older) Ernest remained alone and unloved.

School for a boy in such an unenviable position would have been merciful release. It should have been something to look forward to, a welcome change and an opportunity for finding companionship and making friends. By the time the Bawdens had moved to Hollowcombe, the village school in Hawkridge had been running for a number of years. It was a typical, small, late-Victorian establishment, the twenty or so children drawn from the parish and supposedly remaining there until they were fourteen.

The records give no indication that there was anything untoward about the school or the mistress – the young Miss Park from Taunton – but it appears that something was amiss. Perhaps one or the other failed to meet with the approval of the redoubtable Mrs Bawden. Perhaps, and it is quite possible, her glamorous and fast-living husband took a shine to the young Miss Park, or she to him. Whatever the reason Harriet Bawden took her children away. First, in April 1881, she removed John and James.[5] John, a bright child, had already learned to read and write but not so James who remained illiterate until adulthood when an "X" marked the spot on the marriage register.[6] Frederick, according to the record, was a permanent absentee.

Two years later when Ernest was five and a half and had been at the school for six months, he and the others were withdrawn while the three youngest, although registered, never crossed the threshold. Little Mary-Elizabeth, his younger sister who had just started, was still only three but she was brought out as well. Their mother, in addition to being a strong disciplinarian, was intelligent and well-read, and it must be supposed that the poor Miss Park simply did not meet her high expectations. Neither woman saw fit to complain but Harriet Bawden got her way and, jaw firmly set, marched her children back to Hollowcombe Farm.

Somewhere, somehow, Ernest learned to read and write exceptionally well; of that there is no doubt. His handwriting on his military service record shows a beautifully neat, almost copperplate hand,[7] and his volumes of hunting diaries demonstrate a mature and descriptive prose way beyond what a village school might have been expected to instil.

He read avidly throughout his life, devouring anything to do with hunting and the countryside as well as books about the Empire, politics and current affairs.[8] Harriet had plenty of help in the house and it is reasonable to suppose that she set about teaching her children herself – there could be no other explanation. The young would have learned their three Rs at their mother's knee or, in this case, around the beautiful William and Mary sectioned, mahogany dining room table on which numerous ink stains are still visible.[9]

Ernest must have loathed such close confinement where the threatening figures of John who beat and Frank who glowered menacingly were too close for comfort, while Jessie did no more than turn her back on him. It would have been about this time that Mary-Elizabeth came into his life.

By now desperate for the love and attention that was so lacking, he turned to his younger sister and they became devoted to one another, remaining so for the rest of their lives. Little is known about his relationship with the three youngest brothers at this stage save that there is no record of animosity between them. Neither Ernest nor they had anything to fear from each other.

It was thus his misfortune to have been born right into the middle of a very large family, where the numbers seemed to split into an elder and younger group. His first few years, so terribly important in any child's development, were bereft of warmth and attention. Even making allowances for those brutal far off days, it was hard, but there was *one* outlet, *one* escape – the countryside and wildlife around him. It was to the fields and woods, the moors and streams that he turned for solace and pleasure. Sometimes brother James or

Frederick would go with him, occasionally his father but for most of the time he wandered alone.

Jim Bawden rode and hunted hard whenever he could and made it plain that he wanted his sons to follow him. But there was more to it than that. By now he had built up a small string of racing ponies and was looking for a jockey. One of them, he was sure, would ride well enough but the ponies were small and fast and it was not as easy as their father made it sound. They were all competent horsemen and they all tried but were simply not good enough, added to which the older ones were growing quickly and soon became too heavy.

Ernest, like the others, had been put in the saddle at the earliest possible age – the story of him riding in to the kill at the age of three has become the stuff of legend, but it has been corroborated time and again by family and eyewitnesses alike.[10] The important point about that particular tale is that, from this early moment in his life, Ernest took to both riding and hunting and never looked back.

The impact of the noise and drama of the kill that day could have worked either way; turning him away from such experiences for good or inspiring him. It was the latter. His obituary laid claim to the fact that he had ridden to hounds ever since he could remember, and opportunities for doing so were plentiful. He would have ridden alone or with his father and *his* friends, mostly local farmers whose knowledge of deer and hound-work the youngster would have absorbed.

They would have known what to look for and where to look, what best routes to take and the wiles of the hunted deer. Nothing would have been missed. Ernest, by now an excellent rider, rode out whenever he could but not only to hounds. Soon he would be racing as well, better still he would be riding winners.

* *

Hawkridge in the 1880s and '90s was larger than it is today, nevertheless everyone would have known everybody else. It was impossible to hide in such a community and the village would have been well aware of the comings and goings at Hollowcombe Farm. Like everything else, it would have been part of village life.

The mill down by Slade Bridge over the Danesbrook would have been working then, its huge metal wheel turned slowly by the water that ran from the leat. Dippers and wagtails still flit from stone to stone where the mill used to be and it is here, just a few hundred yards from the farm, that Ernest would have first watched the deer as they came down to drink and first seen their slot marks in the mud and the racks where they crossed the hedges.

Thomas Steer, the blacksmith, ran the smithy just up the hill from the church, helped by his assistant Jacob Adams.[11] Ernest would have brought his father's horses here to be shod, gathering with others around the smoke and the bellows as they waited their turn, listening intently to the news and gossip.

The Lock family, their home and workshops but a short walk from Hollowcombe, had been carpenters in the village for generations, ever since old William Lock came over the moor from Twitchen to learn the trade from James Tout. He was a clever man, was old William; clever enough to marry the master's daughter then take on the business himself.[12]

He was a hard task master and a perfectionist as well, never working on Sundays and stopping only at dusk when a special candelabra would be lit so they could get on with the business of making coffins. Old William trusted nobody and measured himself for his own, crafting it carefully before putting it aside until the day it was needed. When Ernest was ten, an oak gate from old William cost forty-five pence, a wheelbarrow seventy-five and twenty hurdles the princely sum of sixty-five. But a pound in those days was more than two week's wages for a farm labourer.[13]

Mrs Burnell, the dressmaker, and Grace Wensley, the spinner, both lived close to the farm. Next to them were the shepherds, Louis Milton and Bill Mole, then the carter Bill Barnes. The post was brought daily from Dulverton, walked in along the river bank for five miles by Will Beed. He saw it as far as Tom Lock's Post Office (where they sold baccy as well) at which point Frankie Howard took over to do the rounds with the mailbag.

In the meantime, Will Beed would disappear into his shed opposite the forge where he spent the rest of the day cutting hair and mending shoes until it was time to walk home again. Next door to Will Beed, 'Farrier' Baker ran his dispensary for sick animals.

There was no public house in the village; the beer and spirits were dispensed from the carpenter's shop which doubled as an off-licence. Bread came from the bakery at Molland and the fresh meat from Dulverton. Sometimes gypsies passed through, offering towels and pegs for sale, combs and needles, cotton and darning wool. A Mr Yeo from Barnstaple came twice a year by pony and cart bringing with him the latest styles in shoes and boots.

Ernest would have known all these characters as well as the sons and daughters of their neighbours. Although something of a loner later in life, he was never without friends, but he chose them carefully and then kept hold of them. There would have been his cousins, Edwin and Salome, at Cloggs, Mary and Clara Tidball from Parsonage, Tom and Bella Westcott and their cousin Charlie; little John Steer and Freddy Hodge. They, however, had school to contend with, and for much of his early life Ernest would have been by himself.

Already there was a restlessness in the boy, a characteristic that was to manifest itself so strongly later in life. The wildness that was so evident in his family lurked beneath the surface here too – a wildness, or stubborn bloody-mindedness, known to the family as the "Hawkridge wild streak".[1] Hollowcombe farm was no Wuthering Heights but there was an element of the turbulent young Heathcliff about Ernest. He had no interest in the farm – something that would have alienated him further from his brothers – his one abiding love being riding and hunting the deer, and here he was content to be on his own.

It would have been impossible for him to keep pace with the hounds for long on the small racing ponies or farm horses he borrowed from home, so he had to learn to anticipate how the hunted beast might behave, remembering everything he had been told but thinking ahead for himself. He would watch closely, working out the animal's route away from danger, then – riding hard – take short cuts down steep slopes or through the thickest woods, winding his way across bogs or following the tracks of sheep and wild ponies. In doing so he was able to buy time for himself and make up ground, getting closer to the hounds than perhaps he should.

Most of those seeking a career in hunt kennels would, by this time, have begun their apprenticeship. Ernest, however, was a free spirit, learning by himself from the animals, observing their behaviour under pressure, in particular how the hunted deer used water. He had to puzzle things out for himself, worrying the answer through until he was certain. Earlier he had been taught but now the knowledge he gleaned was his own and here, perhaps, lies one of the keys to his greatness.

It is interesting to note who made up the Devon and Somerset Staghounds' hunt staff at this period. In 1889, when Ernest was just eleven, the great Arthur Heal carried the horn, Anthony Huxtable was whip and a young man called Sidney Tucker rode second horse.[14] A few years later the legendary Fred Goss, a friend of Ernest's father, became harbourer. It was a position he was to hold for twenty-six years, by which time Ernest himself would be carrying the horn. It was pure fate that four of the greatest names in staghunting to date had been brought together just when young Ernest was absorbing so much.

For sure he would have watched the hunt servants also, comparing what they were doing with how he knew the deer would react. Even then he would have been developing his own ideas as to how things should be done, perhaps noticing mistakes and shortcomings. These were his formative years and it would have been impossible to have gained so much by sitting in the middle of a huge hunting field surrounded by all the chatter and bustle.

When he could ride no further he would dismount and run, leading his pony at a steady jog for miles on end through the bracken and heather. He was to become an excellent long-distance runner, winning prizes for steeplechases and the mile, sometimes beating the professionals who were lined up against him. But it was always the deer that held his attention; he would have understood that the only way to stay with them in the chase was to think like them, then ride hard taking risk after risk. It is worth remembering here how the great huntsmen introduced in Chapter 1 managed to stay with their hounds.

There exists in any hunting field a strange neutrality among the riders. Men and women come from all walks of life but there has always been an accepted equality among them all in the field, something that is rarely found elsewhere, except where an element of danger exists. Yachtsmen may have it, as do those who climb mountains where courage is the great leveller, but not many others. In the hunting field it is the qualities of sportsmanship and horsemanship that decide who should be respected and who derided. Ernest would have been noticed.

It would have taken time but those who hunted regularly would have remarked to one another that there was a young boy from Hawkridge who could handle himself on a horse. He was nothing more than an unkempt farm boy who kept himself to himself, but he could ride like the wind and knew where he was going. The hunt staff would have noticed him too, either directly or through his father and his farmer friends. Time and again he would have been there at the kill at the end of a long, hard gallop where no pony or feather-booted farm horse such as had been carrying him had any right to be.

For his part, Ernest would have noticed others as well, youngsters like himself who loved to ride out whenever they could. First it would have been a shy nod of the head or raised hand, then the gradually developing friendship with two or more of them riding along together, sharing their bread and cheese and swapping stories. They would have come from the surrounding villages of Exford, Molland, Winsford and others.

Two such boys, both a little older than Ernest, came from Winsford. Harris and Sidney Heywood were their names, farmer's sons from Kemps. A strong and enduring friendship grew between them, one that was to take two of them half way round the world together. They, too, came from a large family – five more brothers and three sisters. One of the girls, Elizabeth-Ann, was later to feature prominently in his life.

Ernest was small – only 5' 5½"[7] – but he was wiry and tough, his weight never rising much above 9 stone throughout his life. He was built like a jockey and it was not long before his father had plans. Frustrated at the lack of ability shown by the others he placed his faith in Ernest, coaching him and driving him on, urging ever more speed from the boy, ever more daring. One moment he would be laughing with delight, the next shouting with anger.

There was an occasion when Ernest took a fall. Far from consoling the boy, Jim flew into a rage, forced his son back into the saddle then, in a fit of drink-sodden madness, and in front of others, he and John tied the boy's feet together under the horse. It was a cruel and senseless act drawing laughter from some, pity from others. The humiliation and indignity must have bitten deeply, aggravated no doubt by the taunts and jeers.

One can only guess at the negative effect such behaviour might have had on his relationship within the family, but on his horsemanship it had the reverse. Where many youngsters would have been put off for life, Ernest became more determined than ever. In less than a year he had won his first race at Larkbarrow[15] on his father's pony "Reago", a quicksilver little mare barely 14 hands 2 high. Ten sovereigns was the prize, a figure that must be multiplied forty times at least to bring it in line with today's values.[16] Next time it was twelve guineas at Minehead then a further ten sovereigns. Soon after he was to win The Farmers' Plate at the first ever Devon and Somerset Staghounds' point-to-point meeting.[17]

Now, suddenly, he had the attention he had craved for so long. It was a false affection, however, brought about solely by success on the racetrack rather than any softening of parental hearts. Nevertheless success it was and the boy was becoming his own man; at last he could do something better than the others, a fact that served only to alienate him further from some in the family. But Hawkridge was getting too small. He had seen a bit of the world beyond and his frustration was beginning to boil.

He craved for more from life but there was precious little in the village for Ernest and his friends. There was nothing to keep them amused on dark winter evenings. There was no public house, girls were few and far between; most of them were sisters or cousins and all were heavily chaperoned. Occasionally there was a dance in the school but it was a serious, well-organised affair supervised closely by the elders.

Old Walter would bring his fiddle, Minnie – his wife – would sit at the piano and off they would go. The more Walter drank the wilder the music became and the better he played, the youngsters making sure his glass was kept full. The highlight of the evening came at the end when they all trooped outside to watch Walter and Minnie trying to get on their horse, the two of them bickering and pushing like children in their efforts to claim the saddle [12].

The Hawkridge streak was bubbling away and they sought their amusement further afield. Withypool – a happy, peaceful little village – became their destination, The Royal Oak public house their target. It lay 4 miles away but that was no odds to those who were bent on mischief. One night they descended fully intending to make a thorough nuisance of themselves but, forewarned or not, the good folk of Withypool reacted immediately and, with commendable vigour, threw out the roughnecks from over the hill.

Unwisely they returned for more, this time getting for themselves a second and more vigorous hiding, some ending up spreadeagled on a set of chain harrows. These unpleasant chains and sharp metal spikes, normally drawn over the grass by horses, are implements not to be tangled with on any account, much less in the middle of a drink sodden rough and tumble.

Hawkridge retired bloodied but unbowed. Hell-bent on revenge, they returned yet again, this time to 'smoke 'em out.' A narrow road runs behind the line of low cottages along the river just over the bridge and this was their objective. After soaking a number of hessian sacks in the river, the smallest – and Ernest was very small – were sent up on to the roofs to place the sacks over the chimneys while the remainder waited by the doors to intercept those fleeing the smoke: Withypool, old and young alike, was not amused.

But that was enough – it was time to move on. The restless, turbulent spirit needed more than that. Riding helter skelter after hounds by day and causing mayhem in neighbouring villages by night was all very well, but it could not last. It would only be a matter of time before the attention of the law would be drawn to yet another member of the family, and the constables of Dulverton knew quite enough already. The challenge was soon to come, but from an unexpected quarter.

* *

The Army in those days stood some way apart from the rest of society, much as it does today. They tended to wear strange clothes and tucked themselves away in barracks behind high walls. One moment they were there, the next they had gone, sometimes for years on end and most probably for hundreds if not thousands of miles. They were difficult to get to know but the Officers and Non Commissioned Officers (NCO's) rode out to hounds whenever they could; none more so than those in the Yeomanry.

A deep bond existed between the Yeomanry regiments and the hunts of England. It had been that way for generations and was to remain so until long after the last horse had gone into battle. The old county yeomanry regiments looked for their officers and yeomen from within their own boundaries. Such bonds are strong, producing a powerful sense of comradeship across all ranks, binding the regiment together especially when they are a long way from home. The same spirit exists today in the county infantry regiments.

Many years later, in September 1915, when the Yeomanry brigade sailed for Gallipoli on board the HMT *Olympic* all the Masters and ex-Masters of Hounds on board sat down to dinner together at a central table – twenty-four in number of whom ten came from the Devon Yeomanry. It was something of a Roll of Honour and the names live on in the Regimental History. The ten were:

Lt Col Sir R. Sanders	Devon and Somerset S.H.
Major M. Greig	Devon and Somerset S.H.
Major St Maur	South Devon F.H.
Major Thynne	Tetcott F.H.
Capt. Hain	Hain's Beagles.
Capt. Sir G. Wills	Dulverton F.H.
Capt. Salaman	Exmoor F.H.
Lt Clemson	Stevenstone F.H.
Lt Scratton	Haldon Harriers.
2nd Lt Hope	Stevenstone F.H.

Somebody produced a horn which was passed round the table and blown by each of them in succession followed by toasts that were drunk to 'Hunting' with great enthusiasm. Such were the ties in those days! It must have been a wonderful and emotional occasion but sad, too, for several were never to see England again. One of those those who died, Major Greig, was killed by a shell within a few days of landing at Suvla Bay.[18]

* *

For the moment those who could hunt in peacetime did so whenever possible. It was fun and as exciting as anything else they did while on a home posting. It was training of sorts and it kept the army in the public eye. Better than that, it was a good time to spot potential recruits. The Yeomanry had to look out for those who could ride and what better place to find them than the hunting field? Those from the towns and cities tended to be hopeless with horses; either petrified at the very idea or else it was all quite beyond them. Training them even to mount and sit properly was a waste of time – and the waste of a good horse as well. Eyes were kept open.

Bawden would have been spotted soon enough, as would the Heywood brothers. Sooner or later an approach would have been made, surreptitiously at first then more boldly, as interest was shown. "Think of the glory," they would say. "Think of the excitement and the comradeship – and the money. The family will be proud of you. And what about the young lady?" Young men with a gleam in their eye never change and exactly the same alluring recruiting patter is trotted out today more than a hundred years later.

Ernest may have paused for a moment but his mind was soon made up. The Royal North Devon Hussars, a glamorous local regiment, was looking for just such young men. Numerous officers had been associated with the staghounds for years. The Fourth Lord Fortescue had been Lieutenant Colonel since 1890 [18] and hunted regularly. He would, for certain, have seen these likely young men. Two more, Major Morland Greig and Colonel Sir Robert Sanders, were both to become Master in the years ahead.

Sometime in the summer of 1894, Ernest Bawden and Harris Heywood rode into South Molton where they met the Recruiting Sergeant under the archway next to the Town Hall. Ernest was just sixteen.

Notes

1. Exhaustive and illuminating conversations with Percy Bawden, Ernest's son (aged 95 in 2003).
2. Hawkridge Censuses for 1871 and 1881.
3. *Memories of a Stag Harbourer.* Fred Goss.
4. Mrs Lorna Stickley, daughter of Ralph Slocombe (whip to Ernest) who grew up with Frank Bawden.
5. Hawkridge school records. County Record Office, Taunton.
6. Winsford Marriage Register. As above.
7. A.F.B 111. Short Service Attestation. National Record Office, Kew.
8. Percy Bawden.
9. Amazing that such a fine piece of furniture should be found in an Exmoor farmhouse. It was a wedding present to Ernest's parents, a further indication that the family were by no means hard up. It is now with Mr Ken Bawden, John's grandson.
10. *The Making of a Huntsman.* Dan Russell.
11. Hawkridge Census.
12. Tom Lock of Hawkridge, gt-gt,grandson of William.
13. Locks of Hawkridge Carpenters' Invoices for 1890.
14. *The Devon and Somerset Staghounds 1907–1936.* E.T. MacDermot.
15. Dan Russell.
16. Compilation of Bank of England statistics, Indices of Cost of Living and Index of Retail Prices.
17. *West Somerset Free Press.* Historical account of D and S point-to-points. 28 Jan 1939.
18. *The Yeomanry of Devon.* Benson Freeman.

Chapter 4

FROM BOY TO MAN

Biographies fall principally into two categories.

There are those in which the subject's life is traced, the moments of drama and excitement catalogued, but little more than that. The reader is left with a fair record of how that particular life ran its course (sometimes barely more than a diary of events) but knows little or nothing of the face behind the mask. What has been portrayed is purely cosmetic, no more than skin deep, and one is no wiser at the end as to why or how that person achieved such prominence or what it was that made him or her tick. The second, however, goes far deeper; its aim being to expose, then examine, the hidden personality.

Each one of us possesses three personalities. First there is our public visage, the character we are pleased enough for the world to get to know (although from time to time it lets us down). Then comes our private personality – deeper and more complicated. We are not so sure about this one, and within the complex jumble of qualities, the sum total of which decides our personas, there are those elements that are best left where they are. And finally there is that third and secret personality which lurks deep within us, which only we know about and which bubbles to the surface only occasionally, more often than not to our deep regret or acute embarrassment.

To chip away at another's façade and expose what lies hidden beneath the surface in order to determine the true nature of the character will always be difficult – whether or not the subject is alive. Most descriptions or anecdotes come from the family, or from friends and associates, and often tell us little more than what is most easily or conveniently remembered. Mostly it is no more than what the narrator wants us to believe. Reports, letters or other documents are often no better, tending to concentrate on certain matters only, leaving much about the subject still unanswered.

The biographer is left with a feeling that there must be more to the subject than that. Something has been left unsaid or there is a suspicion that the truth is likely to be quite different. The picture is incomplete and, even after careful analysis, there remain gaps and question marks.

Ernest Bawden was sixteen when he joined the Yeomanry. Still barely out of boyhood he was, nonetheless, deemed to be a man. Manhood came early then, no allowance was made (or patience shown) for the difficult teenage years around which we tiptoe so warily today. Midshipmen and boy sailors had seen fleet actions by the time they were fourteen while drummer boys of the same age had marched into battle at the head of the thin red line. Sweeps' boys were climbing chimneys at eight as others were hauling carts of coal on their hands and knees hundreds of feet underground. Young girls were often out 'at service' by the time they were eleven or twelve.

By now Ernest's character was well-developed; to all intents he was a man. He was expected to think and behave like an adult and must therefore be judged as such. Riotous youth was given short shrift in those days. Subsequent events might leave their marks or cause changes but, by and large, his die had been cast.

* *

In order to try to get to the bottom of what was emerging as a powerful yet complicated personality, I decided to seek expert advice on all that I had seen and heard. I had arrived at my own conclusions as to how events in his formative years might have shaped his character but that was insufficient. I needed to understand him as well as I possibly could before moving on to the next chapter in his life; in other words before those in the Army got their hands on him. The moment seemed to be right and I sought advice from two disciplines – graphology[1] and psychology.[2]

I approached the former with a measure of caution, aware that those who practise the art are sometimes regarded with unjustified cynicism, the practice even dismissed as something akin to astrology or soothsaying. However I had had first-hand experience of cases where a graphologist had been able to reveal astonishing detail about the subject's past life before going on to analyse the character in question. Selection of high-flying business executives, including the headmaster of a leading independent public school, and assistance to the C.I.D. are cases in point.

I sent two letters written by Ernest. Both had been written fairly late in his career, the second immediately before he retired. Later I called the graphologist – Mr Pendry – and we discussed the subject. It should be noted that he had no idea at all about the person I had in mind except that he was male and was no longer living. He made three assertions about what he had seen then followed up our conversation with a written and more detailed analysis.

The first point he made – and he was quite adamant about it – was that Ernest had suffered from a lower body injury or ailment. This proved to be exactly so: he was struck down by a serious and debilitating complaint before he became huntsman and it was an affliction that was to trouble him for the rest of his life. His second point was that, early in life, Ernest suffered from mother-domination and, thirdly, that he was a hard working, ruthless and determined individual.

The written analysis went much further. Two dominant characteristics prevailed – cruelty and depression. His illness plagued his life, restricting him physically, and he became frustrated, irritable and impatient. He did not tolerate fools. His massive energy had been diverted into creativity, manipulation and this ruthless determination.

Eventually he shook himself free from his maternal domination and became very masculine in most of his ways, except perhaps for his love of tradition and family ties. He developed a paranoid sense of guilt about opportunities which had been lost and a compulsive stubbornness about trivial matters. Everyday decision-making was easy for this man, the report continued.

He was quick, responsive and logical. It was the major decisions which bothered him and he pondered long before making them, often relying upon intuition and circumstances to propel him in the right direction. It was a trait he inherited from his mother and had the effect of slowing his progress somewhat, thereby creating bouts of explosive frustration.

Depression tormented him: he could become so depressed that he actually forgot what feeling happy was like. It must be remembered that the second and longer letter was written just before his last day of hunting after thirty-three years with the staghounds so it is easy to understand his feelings at this time.

To the end he remained unable to tolerate routine or periods of inactivity and if he could not get cracking himself, he was busy organising others. He spent his time dominating everybody and shifting things around. He was difficult to relate to emotionally on account of his secret desire for friction and argument.

Being melancholy by nature, he could surprise everybody by suddenly coming out of his shell and using brute force to influence events. Like all natural leaders he was looking for betrayal and was very mistrusting. One of his lighter attributes was his live-for-today attitude and he would try anything new. The downside of this was his complete tactlessness and lack of regard for safety. He cut corners and hurt feelings, yet would drop everything and come to the aid of a complete stranger, provided that person really needed and deserved it.

In summary the graphologist wrote that he was a ruthless and focussed achiever with a determination to succeed while not worrying too much about others. At home he was a tyrant and had no time at all for underachievers. Deep down he was a traditionalist who wanted everything to remain as it was. Rather a handful of a person, Pendry concluded, but you would not miss him in a crowd!

It is interesting to note that both Ernest's son and a nephew, as well as a second-horseman who served under him, agreed with almost everything that Pendry had identified from the letters. Now armed with this comprehensive – albeit somewhat unflattering – report, I arranged to meet an eminent child psychologist [2].

What I needed to know was which of these characteristics were genetic – part of the so called Hawkridge wild streak and which were behavioural, originating from his childhood experiences. As a prelude to our discussion, I went through his difficult early life at Hollowcombe Farm in some detail, describing the character of his parents and other members of the family.

The cruelty Dr Pamela Durrant attributed principally to inherited tendencies, a fact well-covered in literature on Child Psychology. She felt, however, that there would have been strong interaction between his own personality and his unfortunate environmental circumstances – in essence his personality developed through a combination of both.

It was the survival of the fittest and he, like the rest, had to fight his corner or succumb and allow himself to become overwhelmed by it all. The aggression could have stemmed from the fact that he was unable to impress his father (until the pony racing and, even then, for the wrong reasons) added to which he got no love from his mother.

In so far as his depression was concerned, and allowing for the fact that one of the letters was written at a most distressing moment in his life, Dr Durrant felt certain that the roots lay in his childhood experiences. The failure of parental figures to address the emotional needs of a developing child played a leading role. Neglect – known today as emotional abuse, and a more acute phenomenon – was due almost entirely to his exclusion from family acceptance and the lack of parental warmth. This resulted in a feeling of exclusion, inadequacy and insecurity. Physical abuse, known euphemistically as corporal punishment, would have enhanced this feeling.

She considered also that he, perhaps in line with other members of the family, may have been subjected to some form of sexual abuse. She stressed that such behaviour was widespread (and remains so) in particular where the many children of large families are denied any degree of privacy and who were forced, through circumstances, to share clothes, washing and bathing facilities and beds. She emphasised that it was unlikely that anything more serious than 'messing about' or some quite minor and relatively harmless interference might have taken place, but the effect on such a vulnerable child could have been profound.

The result of any such experiences may have later driven him to seek gratification through dominance of others rather than sexual encounters. While in no way diminishing his desire for female companionship, thoughts of the latter might have been pushed to the back of his mind, possibly even to the point of exclusion.

The ruthless determination that Barry Pendry identified was, Durrant considered, the result of his mother's domination. It created the 'focussed achiever' he spoke about, in that Ernest had always to prove himself. The excitement of the earliest hunting episode when, at three years, he sat on the pommel of his father's saddle and rode into the kill, would have been a dramatic experience for him and would have had a most profound effect on his character. She went further, stating that such an event would have provided a bond with his father in that Ernest realised that riding and hunting was something special in his father's life and he could see a way to winning his father's approval.

Her final point was that the thrill of the chase and the power of the occasion (the noise, the shouts, the baying of hounds and the spectacle of adults apparently revelling in the sight of blood) worked as an addiction or stimulant to his aggressive nature.

* *

It is not necessary to go back over the earlier chapters in order to see how these qualities in his character were brought about. Many were to become enhanced further in the years ahead. What *is* of particular interest, however, is that Ernest Bawden already possessed a number of the qualities that were so essential to the make up of a great huntsman as identified by Eva Dunbar – the fearless riding, the ruthless determination and the focussed mind.

These Ernest possessed in abundance but now there were more – that cruel streak, the desire to dominate and that will to win – such attributes surely the mark of any great hunter, man or beast. Add to these his tough, wiry physique, the hard natural environment from whence he came plus his intense love of hunting and the potential of the man is beginning to emerge. Some of these qualities he brought into the world with him – others, much to his discomfort, were thrust upon him.

It would be interesting to take some of the romantic personalities described earlier by Eva Dunbar and subject them to such an analysis as I have attempted with Ernest Bawden. They would not have wished for such an exposé that is for sure. However, once the veneer had been stripped away, we would have discovered many similarities between Bawden and his illustrious predecessors.

This manifestation of his character has been brutal and unforgiving. The man is not here to defend himself and would, no doubt, argue that he had been taken out of context. For a start, he was born into a tough, often violent, world that we cannot comprehend today. Hollowcombe Farm was by no means the only household where such goings on took place. Indeed James and Harriet Bawden succeeded in bringing up their family intact and without major incident. Not only that but subsequent generations of theirs have fitted easily into the society around them.

Furthermore, everything that this analysis has revealed constitutes his weaknesses, his faults and limitations. It is the sinister third and most easily concealed of his personalities that has been laid bare for all to see; the one that he, like everyone else, would have taken great pains to hide and keep under control. He would have possessed (and most certainly did) many admirable qualities – humility and loyalty, generosity and charm. He was a dignified and private man who drank in moderation only, never gambled and who remained faithful to his wife. He became a pillar of society and a celebrity to whom people warmed rather than shunned.

A balance has to be struck. Ernest's character has been exposed dispassionately in order to see what it was that drove him to the heights that it did, where his fame became truly international. To attempt anything less would be to fail the man. Natural talent would have got him so far but not nearly far enough.

He was not happy at home, neither had he shown any interest in becoming a farmer like so many of his family. Something had to capture his imagination or there would be trouble. Perhaps he made overtures to the hunt in order to see if there was an opening for him in the sport he loved. If so, then his application was unsuccessful and he was forced to look elsewhere – tempted, no doubt, by what he had heard.

Notes

1. Mr B. Pendry, Graphologist. London.
2. Dr Pamela Durrant. M.A.(Hons), D.Clin.Psych., D.A.C.P., C.Psychol., A.F.B.Pt.S.

Chapter 5

Soldier Brave

In 1894 Great Britain could claim to have three separate armies. There was the regular British Army made up of professional soldiers who signed on for a number of years. They lived together in barracks or under canvas and, except when they were on furlough or leave, wore uniform day in and day out. Although answerable to civil law they were subject also to the much fiercer and more draconian military law. They were paid, maintained and equipped by the government of the day for whom they were happy to march off or sail away and do whatever was asked of them, very often dying in the process.

Then there was the Indian Army or 'Sepoy' Army based permanently on the sub-continent and made up of either British Army regular units or Indian units commanded by British officers. Service in India for the British contingent lasted for several years at a stretch. Most English counties raised two battalions of soldiers, one earmarked for home or oversea's service, the other destined to serve in India.

Drafts of time-expired men would be withdrawn from India to be replaced as individuals rather than whole units at a time. The usual tour of duty was for seven years and it was common for the children of officers to be sent home to England for their education, lodging with some maiden aunt in Broadstairs and seeing their parents only very occasionally. The whole business of service in India was a very long-distance affair encouraging those involved to consider themselves more or less a race apart: for certain an army apart from those who lived and served at home.

Lastly, there were the part-time soldiers consisting of the Militia, the Volunteers and the Yeomanry, many regiments of which had been in existence for years. The Devonshire Yeomanry (part-time and mounted) came into being in 1794, exactly one hundred years before Ernest Bawden signed on, while the Devonshire Regiment (regular infantry and part of the professional army) had been formed way back in 1685 – soon after the Monmouth scare.

* *

It has to be said that in 1894 Yeomanry soldiering was neither taken particularly seriously nor regarded as arduous. The prime function of the old volunteer regiments had been the maintenance of security on the British mainland, a task for which, even in the early days, they were hardly best suited – a squadron of cavalry armed with sabres or lances would give any mob good reason to pause for thought but were a serious confrontation ever to take place then there was likely to be a blood bath.

Over the years and before the advent of the police (but even after they came into being in 1829) the Yeomanry had been called upon to restore law and order on numerous occasions. Industrial and agricultural unrest, food riots, mounting guard on shipwrecks and such like were typical events. Usually it worked and trouble was assuaged but there were occasions when over-enthusiasm got the better of the military (such as the infamous Peterloo massacre near Manchester). But now, at the end of the nineteenth century, life had become more orderly and the police well-established. Service with the Yeomanry, while a fine patriotic gesture nonetheless, was regarded by many as something of a pastime.

Nobody had ever made the suggestion that these volunteer units might be called upon to reinforce the regular army as is done today, neither was it contemplated that they might have to serve overseas. However, in spite of these limitations, or perhaps on account of them, the old Yeomanry regiments refused to die. In fact they flourished, soldierly in appearance (and fiercely proud of it) but amateur by profession. Officers and men flocked to join in their hundreds.

As in most regiments, many of the Devon Yeomanry were farmers – gentlemen farmers, yeomen farmers, tenant farmers, farmers' sons and even farm hands. Furthermore, in North Devon, the farming community at all levels was closely interwoven with the world of trade, so the North Devon Yeomanry also included among its members merchants and tradesmen, bankers and shipowners, together with their sons and apprentices.

Many of the great Westcountry family names were well-represented in the order of battle, sons often following fathers into service with the local colours – Dyke Acland, Fortescue, Airlie, Chichester, Clinton, the Devons of Powderham, Hambledon, Poltimore and Rolle to name but a few.[1] It mattered not from whence the volunteers came, the spirit of adventure and desire to serve ran through them all.

By 1894 Devon had two Yeomanry regiments – The Royal 1st Devon Yeomanry from Exeter and The Royal North Devon Hussars from Ebberley Lawn Barracks in Barnstaple – both units numbering in excess of five hundred officers and men. It was to the latter of the two that Ernest and Harris Heywood were directed.

* *

They would have reported with their own horses (borrowed from home), arriving at the Guard Room early on the day concerned. The Guard Commander would have checked their names from his list and directed them to the Regimental Headquarters. Many aspiring volunteers would have turned up with them, for the day would have been one of general attestation.

Ernest and Harris would have glanced around nervously, wondering if they were to pass muster. In addition to the well-presented farmers such as themselves, there would have been wealthy young men, finely mounted. Others would have taken less trouble, looking scruffy and unkempt, mounted also perhaps, but poorly, and many without a horse of their own. Some would be too old, others too young.

The selection process would have gone on all day, the men going before the doctor where teeth and tongue would have been examined as well as eyes, ears and the rest of the body, while the horses went before the farrier and veterinary surgeon – the horse being just as important as the man. Physical and written tests would have been conducted before those remaining went to the riding school where the Riding Master would put man and horse through their paces.

At the end of it all those who had passed would have been formed up and sworn in by the Adjutant. One at a time they would have repeated after him the oath of allegiance, their left hand holding aloft the Bible, their right hand on the Union Flag:-

"I, Ernest Comer Bawden, do solemnly make Oath, that I will be faithful and bear true Allegiance to Her Majesty, Her Heirs and Successors, and that I will, as in duty bound, honestly and faithfully defend Her Majesty, Her Heirs and Successors in person, Crown and Dignity against all enemies, and will observe and obey all orders of Her Majesty, Her Heirs and Successors, and of the Generals and Officers set over me. So help me God." [2]

Strong words but, once pronounced, they were *in* and one can imagine the sense of relief and achievement. Next, and it may have been there and then or at some later date, they would have drawn up their clothing and equipment before attending a recruit training cadre which lasted for two or three weeks. Once that was completed they would have been assigned to a Troop and their life in the Hussars would begin.

But they were very much part-time soldiers, returning home after each spell of duty, when they would put away their uniform and become farmers once more. However, with their pay in their pockets, they had to be ready and their uniform would be hanging up behind the bedroom door. The headquarters in Barnstaple would be run by regular officers and soldiers drawn from the cavalry, but the Troops and Squadrons that made up the fighting strength or 'teeth' of the regiment were all part-time soldiers meeting for a weekend of training once every month or so, for an annual camp of three weeks and the occasional military tattoo or pageant.

Cavalry Week in Barnstaple was the highlight of the year, when the Royal North Devon Hussars showed themselves off to the public with marches, parades, musical rides and mounted games. Cavalry Sunday was the climax of the week, when the population of Barnstaple would double [3] as the crowds flocked in to watch the festivities. Soon after church the special trains would arrive from Ilfracombe, Bideford, Taunton, Dulverton and Exeter. The

Volunteers (Infantry) joined up with the Yeomanry for morning service then marched together through Taw Vale, where the Mayor took the salute.

Sporting events, football, cricket and boating on the river all took place before huge crowds, the Yeomen competing at sabring heads, lemon slicing and tent pegging. It was one huge, colourful jamboree which Bawden loved and at which he excelled. As the Yeomen were paid off in the Pannier Market, prizes were presented to the smartest soldier and the best turned out horse and soldier, both of which he won time and again, the silver flask for his victories in 1899 now held by his grandson.[4] He won athletic prizes also – long distance running and mounted races where his skills learned on Exmoor paid handsome dividends.

He loved the life and, to the Yeomanry, he was a natural soldier full of promise. But so much of what they all did was a charade, nobody having the slightest idea as to how they might be asked to perform were they ever to be called upon to *"defend the Crown against all enemies,"* as they had sworn to do. The tactics of massed cavalry wheeling smartly in line and trotting out to meet the enemy before breaking into the charge had not been used for years, and such information as could be gleaned from the campaigns in Afghanistan, Africa and the Sudan was sketchy indeed. Furthermore, there were those who were beginning to doubt the merit or validity of such tactics. The Yeomanry were stuck in a time warp, hanging on to the past for dear life yet quite unable to see ahead.

The government seemed unwilling to help – incapable even. Weapons and equipment were antiquated, ammunition and saddlery in short supply.[5] The more wealthy officers paid to make up for many of the deficiencies themselves.[3] The one great and enduring strength of the Yeomanry was their spirit and the quality of the officers and men.

However, events were beginning to change, albeit slowly at first. Thousands of miles away in South Africa their regular counterparts were coming ever closer to a major confrontation with the inhabitants, not the native Africans but European settlers of Dutch origin with whom the British government was having territorial disputes. The Boer nation, far from being cowed by the presence of the greatest force on earth, was squaring up and not giving an inch of ground. Ernest and his fellow Yeomen knew little about the matter. News was perfunctory: what had become a problem for the regulars was hardly a concern of theirs and, in any case, it was all taking place a very long way from home. It was no place for them.

Then, suddenly, everything changed and very quickly at that. Within three months a series of events in South Africa shook the British establishment to its very core and the Yeomanry, that much maligned and half forgotten element of the British Army, regarded for so long as a sleepy backwater, was about to be called upon. Soldiering – a matter that had for so long seemed little more than a game – was now to become deadly serious.

* *

The friction between the British and Boer governments, which had been simmering for some time, finally came to a head in the Autumn of 1899. Ultimatums were given by both sides (only to be rejected immediately) and it was five o'clock on 11 October – just at tea time, noted *The Times* – that war officially began.

The British, although far from ready, were spoiling for a fight, desperate to put behind them numerous setbacks and reversals they had received at the hands of the Afrikaners. There existed in England a firm, unshakeable belief that Britain possessed not only the capability but the right to rule over her vast dominions and that nobody, least of all these untidy farmers, could be allowed to stand in her way.[5] Who did these people think they were?

Scarcely anyone believed that the war would seriously strain Britain's resources or that it would last for more than six months. Badly prepared and poorly equipped as the army was, its officers and men felt ready and the nation prepared to address herself to this irritating problem. However, they were all far too late for, even as the military contingent in South Africa was being reinforced, the Boer armies struck.

There followed two months of setbacks and reverses, until, just before Christmas that first year, what was to become known as 'Black Week' brought home to the British public that this particular war was going to be no pushover. In the space of just six days General Gatacre's force at Stormberg was almost annihilated, two days later Methuen's attack at Maggersfontein was repulsed and, on December 15th, General Buller was defeated at Colenso.[1 & 5]

Disaster followed disaster and the nation was stunned, humiliated beyond belief. But then, as is the way of the British after adversity, they reacted swiftly. The War Office issued a notification that the Government would raise a force to be known as 'The Imperial Yeomanry', the aim of which was to beat the Boers at their own game. The Yeomanry Regiments, every one of them, stepped forward eagerly and it was to this hitherto neglected force that the Government turned, just as they had done in the days of trouble before.

The farmers of Britain were called upon to go overseas to meet the farmers of the South African veldt. Ernest Bawden and his comrades were about to be sent into action – they were about to face the ultimate test.

Notes

1. *The Yeomanry of Devon.* Benson Freeman.
2. Army Form B 111
3. *The North Devon Yeomanry 1794–1924.*
4. Mr Gerald Bawden of Hove, Sussex.
5. *The Great Boer War.* Byron Farwell.

Chapter 6

JOHNNY BOER AND THE VELDT

Events in Ebberley Lawn Barracks moved swiftly. Volunteers were needed but the length of service would be for a year at least and longer if necessary, thus those who stepped forward would become regular soldiers in all but name for the duration of their posting. Only the best would do, so there would have to be selection, for the pride and reputation of the unit was at stake.

Letters and telegrams were despatched and the men assembled as quickly as possible, Ernest and Harris Heywood among them. While selection was in progress news came through that the two Devonshire Yeomanry regiments were to provide just one company between them and, of this number, The Royal North Devon Hussars' share was to be fifty. All over the country volunteers were pouring in and, for once, the army was able to pick and choose. Competition was fierce.

The British Army in South Africa was being reinforced by units from the Regular Army but the eyes of the nation were now on the Yeomanry. While the men were of high quality, the equipment was antiquated or deficient but in North Devon, as elsewhere, the regiment and public rallied to those who had been chosen to go to war. Colonel The Lord Ebrington took great personal interest in ensuring that everything the men wanted should be made available, stripping others of their saddlery, arms, clothing and personal equipment where necessary. A county fund was raised to buy more equipment, some benefactors giving as much as £1000. Colonel Shelley arranged that the men should each have a fine hunter to go with him, a new pair of field glasses and other articles.

The uniform was a slouch hat, turned up on the left side, a khaki service dress jacket that was buttoned to the chin, Bedford cord breeches, long puttees, boots and spurs. Each man carried a webbing bandolier holding a hundred rounds and wore a webbing waist belt with frog for the bayonet. The personal weapon was the Lee-Metford rifle and bayonet.[1] But of the sabre and lance, which were still on issue and with which they used to parade so proudly, there was now no sight.

It was the best that could be done in the time. Everyone had contributed what they could, determined that 'the boys' should have only the very best. Civilians and the military alike were caught up in a great surge of pride and patriotism: the men that were to go were pampered and feted as heroes before they left.

* *

On 9 January, after an emotional farewell at Barnstaple railway station where the bands played and flags were waved, the men and horses set off to join the remainder of the force at Topsham Barracks in Exeter. There they were split into four Troops, each of about 25 men under command of a junior officer and sergeant. Ernest and Harris found themselves together in Number 3 Troop commanded by Lieutenant G.H. St Hill, himself a North Devon man.

The Company (now referred to as a Squadron) was commanded by Captain W.E.T. Bolitho, also from North Devon. It was numbered the 27th Squadron and was to form part of the West Country Battalion – the VIIth – together with companies from Dorset and Somerset. Training was carried out until the end of February, when the battalion left Exeter for the Albert Docks in London where they boarded the *Manchester Merchant* (6000 tons) on 1 March. A great deal of ground had been covered in a very short time.

Once on board the Squadron would have had time to settle and collect their thoughts. After the excitement of the last few weeks, boredom would have set in and seasickness taken its toll as soon as they headed down the Channel. Ernest later confirmed that he was a hopeless sailor and detested the whole voyage. There was little for the men to do except P.T. and weapon drill, and suffer the endless rounds of inspections, both of themselves and their horses. Once fresh rations ran out, the food would have been dull – endless porridge and biscuit, tinned or salted meat, potatoes and root vegetables – and there would have been little or no alcohol. They stopped briefly at Las Palmas on the way to take on water, but that was all.

Few of them had ever left home before, in fact many would not even have seen the sea. They would have been homesick, desperately missing family and loved ones, their emotions fuelled by uncertainty as to what lay ahead. By this time Ernest may have met Harris Heywood's sister – Elizabeth-Ann – the girl who was to become his wife. He would have missed her as he would have missed Hollowcombe Farm and the wide open spaces of Exmoor.

Cramped as they were on the lower deck where the two rows of hammocks swung close together, there was scant opportunity for privacy. New friendships would have been forged in the confined space but there would have been arguments also, fights perhaps over cards or space or an ill-judged remark.

But there would have been happier moments, too, such as when they were allowed up on deck together after their meals. Even boat drill would have come as welcome relief to the unsavoury conditions below. Later, after the evening meal, somebody would have produced a harmonica or an accordion and there would have been a sing-song, either spontaneous or organised.

British soldiers love to sing and numbers such as "Good bye Dolly Gray," "Where did you get that hat" and "Ta-Ra-Ra Boom-De-Re" were among the favourites of the day.[2] The crew might have replied with sea shanties. Crossing the line would have been celebrated, the men stripped to their underwear and ducked by King Neptune. Generally, morale would have been high for they were young men off on a great adventure together, the tingle of anticipation ever present.

Every one of them was an excellent horseman and they would have cared deeply for their charges that were incarcerated below, spending as much time as possible down there, soothing the animals as they struggled to keep steady in the darkness while the ship rose and fell to the Atlantic swell before sponging them down in the heat of the tropics as they sailed further south. It would be here when they were alone and well clear of the crowded troop deck that there would have been time for quiet reflection on all that had come to pass and, without doubt, what might be lying in store for them.

* *

They disembarked at Table Bay on Wednesday 28 March (after almost a month at sea) and marched through Cape Town to Maitland Camp, both men and horses delighted to be on dry land once more and eager to stretch their cramped limbs. They were an impressive sight, highly commended by Lord Errol on his inspection who expressed himself well pleased, assuring them that units so well turned out deserved to be sent to the Front![3] But hardly had they time to find their feet than they were ordered entrain and endured a tortuously slow, three day journey to Edenburg, 50 miles south of Bloemfontein. Here operations began. It started to rain, as well, for although it was spring in England here, in South Africa, it was autumn.

It rained for a week, turning the roads to a quagmire and soaking everyone. The men dried out whenever they could but the horses were exposed to the elements and were to remain so until they were spent. As they moved north-east so the land rose until the plains were over 5000 feet and the nights grew colder. The first shots came on 18 April when leading elements of the Squadron clashed with the enemy's scouts. The same occurred the following day and so it went on, inconclusive skirmishing with the enemy always standing off, watching them carefully and waiting patiently for the next opportunity.

The first few weeks of operations must have come as a rude awakening to the yeomen and their horses alike. The veldt was vast, bleak, open and scrub covered; scorched by the summer sun but now cold and wet as winter approached. Nothing they had experienced before would have prepared them for this. Operations consisted initially of escort duties where they mounted advance guards and flank protection for convoys and large bodies of men on the move.

Sometimes the screen would have to cover a frontage of several miles when, suddenly, the men would find themselves out on their own in sections or pairs, fending for themselves and having to make their own decisions. Nobody had prepared them for this either; there were no training manuals and they had to make up their tactics as they went along. Sometimes the enemy would catch them and they would have to learn by their mistakes.

Senior troopers or Lance Corporals were placed in command of these small groups, the officers and senior NCOs were hundreds, if not thousands, of yards away. Ernest was to be promoted Corporal before the end of the year so he must have caught his commander's eye early on and been given some form of responsibility on these marches.

His lonely boyhood, when he spent countless hours in the open, would have taught him much and he would have felt more at home in this country than most, his keen eyes well-used to judging distance and selecting routes. He would have become adept at identifying likely danger spots, even catching sight of the elusive, ever-present enemy. But it was here on the open veldt that the Boer held the advantage.

They were native to the land and knew it intimately, as did their ponies. They were operating close to home, thus had food and water available; not for them reliance on the cook's wagon or quartermaster's stores. They knew the paths and tracks and what lay over the next hill. They were operating among their own people and developed an excellent network for gathering intelligence.

Almost to a man they were hardy farmers used to living off the land and excellent marksmen. The British, on the other hand, were stumbling around in the dark. Maps were few and far between, guides of any use almost non-existent. The land and wildlife were strange, the enemy all around them but there was no intelligence about him or his capabilities. Their lines of communication were long and vulnerable to ambush, their clothing and equipment cumbersome and uncomfortable on the high veldt.

The British horses, superior though they may have looked, were quite unsuited to the terrain and were no match for the tough, little sure-footed Boer ponies. The quality of animal fodder they could find, or what was brought up for them, ranged from adequate to inedible – while the regimental farrier and saddlers, now needed ever more frequently, were often many miles away.

And finally, the weapons. The Boer had the German Mauser, an accurate weapon with good sights and a five round magazine that was *clip* loaded. The Yeomanry, on the other hand, were armed initially with the recently introduced, yet much distrusted, Lee-Metford. It was of marked inferior quality to its opposite number, inaccurate as well, striking the target up to 18 inches away from the aiming mark at anything over a few hundred yards range.

The Lee-Enfield was quickly introduced but its sight remained inferior to the Mauser, added to which the magazine had to be *charged by hand*. Thus after the first five rounds, the Boer could reload and commence firing again far more quickly than his opponent.[4]

The troopers discarded whatever they considered to be non-essential but the load was still formidable. Ernest would have despaired for his horse as daily he put together saddle, wallets and carbine bucket, his bridle, spare horse shoes and nails in their shoe case, rifle and one hundred and fifty rounds of ammunition; bandolier, mess tin and water bottle, rations for man and horse, greatcoat and blanket, numnah, forage net and corn sack. Six months earlier he would have been hunting on Exmoor riding out at little over 11 stone all up. Here, his wretched horse (perhaps poorly nourished and badly shod into the bargain) was carrying almost 20.

If all this was not enough, the Boer soldier was fighting for his homeland, his farm and his family – the strongest incentives of all. Born and bred on the veldt they were big, bearded men, loose of limb, shabbily but comfortably dressed in broad brimmed hats, cord trousers and brown shoes. They rode their ponies easily, looked unkempt, rough and half savage, even their eyes expressing a lazy good-nature, sluggish stubbornness and dormant fierceness.[5] It was going to be a strange, interesting contest, but by no means as one-sided a confrontation as the British had expected.

* *

Colonel Browne recorded faithfully the VIIth Battalion's progress day by day in his diary. Most days were different to the ones before, but a pattern of life for his soldiers began to emerge.

Reveille when on the march would be well before dawn, the last sentry of the night guard shaking the men huddled beneath their blankets, often wet through, sometimes frozen but occasionally (if they were lucky enough) free from the worst of the elements. Bedding would be packed away by some while others went to the horse lines, the men usually working in pairs. Breakfast, consisting of biscuit porridge and a bowl of tea, would be taken quickly before the fires were doused and the column would aim to get underway by four or five o'clock.

Ernest, having been given his orders, would take his small group out to their positions on the screen or flank guard. The horsemen would ride in pairs, each man well separated, each pair several hundred yards apart. He may have been put in charge of two or three pairs whose duties would be to check the route and keep a sharp lookout. It would be up to him to select the most suitable points of observation from which he could best see the land around them. He would have to maintain contact with the main column, for it would be his duty to ride in with any information they had found.

The column would halt around midday, when a further brew of tea would be taken with biscuits or whatever they had managed to scrounge from the villages or farms they had passed. Horses would be held centrally, out of sight from the surrounding high ground and out of the sun or wind. Whenever they stopped, picquets would be put out. This was an exhausting and time-consuming business but it was important, for the Boers would attempt to sneak in close to snipe or cut off stragglers.

The end of the day's march would be signalled at least two hours before last light so that proper defences could be arranged, sentries arranged and the picquets deployed once more. Each man could expect to do two shifts (or "stags" as they were known) of sentry duty during the night, each of two hours duration. It was a long time after a hard day but the punishment for falling asleep or moving around was severe.[6]

Daily life was tough; mere survival and looking after oneself, one's horse and keeping the weapon clean took up several hours of precious time. There were no comforts, no canteens where one might get a cake, a glass of beer, a packet of cigarettes or a hot meal. Mail came through infrequently and it was even more difficult to get a letter out. Where was the writing material? Cuts, sores and shaving nicks festered, torn clothes had to be repaired, split boots stitched or cobbled back together.

The leatherwork and saddlery of the horses had to be kept together also, cast shoes put back where possible and worn ones replaced. Every man had to look after himself. The rifle came first, then the horse and finally, a long way behind, came the man. Discipline was relaxed but the basic requirements and standards of soldiering were rigidly enforced. Mistakes cost lives.

It is interesting to note that the Devons were awarded the clasp 'Diamond Hill' on their South Africa campaign medal. The battle came early during their tour (11 June) but they had very little to do with it, rather they were kept out of the way and did no more than send out a number of patrols to ensure that the battle between General French and some 3000 Boers did not come their way. Of particular sadness to them all would have been the news that Lord Ebrington's brother, The Hon. Lionel Fortescue, was killed in the battle while serving with the 17th Lancers. (See map p. 55.)

Soon after Diamond Hill most of the Squadron left to become temporary policemen in Pretoria. It would have been a pleasant interlude from the interminable patrolling. They would be able to get under cover at last and have a chance to spruce themselves up. More than that, the pay of a policeman was no less than six times that of a trooper, so it was small wonder that most of the men volunteered and Ernest (who usually managed his financial affairs rather well) would have been among them.

By now most of the horses they had brought out with them were spent and remounts from the Argentine taken over as and when they came up to the front. Several of the old horses had been hit by small arms fire or shell splinters, a number had gone down with sickness and the rest were exhausted – a sad and sorry end to the proud hunters from North Devon.

Operations continued relentlessly, the Squadron moving every two or three days. Colonel Browne made no mention of the infamous raids in which property was to be burned or destroyed. In the main, these unpleasant operations took place later in the war when the population was rounded up and concentrated in camps. The Devon countrymen would have loathed such tasks. They would have found a strong affinity with the Boer farmers, knowing only too well how difficult it was to raise stock or cultivate the land and how hard the families must have worked to build up their small homesteads. They would have noticed that much was in common with their own homes and way of life.

"Foraging" yes, that was all part of the game where fodder and carts were taken and cattle rounded up. The Boers took whatever wagons and equipment they could from the British whenever they had the chance also, but the yeomen would have found being ordered to burn and destroy the farms deeply repugnant.

It was after the tour of police duty that two episodes occurred which involved Ernest, both of which revealed interesting sides to his character. The first was on 5 November when the Devons were near Vlakfontein some 75 miles due west of Pretoria. The force, under command of Lord Roberts, were hunting the Boer General, de la Rey, and had been in sporadic contact with the enemy for a number of days.

At the time of the incident the squadron had halted and were having their evening meal of bully beef, biscuits and hot chocolate. It had not yet got dark but, suddenly, a sniper opened up. His first shot so narrowly missed Ernest and those sitting next to him that it knocked the mess-tin he was holding over the fire out of his hand. The other men scattered but young Bawden took his rifle and disappeared. Three hours later, after a shot was heard, he returned having identified the sniper in a tree and killed him. He brought in the dead man's horse with him.

The story, unrecorded in the regimental history, was brought to the family years later by Lieutenant Las Casas, late of 27th Squadron. Ernest had never said a word to anyone and the family were stunned. However, the tale was recorded by Colonel Browne in his diary. He took pains to make careful note of every casualty, both friendly and enemy, and there was only one incident when a Boer sniper was killed by his men – and his horse captured.

To stalk or lie in wait for an enemy sniper to reveal himself, especially a much-respected Boer marksman, and then to commit the 'coup de grace', takes not only fieldcraft and marksmanship of the highest order but patience, determination and ruthlessness, not to mention courage. Had the sniper caught sight of him first then the outcome would have been reversed.

The second incident, and barely a month later, was of a very different nature. The regiment had, by this time, become part of a much larger force that had swung east and which was now operating close to the Magaliesberg range of mountains just to the west of Pretoria. The General's plan was to block one of the mountain passes near a spot known as Nooitgedacht but, unknown to them, they had been spotted by the scouts of a large enemy force who decided to attack them before dawn the following day.

Fire was opened soon after four o'clock, catching the British unawares. For a time there was chaos. Some troops broke and ran, many of whom were cut down by the enemy, but disaster was averted by a number of gallant actions in which elements of the Devon Squadron were involved. In one, Captain Bolitho led a bold attack to secure a ridge from where they could return the enemy's fire and stem his advance. Sixteen of the assault party were killed or wounded in the attempt, including Captain Bolitho who was awarded the D.S.O. [7] for his gallant leadership.

Operational area of VIIth Bn, The Imperial Yeomanry.
May 1900 to April 1901

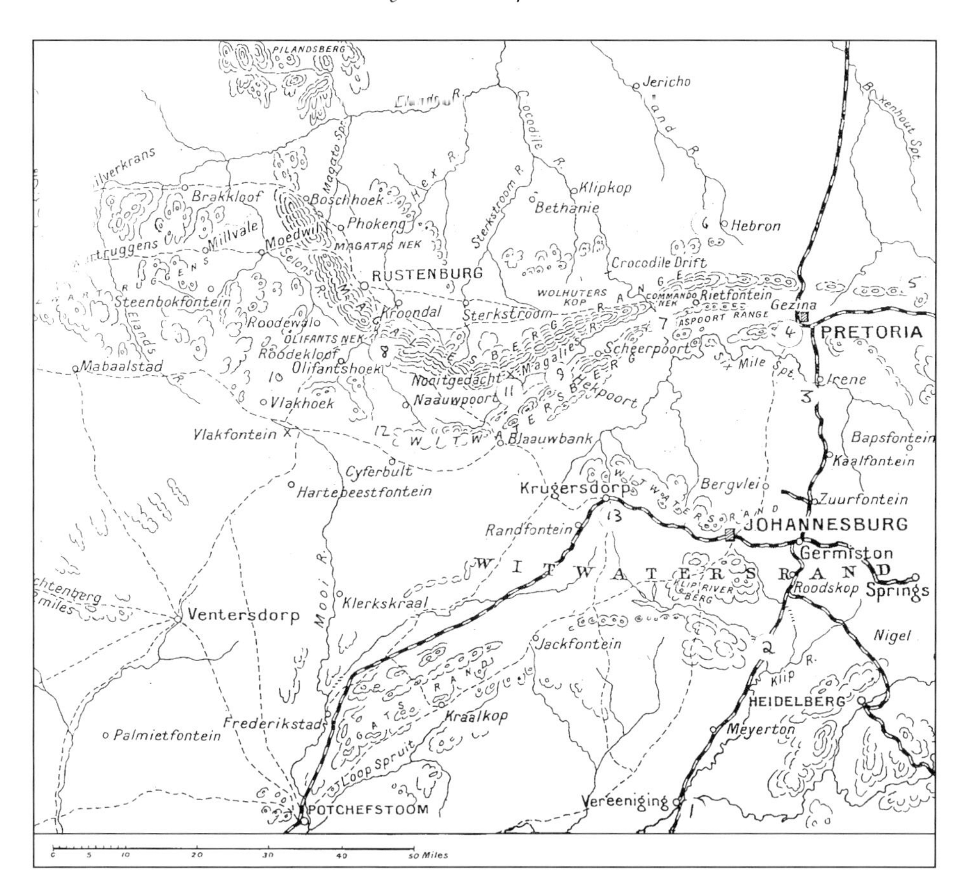

Dates and locations of the principal engagements:

1 26 May 1900. Assault and capture of Vereeniging railway station.
2 29 May 1900. Assault on Elandsfontein where there were 500 enemy.
3 4 June 1900. Capture of Six-mile Spruit in a storm. That night it froze hard.
4 5 June 1900. General Botha surrenders. Devons among first to enter Pretoria.
5 11 June 1900. Battle of Diamond Hill.
6 17 July 1900. Battle of Kameel Drift where the Boers used artillery.
7 23 July 1900. Fighting at Commando Nek against General de Wet.
8 17 August 1900. Assault and capture of Oliphant's Nek.
9 10 September 1900. Battle of Magalies River against 1500 Boers.
10 5 November 1900. Where E.B. stalked and killed a Boer sniper.
11 13 December 1900. Battle of Nooitgedacht where E.B. won promotion.
12 23 January 1901. Three days of operations against General de la Rey.
14 30 January 1901. Capture and occupation of Krugersdorp.

The second action was commanded by a Sergeant Bright who held another ridge with a small party of Devons for several hours, buying valuable time for the situation to be brought under control and until the Boers had withdrawn. For this action he and a Trooper were awarded the D.C.M.[7] It had been a hard day, Colonel Browne noting later that *"they had been under fire for fourteen hours and were altogether twenty-six hours in the saddle. Men and animals were cooked."* Just where Ernest Bawden was throughout this fierce and bloody engagement is not recorded but his documents state that it was on this very same day that he was promoted to full Corporal.

His promotion would not have come as the result of some properly convened Promotion Board where the members were able to sit quietly and deliberate over the names in front of them. Far from it, for to receive immediate promotion such as this on the field of battle can mean only one thing – that Ernest Bawden distinguished himself somewhere in the thick of the prolonged action, most likely with either Bolitho or Bright, where the fighting was at its heaviest.

To be promoted thus would have been close to being put forward for a gallantry decoration, indeed that may have been the case but there were others who were even more deserving. What is beyond any doubt is that on 13 December 1900, Ernest had proved himself in action and he had come through the sternest test of all with flying colours. Here again, the qualities exposed by the analyses earlier had come to the fore.

* *

The regiment moved on the next day, their one hundred and twenty-fifth move after being on the march for one hundred and forty-one days. The constant physical exertion under difficult conditions and with poor food was beginning to tell. By now the horses had been changed three times and many of the men would have been weakened by sickness or come close to exhaustion.

Although many were killed or wounded in battle, the biggest drain on manpower was sickness. Influenza, dysentery, cholera, malaria and typhoid were ever-present and the regiment was hit by a typhoid epidemic early in the New Year when the weather was at its hottest. What little water there was available on the veldt would have been dirty, often coming from muddy scrapes or water holes shared with the wildlife.

Many of the regiment went down with the disease, the Commanding Officer and Ernest included, and several died. That they were physically drained did not help but the conditions of the medical centres and field hospitals were quite inadequate and unable to cope with the numbers that were coming through. Recovery took a long time and many were left with supplementary problems. Ernest's intestine was damaged (a not uncommon side-effect) and he was never able to make a full recovery. Later he was to develop diverticulitis, an ailment which worsened as time went on and for which he should have had surgery. It was about this that the graphologist had been so adamant in his report.

He was determined to rejoin his troop and would have been involved in the unit's last series of operations. In one – one of their largest – they provided the right guard for a mixed force of Imperial Yeomanry, Scottish Horse and New Zealand Mounted Rifles when they carried out a successful raid on a Boer laager capturing a number of men and weapons. In another, part of the Devon squadron remained behind in ambush, for the enemy formed a habit of following them up. They killed two and wounded another whom they took prisoner.

By now operations were becoming sporadic and word came through that their replacements were on the way. Although it would be some time before they left the theatre of operations, events appear to have been brought to an end by the middle of May. Colonel Browne wrote in his diary:

"Friday, May 17th. We marched at 7a.m. to Welverdiend Station, the Yeomanry being the main body. We got in at eleven o'clock and I bid farewell to the VIIth Battalion and caught the train to Johannesburg with Colonel Shekleton. There I saw Lord Chesham and was told to take my regiment home. I dined with Shekleton at Heath's Hotel."

* *

The VIIth Battalion was one of the very last Yeomanry regiments of the first tour to leave the field – they had well and truly done their bit. On 22 May they crossed the Orange River, heading south, before they and a number of other Yeomanry units were held in a transit camp for over a week, where horses and equipment were handed over. Frustrating though this delay may have been, it nonetheless gave them all a chance to recoup some of their strength and mend or exchange their clothing and boots for the first time since Pretoria, almost nine months earlier.

Corporal E. Bawden led his section of men up the gangway of the s.s. *Hawarden Castle* on Monday 3 June. There were forty officers and seven hundred and eighty men on board. Conditions would have been cramped but not a man would have cared. However, they were not quite out of it yet.

The ship stopped briefly at St Vincent where coaling began at once: a filthy, dusty operation in which everything and everyone got covered in thick, black dust. To the horror of those on board, the local Portugese coalers were in quarantine and it was the Yeomen who had to turn to and do the dirty work. Even now, fate had time to play one last trick and the weather broke. The N.E. trades turned nasty and the weather deteriorated badly. For several days, high winds and heavy seas sent them rolling and lurching on their way through the Bay of Ushant.

Nothing, however, could stop their progress and the ship docked at Southampton at eight in the morning on 25 June. They had been in South Africa for almost fifteen months to the day.

Notes

1. *British Cavalry Equipments 1800–1941.* Mike Chappell.
2. Most were songs from the London Music Halls but others like *Good Bye Dolly Gray* (sung by Florrie Forde) came from the American shows. Still more, such as *Soldiers of the Queen,* were written especially for the war. Source. *This England* magazine
3. *A Rough Diary (Kept on the Veldt).* Lt Col P.J. Browne. Sadly he went down with the s.s Waratah when she was lost without trace in July 1909.
4. *The Great Boer War.* Byron Farwell.
5. G.W. Stevens, a British War Correspondent.
6. The days of flogging were over but such lack of discipline was taken very seriously indeed, the miscreants being sent to jail whenever that was practical. If not they were forced to undertake the most exhausting or unpleasant tasks known as 'Field Punishment.'
7. The Distinguished Service Order and the Distinguished Conduct Medal. Gallantry decorations second only to the Victoria Cross, the former awarded to officers, the latter to other ranks.

Chapter 7

HOME AGAIN

Altogether it had been a long time – a shade under eighteen months – since the contingent of fifty officers and men from the Royal North Devon Hussars had first boarded the train in Barnstaple to go off and face whatever was in store for them. They were not regular soldiers who had chosen the Army as a way of life and who were happy enough to be away for years; rather they were part-time volunteers who had answered the call and it is easy to imagine their feelings as the s.s. *Hawarden Castle* inched her way slowly up Southampton Water early in the morning of 25 June 1901.

The yeomen would have lined the sides of the ship talking quietly among themselves or gazing in silence at the glorious, English landscape. Their thoughts would have been either on their families and homes that awaited them or else far away on the veldt remembering those who they had left behind. There would have been a twinge of guilt and unease at these memories, as there always is when those that have been spared think of those who have not. It had been a hard slog; not the unbelievable carnage and horror of the World War that was yet to come, but a very tough campaign nonetheless.

Every man would have been marked by his own experiences, left with memories that would remain undiminished. Casualties had been high, with almost one man in three of the Devons either killed or wounded in action or lost as a result of disease. They would indeed be glad to be home and the great desire right then must have been to get out of uniform, pick up their back pay and return to the life they remembered.

* *

However, not one of them could have been prepared for the welcome that awaited them as soon as the ship docked. Even at that early hour huge crowds had assembled along the quayside cheering and waving as the Yeomen made their way down the gangway. Why, they must have wondered, what had they done to deserve all this? There were welcoming speeches, bands played patriotic songs and the train to carry them home was decked with flags and bunting.

The party that went as far as Exeter was met by a mounted escort of The Royal 1st Devons who later led the march from the Regimental Headquarters to the Guildhall where the Mayor welcomed them on behalf of the city. Major

Bolitho D.S.O responded and a procession formed up under his command to march through the streets to the cathedral, led by the Mayor and Corporation and the Exeter Member of Parliament. Here, soldiers and city alike joined in a service of thanksgiving.

After that they went on to Barnfield Hall where they were entertained to dinner by the City. Each man found himself presented with a five pound note (almost two month's wages for a Trooper in 1901). Everywhere they were cheered to the echo, greeted as returning heroes: a situation they neither expected nor understood. They had won no battle of note, they had withstood no great siege; in fact they had not even repulsed a recognisable enemy. Why then all the fuss? The welcome was quite overwhelming.

* *

Exeter, with all her good intentions, was doing no more than reflecting the mood of the nation as a whole. England, from the monarch and parliament down, was delirious with relief, not that any crushing victory had been inflicted – far from it – but that those returning had been instrumental in stemming the flood of appalling and humiliating disasters of the recent past. More than that they had faced up to the foe and had taken the first steps towards him. They had saved the nation's pride and, for that, the country was jumping for joy.

Lord Kitchener had been sent out to take command of what was now a huge army in the field. His orders were to bring these Boer farmers to heel, but the men who were now returning home, these Yeomen of England, were among the first to have volunteered and who had then held the line until the country was ready. The crowds that pressed around to salute them along the way did so in a great outpouring of gratitude fuelled by relief.

The following day Ernest and Harris Heywood reached Dulverton station where they were met by another crowd, many of whom they knew. As soon as they stepped down from the train, they were lifted shoulder-high and carried to a decorated cart which was pulled by well wishers for more than a mile into the centre of the town and up to the Town Hall where they were publicly congratulated and feted before being sent on their way [1].

For Ernest, a quiet and private man, such adulation must have been agony. All his life he had shrunk back from the limelight, distancing himself from attention whenever he could. Both men knew that not one of those now cheering them on had any idea of why they were making such a fuss. Right now he longed for the peace and quiet of Hawkridge where he could escape the endless handshakes and backslaps. He just wanted to get home.

One can imagine the awkward small talk and uneasy silences in the farm cart on the short journey back to Hollowcombe Farm. He was their son and brother but now, after all this time and as he sat swaying to the lurches of the cart, he had the air of a stranger about him. As they glanced at him dressed in his khaki marching order, with just his pack and a bundle of assorted belongings, they would have sensed a difference. With the noise and bustle of Dulverton behind them nobody knew quite where to begin or what to say. It was the same when they reached home where the rest of the family and friends were waiting.

It was only when they reached the farm that the family saw he had brought his Lee-Enfield rifle home concealed in a blanket. Somehow, in the rush and chaos of the last few days, the weapons had not been properly collected in, and Ernest had decided to 'borrow' his. It was an act of sheer folly. What on earth had been going through his mind? He could not possibly have forgotten to hand it in, and would have been well aware of the dire consequences of such a decision. Was it some trophy, maybe? A reminder of what he had been doing – the nearest he could get to the sniper's scalp? Or was it some sinister indication of the ruthless and cruel streak in the man that had momentarily floated to the surface?

Whether it was by accident or design nobody can say, but the weapon was to remain undetected for more than seventy-five years. He took it with him and kept it hidden away wherever he went until it reappeared briefly in his hands during the Second World War. It then disappeared again before coming to light once more in 1975 and now resides in the Barnstaple museum, the plaque underneath recounting its strange but eventful history in the hands of 6562 Corporal E. Bawden.

The events of the last two years had taken their toll. His mother and younger sister both noticed how he had aged, how his face had grown lean and the eyes more piercing. They detected a tautness about him as he tried to readjust to the new life at home. He had become more abrupt in his manner and there was a now military bearing about the way he walked and carried himself that had not been there before.

Most of the older ones had left home but Mary-Elizabeth, now aged twenty, was still there so were Joseph, seventeen, Harold, just sixteen and Archie, the youngest, still only thirteen. They fussed around him as any family would, glad to have him with them again and proud of him but it was difficult to get him to settle and they would have wondered about him… and it is here that the problems would have begun.

Ernest would not relax and found it impossible to tell them what they wanted to know. Nothing, not even a hint, was said to the family about his exploits. Harris Heywood would have been sworn to secrecy, for not a word was said about his duel with the sniper or their exploits during the battle of Nooitgedacht and other places. The family knew nothing until Captain Las Casas came to the hunt kennels years later.

Such reticence is not unusual and most homecoming soldiers find it difficult to talk and explain, Ernest especially so. Men who have been in battle rarely find it easy to pass on their experiences or their feelings. It is simply not possible to describe the terror and violence of action without appearing to exaggerate and brag, so it is better to say nothing at all. Those who boast the most are the ones who have done and seen the least. Every regiment has its share of braggarts, or 'canteen cowboys' as they are known, but they are usually the shirkers or back-room boys who like to make out that they were there.

Those who *were* there; the ones who had seen the horrors never talk except amongst themselves – only when those across the table know what it is all about. How could a sister or younger brother ever understand? What would they think if they were to know that he, their own brother, had shot and killed not once but several times; that he had seen men and horses mutilated beyond description and witnessed the miserable tragedy of the Boer families and homesteads?

Ernest remained silent. He clammed up, shrugged his shoulders and muttered something indecipherable before getting to his feet and going outside. His mind would have been in turmoil. Was he supposed to be proud of what he had done or was he ashamed of fighting these farmers who were only trying to defend themselves and their way of life? Did he enjoy it all or did the memories sicken him? These thoughts would have passed through his mind yet, in his case, there remained something of an enigma about the strange story of his rifle.

And yet, in spite of this, he would have wanted to talk; he needed to. It would not have been long before he missed the close, claustrophobic camaraderie of the troop. Deep and lasting friendships would have been forged on the veldt. The rough, spartan lifestyle where privacy was non-existent and danger ever-present would have bound them together. They would have done everything together, shared everything between themselves from the last few mouthfuls of stew to the last pipe bowl of tobacco, even the contents of the occasional letter from home.

Suddenly and inexplicably he would have missed it all and longed for their company where he could relax and talk freely. To have to stay silent like this was difficult and he would have hankered after their company. Some would have kept well clear of it all, eager to put it out of their minds, but he missed his comrades just as he found he missed the strangely comforting harsh routine and rigid discipline of regimental soldiering. He was always to feel this way and later returned year after year to the Barnstaple reunions with the Old Comrades.

* *

Once they had finished their short disembarkation leave they were recalled to Ebberley Lawn barracks where their clothing and equipment were withdrawn. It is impossible to explain how or why Bawden managed to keep hold of his rifle – someone had slipped up badly, and the armoury book of registered weapon numbers would have made interesting reading!

That same day they were called forward one at a time to the adjutant's office and given three options. Either they could discharge themselves from the Army and return home free of any further military obligation, or they could sign on for a further period of service – in effect become a regular soldier – or they could revert to their original status as part-time soldiers in the Hussars. The choice was theirs.

Both Ernest and Harris Heywood chose the third option. Ernest's military service record (his Army Form B.111) showed that his original engagement was terminated on 12 September 1901 some ten weeks after they disembarked at Southampton. He was, however, an excellent soldier – his performance under fire and double promotion to full corporal unequivocal proof of that– and, in spite of all he had been through, he really did love the life. He took easily to the discipline and rigours of barrack life and excelled at both marksmanship and equitation.

Many of his personal qualities and skills seemed tailor-made for life as a soldier and for evermore he was to remain something of a military martinet, a feature that was to manifest itself more clearly in the years ahead. He had been a soldier for a relatively short time, yet his experiences – in both peace and war – forged his character. He began to set impossibly high standards for himself and others, developing a fierce pride in ensuring they were maintained. He became focussed (Pendry and Durrant again), determined to succeed at whatever the cost.

Nothing showed this more clearly than his fastidious attention to his dress and appearance, and his obsession with punctuality – both his own and that of others. He had learned to respect authority, yet never was he to become ingratiating or obsequious, and was soon to display a scant disregard for those who failed to give of their best. But it was in the hunting field that his meticulous attention to detail was to later pay such handsome dividends. The late Captain Ronnie Wallace always claimed that organisation, the Big 'O' as he called it, made or broke a hunt.[2] Ernest began to organise his life, living his days in an orderly, regulated fashion; he became a stickler for rigid discipline, leaving nothing to chance.

For a while he remained a Yeoman and his career went from strength to strength. That year he was awarded his National Commemorative Medal for service in South Africa then, three years later, he won promotion to sergeant, progressing remarkably swiftly from humble trooper to that coveted rank. Almost immediately he was awarded his Imperial Yeomanry Long Service and Good Conduct medal (L.S.G.C.). The Long Service medal was instituted in 1904, the year he left to join the kennels. The medal, mounted on a gold ribbon, was awarded only to those who had shown exemplary service and less than two thousand were awarded nationwide.

Success, though, had come at a cost. He had suffered badly from typhoid in South Africa and although he recovered enough to lead a fully active life, his intestines had been damaged. The affliction was to cause him almost permanent discomfort and was to worsen as time went on, occasionally limiting his mobility severely. More of this later but it is interesting to reflect upon the uncanny initial observation of the graphologist, Barry Pendry, when he first read Ernest's letters.

Ernest attended camps and training weekends whenever possible, riding into Barnstaple first from Hawkridge and later from Exford. On 9 August 1902, the regiment was ordered to furnish a guard of honour at the coronation of H.M. King Edward VIIth. The original strength to be found was for two officers and twenty-four from each regiment but numbers were later reduced to just one officer and nine other ranks.

The Royal North Devon Hussars had now reached a strength of five hundred and fifty all up and competition for such an honour was fierce. Ernest, time and again the champion horseman and with a fine war record, would have been an automatic choice for this select body and this was the case. The whole parade was commanded by Lord Ebrington, now Honorary Colonel of the Regiment as well as Chairman of the Devon and Somerset Staghounds, and Ernest (then still a corporal) would have been second or third in command of the chosen few from Ebberley Lawn barracks. It is interesting to note that, at this time, the North Devon regiment *alone* contained no less than nine past or present Masters of Hounds.

Camp that year was regarded as a modest affair, nonetheless over two hundred and fifty officers and men of the Royal North Devons spent the three weeks under canvas high on Exmoor at a bleak spot known as Blackmoor Gate. On one of the exercises the Commanding Officer despatched a flying column of eight officers and two hundred men to ride through the night. They camped the following day at Simonsbath then rode on, their objective being the camp of the West Somerset Imperial Yeomanry. The opposition was encamped near Minehead, a position the R.N.D.H. attacked and whose line they breached before riding back triumphant across the moor.

Witnessing something in the region of four hundred fully armed cavalrymen clashing on the heights of Exmoor in mock battle must have been an astonishing spectacle. One is led to wonder what the hunting field would have made of it all were hounds about that morning, or what might have been the reaction of some lonely shepherd on his pony as rank upon rank of cavalry loomed out of the dawn mist, their horses snorting and their saddlery jingling and slapping.

It was, however, no more than a dying ember of an era that was soon to pass. Economy was biting hard into the flanks of the horse-mounted Yeomanry but, more to the point, so was modern technology. The old regiments were to soldier on for a number of years but the age of the horse in battle was coming to an end. Ernest, Harris Heywood and their comrades in arms had seen all but the last of mounted warfare. The shell and the machine gun, barbed wire and the aeroplane were to put paid to the age of such chivalry.

* *

In 1901, when Ernest was twenty-three, he was a man in his prime. He was single, good-looking and with a fiercely independent air about him, and he had money in his pocket. Most of their South African pay came to them as a one-off back payment for which he would have received something in the region of £100 for his eighteen months service.[3] He had a comfortable home and there was no more nonsense from his brothers and sisters; the tough, battle-hardened soldier was a very different proposition to the lonely little boy that used to get in their way all those years ago.

However, and to be fair, his long break from home had healed many of the childhood family rifts, just as it does with so many families. He grew closer to his parents, his elder brother James offered him a job at his livery stables in Exford and the quarrels with Frank and Jessie, even John, were forgotten. It was altogether a much improved situation, yet the old wounds had left their mark.

He was helping out on the farm between bouts of military training with the R.N.D.H., he was riding the moors again and it was not long before he was back in racing colours. None of his old dash or skill had deserted him and on 24 August, less than two months after disembarking at Southampton, he again won The Farmers' Plate at the Devon and Somerset point-to-point, this time at Hawkcombe Head and on his own newly-acquired pony "Beeswing". He won again at a point-to-point meeting near Minehead and then twice more at Ashwick where the Hussars were at camp.

As soon as Autumn staghunting began he would have been out with his father, no doubt meeting up with many of the officers and comrades from the regiment. There would have been others too, any number of Exmoor friendships from the past would have been rekindled. Harris Heywood and others would have been there also but now there was somebody else – another Heywood had come into his life. Elizabeth-Ann, Harris's younger sister and a face he would have remembered well, was living with her family at nearby Winsford.

Ernest, as quiet and retiring as ever, took his time but eventually they met alone and the courtship began. Such matters were difficult to arrange when there were so many family members about – for the Heywoods, like the Bawdens, were a family of ten, Elizabeth-Ann also the sixth in line. But, in spite of potential problems, the friendship took hold and blossomed.

Later that year, Ernest took up his brother's offer of work, leaving Hollowcombe for ever and moving to Exford where James managed The White Horse Hotel and the livery stables behind. He was given free board and his lodgings were a small room at the back of the hotel, not many hundreds of yards away from the Devon and Somerset stables and kennels. From his bedroom window he would have been able to hear the hounds singing and from the stable yard he would have caught sight of the hunt whenever they crossed the bridge over the River Exe less than a hundred yards away.

The two brothers had always got on well together and Ernest set to work with a will, determined to make a go of it. But sadly, and in spite of all his grand ideas, James remained the same lovable but weak and wholly irresponsible man that ever he was. He still carried his heart on his sleeve and allowed drink and cards to become his masters, all profit from his fledgling business either poured away or pushed across the table to those with sharper minds and clearer heads.

The brothers struggled on, turning out horses on which visitors would ride to hounds but it was not long before the business was in trouble and James came to him. A loan was arranged and the one hundred pounds of his hard-earned wages as a soldier were handed over on nothing more than a handshake (an act of folly which Ernest never forgot). For the moment he was prepared to trust his elder brother but, were he to know it, he was never to see a penny of his money again. That was for the future but, right now, life was beginning to look up and Elizabeth-Ann, a bright and comely young woman of the same age, was happy to accept his advances. Their courtship developed.

Ernest moved cautiously. Seeking to avoid as much attention as possible they arranged to meet in secret, high on Winsford Hill, as far away as possible from the multitude of preying eyes and village gossip. It was a wild and desolate spot, close to the crest of a windswept ridge where a group of gnarled and bent trees crowded together as if to seek shelter from the elements.

The rendezvous they chose was the same spot as a Celtic chieftan had selected almost two thousand years earlier when he set into the ground a great stone as a memorial to King Caractacus. Caractacus, a forbear of his, had fought valiantly against the might of the Roman legions before he was captured and paraded through Rome in chains in A.D 51. *"Carataci Nepus"* was the name engraved on the stone recalling the valour of the King of Silures and it was here that the lovers chose to meet. Elizabeth-Ann either walked the two miles or rode up on a farm pony while Ernest, for whom the distance was much further, borrowed one of his brother's horses.

The Caratacus Stone, as it is known, is set in a beautiful spot high on the Exmoor hills and it is difficult to imagine a more romantic setting for their courtship. Ernest, as immaculate as always, would have ridden out in his best clothes or perhaps, if he had been away soldiering, came dressed as a sergeant of the Hussars, while Elizabeth-Ann, her long, dark hair ruffled by the breeze and her cloak wrapped round her for warmth, waited expectantly for her man. They would have been quite on their own, just the wild ponies and moorland birds for company.

For two years and more they lived like this. Ernest at the stables, trying desperately to see his brother through crisis after crisis, would have stolen away every now and then to hunt or race. Meanwhile Elizabeth-Ann, their courtship still a secret, would have kept her own counsel, quietly waiting for matters to develop as she was confident they would. They met whenever possible, easy enough during the summer months but difficult in winter when the nights were long and the stables were working hard while hunting was in progress.

There were, however, others who had noticed Ernest's proximity to the kennels. Sir Robert Sanders, by now a Major and Second-in-Command of the Royal North Devons had been Master of Hounds since before the war. If he had not noticed Ernest earlier (and almost certainly he would have done) he would know him well by now.

In all probability he would have won money on him at the military races as well as seeing him time and again in the hunting field, no doubt seeking his advice on which way the deer had gone or the best line for him to take across the soft ground. Lord Ebrington, soon to become the Fourth Lord Fortescue, would most certainly have known him, and very well too, having been his Commanding Officer at the Coronation procession two years earlier.

Finally, Sidney Tucker, now huntsman, would have recognised him. Not only would Ernest have been known to them all, he would have been highly regarded as a horseman as well. The current whipper-in, Fred Barber, had been forced to resign through ill health and the hunt was on the lookout for a suitable replacement. The three of them would have discussed the matter.

Bawden, so it seemed, possessed all the right credentials and they needed to search no further than a few yards down the road. It was Major Sir Robert Sanders, the Master himself, who went around the back of The White Horse and into the stable yard. The 1903/4 season was just finishing and the new man would be able to move straight into the kennels.

The pay was around a pound a week plus the roof over his head together with coal, wood and lamp oil. "Would you like to consider it?" the Master asked. For Ernest Bawden it was the moment he had been waiting for. It was the start of a great, new adventure – a new way of life – and he took the job there and then.

For the Devon and Somerset Staghounds, however, it was to be the beginning of a whole new era, an era never to be surpassed in the long history of the hunt. In fact it has been widely accepted by field sport commentators of the day that the staghounds and staghunting on Exmoor was to become the finest hunting that could be found in the country – perhaps among the finest of all time.

Notes

1. Recollections of Mr Percy Bawden.
2. Captain R.E. Wallace. Exmoor archives CD.
3. *A Rough Diary*, Lt Col P.J.Browne C.B.

Chapter 8

HUNTING THE DEER

Exmoor, in 1904, the year Ernest Bawden was asked to join the hunt, remained very much a far-off and forgotten corner of the land. Roads, such as existed, had improved but the rugged landscape and uncertain weather dissuaded all but the most determined and adventurous visitors. Victorian technology had taken its time to filter that far west. Years earlier the advent of the railways had laid bare the English countryside yet the high moorlands, remote and sparsely populated, had escaped such indignities.

By 1880 lines from Taunton had reached Barnstaple and Minehead; ten years later further inroads had been made from Exeter to Dulverton while, from Barnstaple, a thin finger had crept out as far as Lynton. Civilisation, if that is what it was, had surrounded the moors like the incoming tide encircles a rock. The few local roads 'up over the top' remained little more than tracks. Exmoor, like the rock, remained proud and unconquered.

It was as if the modern world stopped at the stationmaster's office. Visitors would alight onto the platform behind the smoke and hissing steam then struggle through the ticket office to emerge at the edge of a world time had passed by. In those days there was no motor transport to meet them. Further movement was on foot or, if they were lucky enough to be met, by horse, pulling either cab or cart, or as a simple beast of burden. There was no electricity to lighten the darkness of the Westcountry streets, neither were there telephones or other methods of communication. Once the carriage doors had clanked shut and the train had gone, a silence and sense of calm returned.

1904 was still a very long time ago. A government paper that year concluded that rural lunacy was on the increase, a fact, according to the authors, due entirely to the tedium of life in the countryside. True or not life in the south west remained hardy and backward – primitive even – compared to life further up the line where the first mainline electric train had begun to run from Liverpool to Southport, and where Mr Rolls had just met Mr Royce.

* *

Ernest Bawden could count himself fortunate that he had caught the eye of the hunt. Life with the staghounds would be a challenge but it was a prestigious post and he wasted no time.

He and Elizabeth-Ann decided to get married before the new season began at the end of July – it was now early May. The accommodation they had been offered was sparse and they needed to get themselves established while there was still time. As he severed his links with brother James at The White Horse so he asked for his loan to be repaid, but there was nothing. James was heavily in debt. Unbeknown to his brother, he had arranged a further loan from his father through the South Molton solicitor Frederic Day for more than twice the amount he owed Ernest. His Exford property had been mortgaged as security and the larger debt would have to be attended to first. Ernest would have to wait.

Time was against them and a family church wedding was beyond their means, so they went instead to the Registry Office in Dulverton. It was a strange decision, by no means popular with other members of the two God-fearing families. Even allowing for the difficult situation in which they found themselves such behaviour was not readily accepted.

But for Ernest it seemed the obvious solution. He hated the limelight and would have relished the chance to avoid being the centre of what he saw as unnecessary attention. Later, and when at the peak of his fame, he learned to accept such interest but he never found it easy and most certainly not now. Furthermore he was not a regular church-goer, thus the simpler and less fussy civil ceremony appealed to him.

Elizabeth-Ann obliged and on 21 June 1904 they became man and wife. The ceremony was witnessed by Ernest's father but Elizabeth-Ann was represented by Frederick, one of her elder brothers, rather than by her father. There is no further record of the occasion neither are there any photographs – by now a popular novelty. With the opening meet of the 1904/5 season a little more than a month away they moved immediately into the semi-detached cottage at the kennels, the new Mrs Bawden now very much part of the team.

Not only was she to demonstrate remarkable fortitude in her role as wife to her husband but was soon to become the unpaid and unsung member of the kennel team. She was bright and well-educated at Edgehill boarding school in Bideford, thus more than capable of maintaining the records and kennel accounts. She played her full part with the hounds as well, generations of the less fortunate ones, either weakling puppies or veterans wounded in the hunting field, owed their lives to her nursing skills. Rarely was her hearth free of a straw-lined box of tiny whelps or her kitchen free of hounds looking sorry for themselves.

The marriage itself was to prove enduring. Ernest, for all his volatility and the high-profile career he had elected to pursue, quite rightly (and very sensibly) placed his long-suffering Elizabeth-Ann high on a pedestal. "Missus", as she became known to him and him alone, quietly ruled the home, her husband never attempting to challenge her position of authority, as he was to do with so many who crossed his path.

Quietly spoken, unruffled and unflappable, Elizabeth-Ann remained both central and essential to his life, a fact he undoubtedly recognised. He, in turn, although demonstrations of affection never came easily, adored her and remained faithful to her throughout their long marriage.

* *

It is impossible to delve further into his career without looking briefly at the life surrounding a successful hunt a century ago, and a pack of staghounds in particular. There are many differences between hunting the fox and the deer and not every reader will be familiar with all that is necessary to appreciate the extent of Ernest Bawden's greatness.

Even the simple mechanics of such a profession are difficult to assimilate, while the traditions and rituals, reaching back into the mists of time and couched often in mystery and mythology, seem barely comprehensible to the onlooker; the more so if he is a city dweller. *"A man that has never tried his hand with hounds has not the slightest conception of the undertaking."* So wrote R.S. Surtees in 1845,[1] an axiom that remains as true today as it did then.

The ways of a hunt are bound by knowledge, tradition and skill. Routine, organisation and regimentation are the bywords, points emphasised time and again by the likes of Ronnie Wallace. The huntsman reigns supreme in his kennels, controlling the duties of his whips, the kennelmen and any other labour employed by the hunt. He is responsible directly to his Master for the high standards and good organisation of the place in which up to one hundred hounds (known as "fifty couple" in hunting parlance) live. It is a responsibility equal in importance to ensuring the performance of the pack in the hunting field.

A further responsibility, and something not always appreciated, is that of selecting and preparing hounds for breeding. Every hunt should know exactly what is required for their own particular country and make a concerted effort to establish their own bloodline. Buying-in hounds or accepting drafts from elsewhere is a stop-gap method of quality control for there is nothing like one's own well-proven genes – hounds bred to do a particular job. Every hunting country possesses subtle yet discernibly different requirements.

The Master, most easily described in today's commercial parlance as the Chief Executive, is answerable to the Chairman of the Hunt Committee for the running of the pack and for its good name among the community throughout its hunting "country." The respect shown by the great Hugo Meynell, Tom Firr's Master of the Quorn, for the yeomen and farmers of his country was legendary. A note penned by him would invariably accompany the Secretary with his compensation for the damage or inconvenience suffered by landowners, and he was forever holding up hounds at the gate of some farmer whose presence he had not seen in the field and whom he judged would now be hurrying to join them.

"Oh ye Masters of Hounds," Nimrod cried. *"In your haste, bear this in mind! This is the way to preserve your country!"* Meynell, and others like him, not only looked after their own followers but appreciated that not everybody welcomed

their hounds. Much time and trouble was taken over those who, for whatever reason, felt this way. It was a matter those bygone Masters of hounds considered to be well worth the effort.

Diplomacy and public relations were important in those days; a matter fully understood later by Colonel Walter Wiggin when he became Master of the Devon and Somerset and later still by Colonel Michael Murphy. Today, when the eyes and ears of both public and media remain ever-open and tuned finely towards the hunting fraternity, such qualities are more important than ever.

The appointment of Master is high profile and prestigious. He is very much in the public eye whether he likes it or not. It is to him that this same public will turn either for their sport or, more likely, to air their grievances about any matters for which they hold the hunt responsible. To be successful at his job, a Master needs vision and understanding – compassion even – and should aim to spend almost as much time among the sensitive and egalitarian society who live in his country as he does enjoying himself in the hunting field.

Today, indifference to the views of the general public will be interpreted as insensitive and arrogant; ignorance dismissed as inexcusable. He may claim that he has a staff to do this for him but that is not good enough; furthermore, he may find himself surrounded by members of the hunt fraternity who choose to tell him only what he wants to hear. This is dangerous for it must be his own antennae that are tuned constantly towards the public at large.

He must be right on top of his own public relations; it is an exercise that is constant and ongoing. Anything less and the support that is so essential to the hunt will simply ebb away. The lot of the Master, while it may seem glamorous to those who follow the fortunes of the hunt, is a difficult one, made easier only when he can call upon the services of a diligent and perceptive Hunt Secretary.

Just as important to the Master as his kennels are his hunt stables. Hunts vary in size but usually between ten and thirty horses are kept (in those days the D and S had twenty-four). They are the responsibility of the stud groom or head lad and his staff. The huntsman and stud groom should work closely together, their combined efforts bearing directly on the performance of the hunt for whose good name they must both willingly give all. Disloyalty and self-seeking, such plagues in modern society, have no place in the hunting world.

* *

The whipper-in, which Ernest had just become, is the huntsman's assistant and understudy both in the kennels and in the hunting field.[2] When Ernest arrived he was the only whipper-in. Later there were two, a more usual practise which remains to this day.

It is a job which the successful man might expect to do for years, either until he was offered the horn on the retirement of the huntsman, or he moved elsewhere, or until he was passed over for one younger and more competent. Just as now, the whip played a key role in both field and kennel where the highest of standards were demanded; no Master would tolerate sloppy behaviour or incompetence. The man would be removed forthwith and the authority to do so would lie with the Master who would have been nearer to the case, rather than with the more distant Hunt Committee.

Back in 1904 there was no route to appeal for unfair dismissal and, once out, no unemployment or housing benefit. Competition would have been fierce as well. Many hunt servants came from families who had served for generations, others were selected from kennelmen, grooms or second horsemen whose eyes and ears were ever open for the opportunity to present itself.

While the roles of both men may be seen as complementing one another and whose breakdown of duties frequently overlap, it is said that a good whip rarely makes a good huntsman, something argued persuasively by Surtees and Nimrod.[1] It often goes, claimed Surtees, that there is better sport and more kills with a moderate huntsman and an excellent whip than with the best of huntsman who has no such (excellent) assistant.

Sometimes this might be the case but the vast majority of huntsmen have secured their appointment only by proving their worth year in, year out beforehand as whipper-in. Which Master, in his right mind, would not reach out for the most successful understudy he could find when choosing a replacement for his huntsman?

Such generalities apply to both foxhunting and staghunting and are confined principally to life in the kennels. Certain duties in the hunting field are similar, of course, but there are differences as well, a number of them significant. There are many who think – and there are some who do not bother to think at all – that staghunting is similar to foxhunting and that it is nothing more than a bigger, and perhaps longer, event. Not so.

Practically everything imaginable (except their wild status) about the fox and deer is different. While the deer are gregarious creatures of habit, the fox is a loner who lives on his wits. One is vermin, the other game. The breeding habits and social behaviour differ markedly as do their daily and annual life cycles. One could go on but the point is obvious and has been made.

The wild red deer of Exmoor belong to nobody save the person on whose land they stand. There are no official guardians of the herd (as there were in days gone by), nobody attends to their needs, neither does anyone exercise control over their numbers. Today the herd totals around three thousand head.[3] They roam free and eat whatever comes their way but nobody pays compensation to the farmers and landowners for this huge bill of fare or the damage done to fences and crops.

Nobody cares at all; nobody, that is, save for the three packs of Westcountry staghounds[4] in whose interest it is that this healthy and well-maintained herd is preserved. Visitors flock to Exmoor in their thousands, delighted to see the wild deer roaming free yet very few of them ever pause to consider how or why it is that they are there and in such abundance.

The existence of these beautiful creatures is thus entirely in the hands of farmers and landowners, and of the hunt itself. All are dependant upon one another for the maintenance of a healthy herd and without their combined efforts the deer would die out, trapped and shot as vermin or poached for venison. It is as though a great network of goodwill covers the moor like a protective blanket. The people of Exmoor know that the fate of the herd is in their hands. They live among the deer and are fiercely proud of what they have been able to achieve.

At the centre of it all lies the hunt and it is through this great web of support and information that it is able to set about its business in a proper manner. The deer they hunt are either killed cleanly or they escape scot-free and go on their way unharmed. There are no half measures – wounding or maiming – as with the gun. No matter how expert the marksman may profess to be he can never guarantee to kill swiftly and cleanly in the wild.

Wounded deer hide themselves away, the horrors of gunshot wounds thus out of sight and out of mind to those who advocate such methods of control. Were the crippled animals to be seen by the public or were they to howl in pain there would be an instant outcry, the crass stupidity of such action immediately apparent. It is this single, stark and inescapable fact – proven time and again down the years – that those who decry hunting either cannot or do not wish to digest.

The deer are hunted throughout most of the year, the three seasons running almost one into the next. First, and beginning at the end of July, Autumn stags are hunted. This is followed in November, after a short break, by hindhunting which goes on until the end of February when Spring staghunting takes over until the end of April. The three seasons, with only May, June and July as close, last for almost nine months rather than the five or so of foxhunting.

* *

The stag to be hunted – one of the right age and known as the warrantable stag – is selected with care, while hinds are taken more or less as they are found, as is the case with the fox. It is here that the principal difference between the two types of hunting – and thus the duties of the hunt servants – becomes apparent. The identification and selection process requires immense skill and a deep understanding of deer. Only very few possess the knowledge and field craft that has taken a lifetime to accumulate – the Highland ghillie or native tracker are the nearest equivalents. On Exmoor such a man is known as the harbourer.

He, through his understanding of the deer, his familiarity with the ground, his stalking skills and his patience, as well as his knowledge of venery, identifies a suitable stag. Once found, the harbourer must keep a close eye on its whereabouts and report his findings to the Master at the meet. His final task is to help the huntsman identify the animal, perhaps lying in thick cover and in the company of several others, then help him to rouse up the beast and set him on his way.

In his excellent book,[5] Fred Goss, arguably the greatest harbourer of all time, states that it was his policy to find a stag as near to the meet as possible, to select one he considered easy to dig out of his bed, and one that was lying as near as possible to the line of a good run – deer often taking traditional lines across country. How easy this sounds and yet how difficult it is to achieve!

Goss writes about no less than *seventy-two* points he looks for in identifying the presence of deer – many of which are ambiguous or even contradictory. Most are visual, either of the deer itself or the impressions of its slots (hoofs) in the ground. The size and shape of the slot mark will vary according to the soil in which it is imprinted and the weather (rain or wet ground blur the edges of the impression).

Irrespective of this the harbourer must be able to tell the age, weight, sex and health of the animal by the slot marks in addition to whether it is a woodland or forest (moorland) deer. He must be able to say how long ago the animal passed that way and whether or not it has moved on or has remained in the covert. Finally he must be able to pinpoint the exact location of that particular deer within the covert. It is indeed a job requiring immense skill and one where accuracy and honesty are so important.

It is a job best done at dawn or dusk when the animals come out to feed. It is a lonely job that has to go on whatever the weather, the harbourer forever dreading the day when he cannot find a suitable beast for the hunt. Deer, as Goss remarked ruefully, appear to have a divine sixth sense for impending danger: what was there for certain the night before so often had long gone by dawn.

* *

As soon as he has reported his findings to the Master at the meet the two of them then confer with the huntsman as to the best plan of action. Ernest Bawden and his Master – Colonel Walter Wiggin – always went one stage further, plotting for hours together by lamplight in the huntsman's cottage the night before. So determined were they that nothing should be left to chance, every possible option for the following day was discussed and plans made before they ever knew what the harbourer had in store for them. He, the harbourer, would be many miles away by this time, enjoying the hospitality of some friendly farmer and his family, preparing to rise long before dawn in order to complete his task.

At the meet Ernest used to wait impatiently for the Master to summon him to join them, eager to hear about what had been harboured and perhaps a touch jealous of the harbourer's few minutes of private consultation with his Master. Once the Master was happy with the plan for the draw, the pack, usually numbering twenty or so couple, were then kennelled at a nearby farm (today they are kennelled on the hunt lorry, ready to be deployed by road if necessary).

It is at this point that a small number of "tufters" – five and a half or six and a half couple of hounds – are drawn from the pack.[6] These hounds, hard working, experienced and sagacious, but above all obedient, then go with the huntsman and harbourer to draw through the area where the stag is known to be. It is up to this small team to identify and rouse up the deer and to force him from cover. Much more of this later when the analysis of Ernest Bawden's diaries will show how he set about this difficult task.

Once the selected deer is on its way the pack are fetched and 'laid on' to the line. The hunt is now underway. The scent of a deer is far stronger than that of a fox and a well-hunted pack of hounds can run anything up to an hour or more behind their quarry whereas ten or fifteen minutes is long enough for the line of a fox. The reaction of the deer will be addressed in the later chapters when, again, Bawden's skill will be examined. However, a number of points need to be borne in mind.

First, the animal does not rush off in a wild panic. More than likely his progress appears to be little more than a nonchalant saunter, the hunted deer frequently stopping and starting and very often running deliberately into others. It is up to the huntsman to keep the pack on to the right beast, to force him away from the herd and onto a specific line.

And this is the second point. Whereas a fox might occasionally take a well known line, it will be more likely to select whatever course the situation demands, knowing exactly what is afoot and making for the safety of his earth or a distant badger's sett. Deer, on the other hand, often (but by no means always) selects a particular line frequently using the wind to their advantage. Ernest's hunting diaries show that the hunted animal will be most likely to run into the wind. On occasion though it will run with it and even across it – the huntsman can take nothing for granted.

Third, and this is difficult for the foxhunter to appreciate, is the length of the chase. Many runs have lasted for three hours or more covering distances of 12 miles as the crow flies but 20 or 30 – more sometimes – as hounds ran. If that is not enough, the rise and fall of the steep Exmoor combes, sometimes totalling thousands of feet in all, should be considered as well. For this the hunt staff each use two or three, sometimes even four, horses.

Ernest Bawden once used five. On one occasion when his horse was "cooked", he took up an offer of the mount from a lady who was riding side-saddle and was still there at the end. On another, he rode into the kill on a horse borrowed from the Dulverton Foxhounds into whom they had all bumped in the middle of the chase.

Sooner or later the deer will run to water. It makes for water quite deliberately either when it is tired or when it decides to throw off the pack. It will either lie low in a deep pool in an attempt to evade its pursuers or else it will move up or down stream, perhaps for as much as a mile or more, before emerging again and continuing on its way. Having studied the *hunted* deer since early childhood, Ernest well understood all this. Even by the time he came into hunt service he knew the deer better than most and it was a subject he was to study for thirteen long seasons more as whipper-in. When, finally, he came to carry the horn his knowledge of the hunted deer was in a class of its own.

The end of the chase comes when the stag can run no more and turns to face the pack – it is "at bay". The occasions Bawden recorded of hounds savaging their quarry during his thirty-three years hunt service are very few and far between.[7] He took it as his bounden duty to get there quickly and regarded such rare instances when he did not manage this as a personal failure. Usually the hounds are disinclined to close with the stag, preferring to stand off and bay until the huntsman arrives. So quick was Ernest across the countryside that he usually arrived with the pack and, almost inevitably, way ahead of the field.

Today the animal is despatched instantly with a folding twelve bore shotgun, firing S.S.G.[8] at point blank range. It was not ever thus. In Bawden's day he dismounted and went in after the deer with a short-bladed hunting knife. It was a highly dangerous business. Sometimes alone and unaided, often struggling through icy, turbulent water way above his knees and with his boots slipping on the rocks it was man against beast. A big Autumn stag, the size of a pony and using the great sweep of his antlers with murderous intent, presented a formidable opponent. To close with such a beast fighting for its life called for courage of the highest order.

Ernest was once gored badly in the leg above the knee. On another occasion, the cornered stag charged his horse before he had dismounted, goring the animal in the flank and thigh. In order to kill quickly and cleanly the huntsman had to plunge his knife into the base of the throat just above the breastbone where the blade would sever the jugular and cut off the blood supply to the brain.[9]

It was a small target, little bigger than a clenched first and, to be sure of success, the huntsman had to get very close indeed, the two of them eyeball to eyeball, breathing each other's breath. Death was almost instantaneous. Ernest insisted on the animal being dealt with quickly and often sought the assistance of those who were there, either by getting them to lasso the antlers with a short rope he carried or by somehow holding on to the stag's head. There was no glory or ceremony about it, every effort was made to get the job done properly. He later wrote of his disgust when those with the gun failed to make a clean job of it.

The above, no more than a brief sketch, alludes to a number of the principal differences between stag and fox hunting and to the problems likely to be encountered by the huntsman and his whipper-in. It also hints at the skills required to get the chase underway and then, once on the move, to keep it that way. Eva Dunbar (back in chapter one) wrote of what it took to make a great huntsman. What she had to say about the foxhunter is just as relevant to the staghunter.

Ernest Bawden already possessed many of Eva Dunbar's essential qualities. One of his great advantages was that, since early childhood, he had been able to study the craft of the huntsman and the battle of wits that took place between him and the deer. The early years at Hawkridge had made for an excellent apprenticeship which was to serve him well.

However, and this is an interesting point to consider, Ernest had no knowledge of or experience with hounds until he entered the kennels, and he was recruited at the relatively late age of twenty-six. Many huntsmen began their careers as kennel lad or second whip when still in their teens and, by the time they were Ernest's age, would have built up a close relationship with the pack. An affinity with the pack was *the most* essential quality of all – without a deep and mutual understanding between the hunter and his hounds there could be little chance of success.

It is a subject which must have taxed his mind severely for he would have long since appreciated that success in the hunting field must be due principally to the huntsman's ability to transmit his wishes to his pack. Furthermore, once engaged as a whip (and he was the only one), he had to understudy the huntsman; thus he had to get to know them well, every one of them, and without delay. Were tragedy to strike in the middle of a hunt or illness intervene, it would be his duty to take over the horn.

There would be no excuses if he were not to rise to the occasion including his ability with the horn itself. His life as a whip was going to be a demanding but essential step towards his life as a huntsman.

Notes

1. *The Analysis of the Hunting Field.* R.S.Surtees.
2. Captain E.R.Lloyd. President of The Devon and Somerset Staghounds.
3. Official Devon and Somerset Hunt figures.
4. The Devon and Somerset, The Quantock and The Tiverton Staghounds.
5. *Memories of a Stag Harbourer.*
6. A legend which has now become a tradition in that an *odd* number of tufters are always used (in this case eleven or thirteen). And why? Because, so the story goes, it is always that one *odd* tufter which finds the deer.
7. Hunting Diaries of the D and S (1917–1937).
8. The cartridge contains just a few ball-bearing sized pellets designed to kill larger than usual game, hence S.S.G.
9. The animal lost consciousness almost immediately as the flow of blood to the brain was terminated, after which death came painlessly.

Chapter 9

Servants of the Hunt

Saturday 30 July, 1904. Molland Moor Gate.

"It is nine o'clock of a fine, bright morning.........all eyes are centred upon the new whipper-in, Ernest Bawden, wearing the scarlet and silver for the first time."

So wrote the ubiquitous "Ware Heel!" then hunting correspondent of the West Somerset Free Press.

* *

The huntsman in 1904 was Sidney Tucker. He was not an Exmoor man but had begun service in the kennels as second horseman in 1885, when Ernest was just seven and riding to hounds whenever he could. In 1890 he was appointed whipper-in before finally succeeding Anthony Huxtable in October 1901.

By the time Ernest became whip, Sidney Tucker had already established for himself a reputation as one of the very best to have carried the horn for the Devon and Somerset. This reputation was to continue. He was a great huntsman;[1] a better example and mentor Ernest could not have found, but neither could he have come across a more difficult act he would one day have to follow.

The Master at this time was Major Sir Robert Sanders – of the R.N.D.H. – who was later to become Lord Bayford. He was more than satisfied with his huntsman and, once he had secured the services of Ernest as whip, must have known that his pack of hounds was in good hands. Indeed so, but Sidney Tucker and Ernest Bawden were two very strong characters.

It was a brilliant combination – the deer had no chance said many – but the relationship was not always easy. Cohesion in such a tight–knit community, rather than dissension was essential but the two were to have their differences. It was none other than the huntsman who pressed Ernest to resign from the Yeomanry claiming, quite rightly, that there was not enough time to do both jobs properly. It was a decision that hurt, for Ernest's pride as a soldier remained as strong as ever and it would have been with a heavy heart that he rode into Barnstaple to sign off.

Life began quietly. Ernest knew he had much to learn and worked hard and willingly, spending as much time as he could with the hounds. The pack of the day was fit and of excellent individual quality but they were an assorted group. The hunt had made little or no effort to breed their own line in order to deal with the requirements of hunting deer on Exmoor. The Devon and Somerset had, for years, relied too often on drafts from other packs: the usual note attached to the collar being that the hound was too big for the country concerned and that the donors felt it would suit the needs of the D and S. It seemed an odd approach, and remarkably amateur, to the considerable problems presented by Exmoor and the deer.

Hounds had to be of a good size but not too big. Many held the mistaken belief that just because the deer was big and ran a long way, hounds had to be much bigger than usual in order to cope. There is an optimum size for dealing with the gruelling runs and steep climbs and the eventual shoulder height settled at around 23 inches.

It was stamina that was of the essence; stamina and tongue. Not only did a pack that ran mute lack flair but it became unmanageable when fog descended. Furthermore, hounds running silently were a menace once they disappeared into the deep V-shaped and thickly wooded combes where visibility became severely restricted by the trees and scrub. The hunt staff had to know where hounds were and what they were about. If they could not see them they had to hear them; the hounds needed to speak.

Mr E.A.V. Stanley, the wealthy and colourful Master who succeeded Lord Bayford, saw this and began to establish his own line but it takes time for the results to be proven and when, after just two seasons, he left to become Master of the Woodland Pytchley, his ideas were largely forgotten. Ernest, however, saw this need, appreciating at once the importance of the D and S breeding their own line.

He sought, in particular, hounds that would stick with the hunted deer rather than chopping and changing as so many imported ones tended to do. He knew it could be done and always considered there was something second best in having to accept drafts of hounds that were not wanted elsewhere, however generous such a gesture might have been. He was determined about the importance of breeding but was going to have to wait many years before he was given the chance.

During his short tenure, Stanley set about improving the quality of horses also. His predecessor had seen to it that he, his huntsman and the whip should each have three mounts but they had to be of the right calibre and suited to the terrain if they were to see the long days through. Before agreeing to a new purchase, each animal was tested severely by being ridden hard down the steepest hillside pell-mell.

It was a task entrusted to Ernest, who later claimed that no animal ever turned head over heels when ridden hard down over the steep, rather they would simply collapse or sit on their haunches and slide! He never sat back but always leant well forward over the withers, his body almost horizontal, the reins slack in his hands as his mount crouched momentarily before leaping forwards and onwards down the precipitous slopes.

Here, were any further evidence required, is another example of Ernest's superb – and quite fearless – horsemanship; an attribute that was later to enable to keep him in permanent touch with his pack if not the stag itself. Those who live on Exmoor and consider this an insignificant matter (perhaps claiming to do it as well themselves) should test their nerve on the high banks to the west of the Barle above Landacre Bridge or Cow Castle, or else on Exe Cleeve at Warren Farm. However, beware – the ground is very steep and Ernest rode very hard!

He never liked the larger horses used by the hunt, preferring instead an animal of less than 16 hands. He was a small man himself, never more than nine stone, and felt more comfortable on something akin to his stature. Of greater importance, though, he claimed that a smaller animal tended to be more sure-footed and easier to manage in the thick coverts into which he was bound to go. More than once he was swept from the saddle of a large horse when unable to duck beneath a low-hanging beech branch.

His favourite of all time was "Jenah" (his spelling), a wonderful little bay mare of scarcely 15 hands that was to serve him so well and whose deeds appeared in many a hunting article.[2] Understandable though his request was, his preference presented the stables with a problem for they liked to rotate the horses and if Ernest needed *one* smaller animal then he really needed five or six of them to see him through the season

There is no record of how he won the affection of the pack. All that can be said is that the hounds worshipped him. Such a deep affinity with dogs (or any animals) is a gift bestowed upon very few. It is a touch that many like to believe they possess on account of how happy the family pet appears to be with its luxurious standard of living and constant attention. There is, however, a world of difference between such a one-to-one relationship and that needed to win the trust of more than a hundred hounds, each one of whom possesses an entirely different character to its neighbour on the bench.

Just as with any large group of human beings, every hound is different. There will be the affectionate, the surly and suspicious, the garrulous and the shy. There will be those who are bold, timid, noisy or silent. Some will welcome attention, others draw back suspiciously. The whipper-in must, without fail, know each one by sight and recognise instantly the sound of its voice. He must understand each individual temperament both in kennels and in the field, where he must appreciate how and where they work best.

Not only this but he must win first their respect, then their obedience and finally their affection. It is indeed a long way away from the owner of the family pet who, on account of the much-pampered pooch wagging its tail and grinning mawkishly, believes he or she is a "doggy" person and has a way with animals.[3]

Ernest Bawden won over the pack, gaining its complete confidence and trust. He identified the strengths and weaknesses of each hound where this was important to stag hunting and began to select hounds from whom a suitable line might be bred. In the hunting field he held their undivided attention. Commentator after commentator watched this extraordinary affinity develop, none more so than George Scoins, the third horseman.

"They were putty in his hands and, in the field, as obedient as soldiers. He never used the whip and rarely raised his voice. They knew what he wanted to do and seemed desperate to please." Scoins recounted a party piece when Ernest would stand with his back to the pack and drop a piece of biscuit behind him. One hundred heads would be cocked in anticipation but not one dared move until he called them forward one at a time, each passing the tasty morsel but none seeking to snatch it up. Suddenly he would call out a name and a body would move through the pack to collect its reward.

It is difficult to appreciate fully the depth of this affinity between Ernest and his hounds. These were no circus animals neither were they some collection of trick-trained family pets whose bodies had been softened and senses dulled by domestication. They were a pack of hardened hunters, kept deliberately in sympathy with the wild rather than the civilisation around them. Lean, fit and hungry they answered to no man save the one they acknowledged as their master. Had any other huntsman attempted such a demonstration with his hounds there would have been a mad rush of bodies accompanied by a deep rumble of growls as they pressed forward to tussle over the scrap. Not so here.

This rapport between Ernest and the pack was the last and most crucial of the essential requirements – the bond which allowed him to communicate his intentions in such an uncanny fashion. The pack respected him, held him in awe (feared him almost) but adored him and would react instinctively to his voice and, later, his horn. As Scoins avowed, they *"were desperate to please"*.

Those who know their hunting will acknowledge that another great huntsman, Captain Ronnie Wallace, inspired such trust and devotion from his hounds. The young Wallace first hunted with the Devon and Somerset at the beginning of the 1930/31 season when he was a schoolboy of ten riding his pony "Bunty".[4] Years later, he would visit Ernest and they would sit for hours swapping stories. He regarded the staghunter's work with hounds as "pure genius".[5] *"All I can ever do,"* he remarked when in his prime as England's premier Master Huntsman, *"is to attempt to emulate his brilliance in the kennels and the hunting field."*

Wallace described the affinity between a huntsman and his hounds as an invisible string which is very fragile with some, a bit like a parcel string with others, and with a very, very few, as thick as a rope.[6] If you have that ability to interest dogs, he went on, you can be a huntsman. If you haven't, you should try another profession. Witnessing these two sitting together and chatting away as master and pupil would have been a moment to savour!

⁂

Ernest and Elizabeth-Ann settled easily into their new way of life. Friends and family were in abundance either in the village of Exford itself or within close proximity. On 28 October 1908, their first child – a son they christened Percival Ernest Heywood – arrived. Percy, as he became known, was to be their only child, a fact that remains a mystery, for both parents hailed from large families, each of whom in turn produced their own children.

Percy had no less than eighteen uncles and aunts (nine on either side) and an almost unbelievable tally of seventy-seven first cousins [7] yet he remained just the one. He is confident that there was no medical reason for this, neither anything more sinister rather that it was his parents' own choice and most likely that of his mother.[8]

Life was hard but good for the couple and Exford was a happy village. Ernest was secure in his job – indeed as the fame of his hounds spread, so he too became something of a local celebrity – yet they elected to have just the one child in the days when such a decision would have been regarded as the exception. The most likely reason was that Ernest could not forget his own miserable childhood in which he experienced the dangers inherent in a large family. Did he and Elizabeth-Ann, therefore, decide to limit the family or was it something deeper? Did Ernest, perhaps, retain some memories of his own childhood intimacies with his siblings that he would rather forget, or were his relations with Elizabeth-Ann somehow governed by past experiences?

As it was, Percy, the single child, grew up experiencing a lonely and largely unhappy early life. Although spared the abuse and violence his father knew, the boy never seemed able to fulfil his father's high expectations, often finding himself at the receiving end of sharp and, in his words, unjust exchanges. He had no interest in hunting, riding or other field sports, developing instead a keen and enquiring mind that led to a career in mechanical engineering; a subject his father knew nothing about. Ernest could never understand why his son failed to love hunting or what made him take that particular course through life. It grated and made for difficult times.

Happily, though, the boy loved his mother deeply and it is due to their close relationship that the rapport with his father never reached breaking point. She was forever the buffer and conciliator between the two. That said, early life around the kennels was as much of an adventure for the youngster as it would have been for any child and, even now, he is able to recall life in the whipper-in's lodgings.

His father, although rarely able to relax fully, nonetheless enjoyed his private moments. Early in life he had developed a love for music and had learned to play the violin. He would sit for hours in front of the parlour fire with "me fiddle" playing sentimental ballads and romantic pieces. On these occasions, Missus would disappear, preferring instead the confines of her kitchen or, better still, she would go visiting – leaving Percy to sit listening at his father's feet. Whenever he found the time, he read avidly, devouring anything to do with natural history, the military or the British Empire and everything but everything to do with hunting.

The Bawdens preferred the quiet life, entertaining and going out occasionally to family and friends. Sunday lunches were their favourites or whist drives in the evenings whenever time permitted. Neither smoked, and they drank only occasionally and when in the company of those they knew. Ernest made a point of shunning the local pubs and bars where he was afraid of being waylaid by the "the ne'er-do-wells and timewasters" as he referred to the regular customers.

He would have remembered only too well the many occasions during his childhood when the effects of drink struck hard but it is interesting to note that Nimrod saw alcohol as being the greatest vice, and thus the enemy, of hunt servants – an observation penned almost a hundred years earlier. As well as those who might wish to show their gratitude for a good day's sport, he wrote, there are always those who seek to ingratiate themselves with a successful hunt servant of a famous pack, bottle and glass being their calling cards.

However full his life now became, Ernest retained close links with the Yeomanry. He joined the Old Comrades, taking time off to attend the Regimental Reunions in Barnstaple, and became a stalwart of the veterans' shooting team. The National Rifle Association held its annual meeting at Bisley during the summer months when, as luck would have it, there was no hunting. He would take his short leave then and travel up to Surrey with the others for the competitions. It was there that he won the much coveted N.R.A. silver spoon for scoring the maximum possible at 500 yards on the famous Century Range.

Another annual favourite was the Aldershot Military Tattoo when a party of them would travel up and back in the same day, leaving long before dawn and returning before dawn the following morning. He became a founder member of the British Legion (now The Royal British Legion) when it was formed in 1921, attending meetings and reunions and making a particular point of marching proudly with them behind the banner and village band to St Mary Magdalene church on Remembrance Sundays. Those years in the R.N.D.H. had left their indelible marks more than ever, so it seemed; his appearance, bearing and manner was that of a military man.

Ernest was beginning to emerge as a popular and highly respected member of village society yet he still remained wary of too close an association with the church. His religious upbringing had been strict, his mother ensuring that regular attendance at St Giles' church in Hawkridge was both a discipline and duty, and regular attendance should have been second nature. Furthermore, the presence in church of someone who was now becoming a public figure would have been expected in the years before the first war and particularly in Exford, the home of the D and S.

Perhaps he had seen enough and valued too much his limited free time, electing to limit his presence to the great festivals of the calendar or when there were "proper" hymns on the service sheet, as he called them. "Onward Christian Soldiers", "Fight the Good Fight" and others of a military flavour appealed greatly and would tempt him when the sharp clear voice that rang out across the combes would be given full rein. Paradoxically he loved Christmas, always insisting that the carol singers should include the kennels on their rounds when he and Elizabeth-Ann would entertain them and the other hunt staff.

* *

As one season ran into the next, Ernest was learning the ways of the hunt, either by watching Sidney Tucker or by working out for himself how the job might best be done. His confidence grew as did his desire to see his own ideas put into practice. However, the huntsman would have none of it and a tension between the two of them began to be felt.

Ernest knew a great deal about the sport and it would have been galling indeed for him to be ordered to do something he thought might be unwise or which he considered should have been done differently or, worse still, something he felt was wrong. Where to stand at the side of a covert or the head of a valley, for instance, when and how to lift hounds on to the line, how far to cast up or down water; there would have been times when each man held their own strong but differing views.

It was Tucker, though, who was the man in charge, and a firm one at that. Once, after words had been exchanged, Sidney handed Ernest a horn and ordered him back several miles to collect up lost hounds after a long day. The whipper-in duly arrived home well after midnight, leading his tired horse after a 15-mile hack back to kennels but with his mission completed. Nothing was said but the wound began to fester.

Clashes of wills between strong characters are difficult to ease when there is no mediator; it is the same anywhere. Tucker was quite within his right to keep the upper hand. He was a vastly experienced man and Ernest, undoubtedly brilliant and impatient as he was, should keep his place. Furthermore, obedience in a hunt servant must be instant and unquestioning, or confusion will reign.[9]

One day matters came to a head. The subject of the dispute has long since been forgotten but Percy, Ernest's son, remembers a violent clash of words when the two men squared up to one another, both incensed and boiling. "I'll kill you Tucker, so I will," his father raged. "I've shot better men than you." Tucker stood his ground and, quite correctly, reported the incident. The following day both were hauled before the hunt committee and a formal warning was issued. Either they could work together and in harmony or one would have to go. It was an ultimatum and no time was allowed for reflection.

Happily the incident cleared the air and the two men later reached out and shook hands. They worked well together from then on but it is difficult to see how either would have been able to forget such an unsavoury moment. Ernest was lucky in that Sidney Tucker was a man of some stature – big enough to put the matter behind him – for there is little doubt that it would have been Ernest, the junior man, who would have been told to pack his bags had there been another showdown.

The pride and desire for complete professionalism was evident in Ernest but there was displayed also in this incident a sensitive and prickly side to his character, something he would have to watch. It is quite possible that one of the leading hunt figures took him aside and appraised him of this. He had his supporters and perhaps the redoubtable and highly respected Mr Froude Hancock or the Hunt Secretary warned him that nobody was indispensable. Perhaps the wise and fatherly Fred Goss had a quiet word where it was needed most. Mercifully, though, the dust settled.

Year after year the hunting provided by the Tucker-Bawden combination was of the very highest order, E.T. MacDermot [10] recalling run after glorious run in the years leading up to The Great War. Maintaining such quality would have been tough on both men and, throughout all this brilliant success, Ernest was plagued by his old Boer War illness which refused to leave him. The bout of typhoid fever had left its mark.

This, in time, turned into diverticulitis, a miserable and painful stomach complaint in which the digestive system finds it difficult to manage. In simple terms what began as a severe stomach ache would sometimes develop into a situation where the bowels could no longer cope – suddenly and without warning the sufferer would be taken short.

Difficult enough under normal circumstances, such moments were nothing short of a calamity in the hunting field where some sort of cover had to be found and quickly. Anyone who has attempted to answer a sharp call of nature in full hunting rig well knows that knee-high hunting boots make it almost impossible for cord breeches to be cleared out of the way. The poor man had virtually to strip and position himself carefully while retaining control of a fired up and impatient hunter eager to get back into the chase.

For Ernest, a proud and private man, such moments must have been a nightmare for not only was he indisposed in an embarrassing situation but he was being left way behind by the hounds or whatever task the huntsman had asked him to undertake. He was to suffer increasingly more difficult attacks as the years went by, something that might go to explaining his devilish hard riding where he strove not only to keep in touch with the hounds and deer, but to 'get away from they damned lot' and buy himself a bit of time should a crisis arise.

Hunting was now his whole life but he continued to remain a soldier at heart and it was thus no surprise that when war loomed once more his loyalty wavered. By this time Major Greig, an old R.N.D.H. man, was Master and several other members of the committee had strong connections with the Yeomanry. Matters worsened and, when eventually war broke out, the future of hunting looked bleak.

Four days after war was declared, and while hunts up and down the country were debating what to do, the Devon and Somerset found themselves late on their way home after a successful day. By this time it was dark and as they made their way over Brendon Hill, the moon appeared lighting the way for them. Suddenly, far out to sea the searchlight of a patrolling gunship could be seen eerily probing the coastal waters.

It was an omen that brought the situation home to the party, for three days later Major Greig and the two sons of the Secretary were under orders to proceed to their respective regiments of Imperial Yeomanry. All three were killed: Morland Greig and Guy Everard in 1915 and Christopher, Guy's brother, a year later. Their father, Philip Everard, was to suffer yet a further blow when his only son-in-law was also killed. Grenville Fortescue, too, another member of the great family that had played such a part in hunt life, gave his life in 1915. The Great War had reached them all.

Only a week later Lord Fortescue presided at a meeting at The George Hotel in South Molton. The large gathering was in sombre mood as it supported unanimously the motion to discontinue hunting, that fourteen couple of hounds were to be destroyed and that the hunt horses would be offered to the Yeomanry, probably the 1st Devons.

It was a time full of dread and uncertainty yet Ernest knew where he had to go and immediately volunteered his services. To his horror his request to rejoin the colours was rejected. At thirty-six he was considered to be too old and he had been down graded medically. He was distraught, complaining bitterly that his experience would be required, but it was not. This was just as well for those left behind for, despite the earlier motion, hunting was set to continue throughout the war.

It was a desperately difficult decision, for nobody could bear the thought of appearing to enjoy themselves while the country was at war. It was, however, the right decision. Those going off to fight, and there were many who were closely connected with hunting, beseeched those remaining behind to continue, to keep things going. If every joyous activity and pastime were to be curtailed as some mark of solidarity with those who were away, then the morale of the nation would suffer accordingly.

That, of course, was the last thing that servicemen wanted. Many of those who joined up looked forward to hunting when home on leave and, in any case, what was the point, they asked. If hunting were to stop then the hounds and horses would have to go and, as far as Exmoor was concerned, the herd of deer would suffer as it had in times past.

The *West Somerset Free Press (W.S.F.P.)* had for years reported hunting activities but such articles were now stopped, only the occasional short notice appearing where, before, columns of reports on the activities of all local packs were written up weekly. To continue to write about the sport, it was felt, would be glorifying something that should now be regarded as nothing more than a working necessity. And how could hunting reports appear alongside such terrible accounts of the war?

For example, in September 1915 the W.S.F.P. reported that a serious accident had occurred in the hunting field when a Mr Kirkham of Worcester fell heavily at Brushford while riding out with the Devon and Somerset. It was a perfectly normal short notice that would have usually appeared alongside the hunting reports. But that was all, there was no other mention of hunting.

However, on the preceding page of the newspaper, a large article gave the first year's casualties for the war. There had been a total of 381,983 British servicemen killed, wounded or missing since August a year earlier of which 79,957 had been killed (or over *two hundred* a day). Casualties, so the statistician announced, had now risen to more than 10,000 a week. It is hardly surprising that, while hunting struggled on, it did so on a much subdued scale. At almost every meet the whole gathering would pause in silence to remember yet more names of those who had been lost.

Every hunt went through difficult times, no more so than the Staghounds. Money everywhere was tight (everything possible going to the war effort), packs were curtailed and the numbers of horses reduced. Masters, Secretaries and hunt servants went off to the war, so many – like Major Morland Greig and the Everard boys – never to return. After Greig's tenure the hunt was run by a committee which, while essential at the time, was hardly the best way to run such a business. In 1916 a Mr William Badco, a shipping magnate who was living temporarily in Minehead, took up the mastership and it was during this period that Sidney Tucker retired.

The decision was in no way due to his relationship with Ernest. The two had long since put their differences behind them: Sidney Tucker was always made welcome at the kennels and his presence at the future Puppy Show became a regular feature. But he was well over sixty by now and had been with the Staghounds for more than thirty years. While other huntsmen have gone on for longer, the very long seasons coupled with the hard riding and widely variable weather of Exmoor had taken its toll.

Nimrod was quite clear in his mind that, after he had reached the age of sixty, a huntsman began to slow down. He could soldier on for a while, surviving on instinct and experience, but the signs would be there. The Master would have to steel himself against sentimentality and be prepared to make a hard decision or the sport he was offering would suffer. It was one thing simply to ride to hounds even at seventy or eighty years of age (and there are those who do so today) but it was quite something else to carry the horn with all the enormous physical demands that such a business demanded way back in 1917.

Sidney Tucker had been immensely successful and left a legacy behind him. As Ernest carried the horn forward into the following season, he would have been well aware of what was expected of him.

Notes

1. Exmoor, sporting and otherwise. H.J.Marshall.
2. He referred to her as his 'tufting pony' because she was so handy in thick cover. Years before the Hunt had special ponies for this purpose but the practise had long since been discontinued.

3. A huntsman must be a "doggy" person. An unelegant but apt description given to the author by no less than five present or ex-huntsmen.
4. Hunting Diaries. Captain Ronnie Wallace.
5. Captain Ronnie Wallace. Oral History. CD1.
6. *Ronnie Wallace. A Manual of Foxhunting.* Michael Clayton.
7. See The Family Tree at Annex A.
8. Mr Percy Bawden. Recollections.
9. Nimrod and Surtees.
10. *The Devon and Somerset Staghounds 1907–1936.*

Chapter 10

BEGINNER'S LUCK!

August 1917 found Ernest Bawden as ready as any man would ever be. His natural skills had been honed by year after year as whip and he could have had no better tutor than Sidney Tucker. He knew every inch of the huge Devon and Somerset country, every danger spot and precipitous combe, the shallows and fords across rivers and every path that twisted through the dense woodland.

Everything, so it seemed, was in place for him to make a fine start and it has been suggested that even luck was on his side. This was not so. In the event the first few hunts of the season were inauspicious affairs with only one kill in the first eight meets after which progress was often sluggish. All very unfortunate for the new huntsman but an examination of his extensive diaries highlights a number of reasons for the situation, none of which were within his domain. And this is the huntsman's lot; factors way beyond his ken lurk in the hunting field, any one of which can make or break the day, and a combination of which can prove disastrous.

In Ernest's case his particular problem was the paucity of deer. Times were hard in 1917 and throughout the war the deer had been poached in hundreds for their meat resulting in a dramatic reduction in numbers. He wrote frequently about their poor state of health and occasions when the deer they caught had been wounded by gunshot or where the wires of snares had bitten deep into their flesh.

But there were other reasons. Autumn came early that year, low temperatures bringing the thick fog that precludes hunting. He wrote about days when suitable deer were hard to find, of others when deer refused to leave cover or when hounds "rioted". And it was not just in his first season that he was plagued by misfortune. The following September at Highercombe things went badly wrong. The month after that a tough old stag fought for an hour when at bay as Ernest attempted to close in to despatch him. Later he wrote of a day that never got going, when the deer ran from covert to covert and when the stag, once it was finally at bay, gored two hounds.

Such a start, unfortunate though it was, showed clearly that even the best of huntsmen were at the mercy of fate. A career has to be judged in its entirety, looked at year upon year; in Ernest's case all thirty-three seasons of his hunt service taken together. He had his days of luck, just as he had his nightmares, but to call him *lucky* is nothing less than mischievous... or envious.

* *

The first enemy of all huntsmen is the weather, for there is simply nothing to be done about it. Whereas the hunt follower has the option of looking out of the window and going back to bed, the hunt servant has no such choice – he has to be there whatever dawn brings rattling against the windowpanes. Lashing rain, driving hailstones or feathery sleet backed by the razor-sharp nor'easter: all must be faced week after week and with a cheerful countenance. And it is no different in August when the burning heat of high summer has to be suffered deep in the airless combes into which the huntsman goes in full hunting regalia.

It is only when the weather makes hunting impossible rather than uncomfortable, that the days are called off. One reason is fog, when it blankets the countryside. Deep snow is another and the third is frost – when the ground is too hard, the surface cutting the hounds' pads while remaining too slippery for the horses. These are the only exceptions.

Time and again Ernest wrote about day after day of sheeting rain when the land became waterlogged and even the higher reaches of the Barle and Exe had turned themselves into raging, unfordable torrents. Out they would have to go, to meet their commitments to the hunting field. One such occasion was a memorable day early in his second season. *"It was awful,"* he wrote. *"Terrible weather, torrential rain and a howling gale that uprooted trees and damaged buildings. The deer, when we managed to find one, then ran into hinds and finally the field got out of control and overran the hounds."* Difficult to imagine anything worse, yet still the show had to go on when every sinew was crying out for the miserable day to end.

Another day just a month later was much the same. *"A dreadful day at Yarde Down when a terrible gale of wind and torrential rain raged all day and night beforehand and then on the day itself. The weather was too awful to describe, no one could hear anything or hardly hold one's head up against such fearsome elements."* Reveille that day was at four a.m. and the steady hack out to the meet into the teeth of such weather took well over two hours. Precious little luck there!

Then there were the great August heatwaves of 1911 followed later in '21 and '22 when temperatures rose into the nineties day after day. They tried to ease matters by starting earlier, even giving the hunt servants white caps (see photo), but it was of little use for the hunt still lasted all day. On days such as at Cuzzicombe Post on 30 August. *"Another cracking August staghunt and he got away at the end of it all! A twelve mile point followed by a sixteen mile hack home reaching kennels at ten thirty in the evening. The day was more than twelve hours in the saddle."* Imagine the state of the horses and hounds, the latter having done fifty miles or more with the temperature in the eighties.

Descriptions of severe weather conditions in January and February are commonplace throughout his diaries. Unless the snow was deep *"filling the lanes and gateways"* they struggled out to do whatever they could, only the harshness of the frost or thick fog sending them back home when they were quite unable to provide sport for those who had come to meet them. It was the weather that always held the trump cards and Ernest never had better or worse luck than the next man.

All he could ever do was to try to make something out of nothing. Whenever he was allowed to he did just that, such as at Cuzzicombe Post one February. They had roused up the hind and were going for the pack when fog descended. Ernest was given the nod and they hunted almost blind for five hours before making their kill.

* *

The second dread of staghunters is failing to keep hold of the right deer. Foxes might be switched; Ronnie Wallace and others often allowed this in order to keep the day moving along. However once the correct deer has been sent on its way it is customary to stick with the animal and not allow the pack to switch to a fresh deer. Stags, but hinds in particular, are inclined to make for other deer then see it as their business to mingle with them becoming the devil's own job to separate.

Trouble may well begin at the draw when the selected deer will duck and weave in and out of the coverts, forever joining up with others or doubling back to those just left. Older stags will root out the younger ones, trusting the hunt to be satisfied with what they see in front of them, then lying low themselves, sometimes even until the huntsman rides right up to them.

Ernest knew all about this long before becoming even the whipper-in, refusing to be hoodwinked or satisfied with anything but the best that was available. Once he had the deer up and away, he would often keep it in sight, anticipating or out-smarting whatever the animal had it in mind to do. He possessed the skill of a harbourer in slotting the animal and would frequently dismount to check the slot marks, somehow managing to identify those of his deer.

Another priceless gift, developed since he was a boy, was his ability to recognise the deer he had selected, even from a momentary glance as it flashed past a gap in the hedgerow or as it ran among others. Where other huntsmen might pause, he rarely wavered, his mind made up in an instant. One hind looks remarkably like the next, the more so her slot marks, yet he managed and only occasionally admitted to having switched from the hunted animal.

He was forever to remain convinced that some hounds were better at keeping on to the scent than others who allowed themselves to be distracted too easily. As soon as he was allowed to breed his own blood line, he made this one of his principal requirements. It took six or seven seasons but, by the mid-'20s the Devon and Somerset pack ran true when Ernest was able to tell by the tone of their voices alone if they were still with the original deer or had switched to something fresh.[1]

Once Ernest's pack was on to the correct line he made sure they kept at it by keeping right up with them, maintaining pressure on his quarry and denying it time to think. It became a battle of wits, a duel between the hunter and the hunted, lasting perhaps for several hours. Sometimes circumstances would decide the outcome but, more often, it would be the huntsman's ruthless determination that saw the day through.

The merits of pressing so hard had to be judged finely, for such tactics inclined to put him far ahead of the field, especially as he would by now be on a fresh horse. Often he found himself so far ahead that he had to hold hounds for a time, allowing the field to catch up and pause for a breather before he let hounds run on again. Occasionally he missed his second or third horse and had no option but to ride on with a tired animal, pushing it as hard as he dared. Then, without hesitation, he would dismount, slacken the girth and slip the irons before jogging steadily after hounds, leading his horse and giving it time to recover.

Sometimes he would run for a mile or more keeping up the steady pace through sedge and bog or bracken and heather. He asked for, and got, boots especially adapted, slit up the middle and laced which gave his feet more freedom of movement. It was a remarkable performance, for cross country running on Exmoor in smooth-soled hunting boots with spurs can never be easy and Ernest had to run in full hunting gear carrying cap, horn and whip and leading his horse.

Bad enough for a fit youngster in his twenties, yet Ernest ran like this throughout his career – up to and beyond his sixtieth birthday. He always claimed it was worth the effort for, once the horse had caught its breath, it allowed him to get up with the hounds again. One can just see the look of grim determination on the lean, sweat-streaked face as he jogged on. What other huntsman has ever done that?

* *

Every staghunter knows that, sooner or later, the deer will make for water. Here lie a number of problems and it is here that the true skill of the huntsman is tested. Why, Ernest would ask himself, had the deer done this and what was on its mind? Was it simply to refresh itself and press on, or to disguise its trail or was it to stand at bay? The angle the deer hit water was important as it gave some clue as to the subsequent direction it might have taken. Inevitably Ernest was either close enough to witness the deer actually going to water or else he learned it from his hounds.

By this stage he would be thinking like the hunted animal. But in order to read the situation as he did, he had to know the rivers well, every one of them, deciding immediately the location and nature of the next obstacle in the water that would force the deer to emerge and take a fresh line. He knew their ways and was supremely confident in his judgement, yet again rarely having to pause before making his decision on where and how to cast. However, to do this and then capitalise on his decision, he needed the right qualities in his hounds; for to try one without having the other would have come to nothing.

Obedience, skill in the water and steadiness were what he required. All such qualities were exemplified by the rare affinity he had with his pack and which made him the master craftsman at working water. Time after time his diaries tell of casting up or down stream for a mile or more; once he wrote dismissively of a *"lucky cast that was for nigh on two miles and took an hour"*. Dick Lloyd, who remembers watching him as a boy, describes how he somehow managed to keep the pack more or less together and split equally on both banks of the water as well as working others in the water itself.

Slowly, yard by yard, with nothing left unexplored, Ernest would work the hounds up or downstream. Overhanging branches and rocks would be checked, shingle banks covered, walls, banks and dense cover searched thoroughly – sometimes just the once, sometimes again and again. The pack knew what was wanted and how it was to be done. Difficult enough on a fair day with time in hand and a fresh horse, but very hell itself when the horse was dead beat, the whole body was ice-drenched and limbs frozen numb, and when darkness threatened and the kennels were more than two hours away.

He never fussed his hounds – rather, spoke to them quietly in a matter of fact manner as one man would chat to another; leaving them to think for themselves until, at last, one spoke out telling him what he wanted to know. Sometimes the lead was false and he would cast again, knowing instinctively which way the deer had gone. Only occasionally, and reluctantly, would he lift them and try further on or elsewhere. It was hound work of the highest order but hound work that had begun in the kennels when the sires and dams of those now working for him had been so carefully selected.

Other huntsmen worked the hounds in exactly the same fashion, for that is the only way to hunt deer. The difference was that so often Ernest would pick up the line where no other, before or since, has been able to. It was a gift like a sixth sense or the delicate touch of a great artist: nobody could say how it was done, least of all the artist himself.

* *

Ernest always rode two horses, sometimes three, as did his Master and the whips. The pre-positioning of the second and third animals was all-important and was entrusted to riders who were old hands and who had won Ernest's confidence. For those following, who had but one horse, the animal needed to be properly fit or the day would be lost before it had begun, and it remains the same today. A good run with the staghounds is unlike anything but the longest – and often the fastest – of foxhunts.

George Scoins, who rode horses for Ernest, recalls how the huntsman would brief him on the most likely line and where the best short cuts lay. It was George's job to anticipate where the hounds would run and where Ernest would want to change. It was a difficult decision and few excuses were accepted if George missed the rendezvous leaving Ernest with a horse that was "cooked".

No sooner had they met at the rendezvous than George would dismount and hold the horses side by side while Ernest sprang nimbly from one saddle to the other and was off without a moment's thought. *"Take good care of her, lad. She's beat,"* he cried over his shoulder one day. George loosened the mare's girth, took off her bridle *(yes, exactly that)* and let her blow before beginning the long, slow walk home. An hour later the hunt came by having backed on its tracks. There were only a very few left by then and most of them well behind Ernest as he sped past the horse and groom.

"Never gave me a second glance," George recalled. *"T'was much later, though, when I was working 'er down in the stables that Ernest came by. Used to do this sometimes so 'e did. When 'e'd finished hounds 'e used to come down to the stables, sometimes, just to see what was what, like. Stood there watching me workin' on the little mare.....never said nuthin' mind, just drew out his wallet and gave me ten bob.*[2] *'Arf my week's wages in them days."*

Ernest rode his horses hard, very hard, but he had no choice. Tom Firr of the Quorn did the same, Tom Goosey and Will Goodall as well, for they *had* to keep up with the hounds whatever the cost. There could be no half measures when hunting hounds, anything less and the pack would be out of sight. That said, such men cared deeply for their horses, none more so than Ernest – and his reward for the young groom who had taken such care said it all. He was never to forget the day when he had to see the whole hunt through with his favourite "Jenah." The little mare did him proud but died two days later causing him to grieve bitterly. Yet still he was never to let up.

* *

Those who hunt today consider that cars and foot followers are a modern phenomenon, an evil those hunting in earlier times were spared. This is not the case – they have been around for a long time. Ernest hated them, first writing about *"They motors and foot people"* on 8 August 1923 when the meet was at Cloutsham. It was a subject that caused him much angst and by 1930 he was continually grumbling about having his deer headed by cars or the line blocked before he had got there.

The problem was nothing like it is now but in those days it was something new and what was but one tiny black spot on a white canvas would have irritated him intensely. What he would have made of the meets today with the rank upon rank of horseboxes, with the hundreds of cars lining every road, with the scramble-bikes and the quad-bikes and the mobile phones, one can only imagine.

However, were he here today then he would have had to have taken care. In his day the hunt was more than adequately provided for, the income and funding of various expenses sometimes underwritten by men of great wealth. Not so now when the hunt has to guarantee everything from the caps and subscriptions it collects. It is these much denigrated car and foot followers whose wallets make up part of the hunt salaries; and it is a something no horseman should ever forget for, without them, his cap for the day or annual subscription would be that much higher.

Also it must be remembered that those mounted are not the only ones who have the right to enjoy the occasion. The sight of the stag breaking cover is just as memorable to those standing on the back of a Landrover or perched high in the hedge as it is to those fortunate enough to be mounted. So is the sight of Donald Summersgill, today's huntsman, working his tufters or laying on the pack, or working hounds up water. It is a joy to watch and a moment to be savoured by everyone. Every hunt has their foot followers, many showing extraordinary endurance and enthusiasm, none more so than Archie Pape, one of Ernest's North Devon Hussar comrades from South Africa.

He wrote in his diary of a memorable day when he and a friend caught the train from Axminster to Minehead. They then cycled to Porlock before setting out on foot up Porlock Hill to the meet at Hawkcombe Head when the Master, Sir Robert Sanders, was carrying the horn. That little walk-in of 5 or 6 miles after their cycle ride and the fifteen hundred feet climb was just the start of it for they followed the whole day, ending on the beach below Glenthorne at dusk when Archie took the stag in the water with his penknife. After that they climbed all the way back up the cliff, walked back into Porlock, then cycled hard to catch the last train home, arriving at Axminster sometime in the small hours.

What extraordinary dedication to hunting! He described it graphically in his diary, the blood still coursing freely through his veins as he wrote. *"At last he came down to the beach. I and another chap collared him by the antlers… but he upset the other chap and ripped my coat right up. However, in the surf, he fell over a rock and a lot of chaps as well, me among them. I… cut his throat with my own knife… this instrument now hangs in my room as a hunting trophy."* Not for the faint hearted, Archie Pape's complete story is told at Annex D. He was at it again a week or so later when Sidney Tucker gave them some liver from both stags killed, and Ernest sent them the stag's tushes which remain with the family to this day.

Car and foot followers are often seen as the poor relations, an aside not entirely fair yet the sheer numbers today do themselves no favours, least of all to the landowners across whose land they see it as their right to drive, or to the public at large who find the roads in every direction blocked and progress impeded. It is difficult to adjudicate for they are an essential part of hunt fabric and who could deny the likes of Archie Pape their "Day of all days"?

* *

The vagaries of the weather, finding the right deer or riding on to the point of exhaustion; there is not much to be done about any of them. Even the very best of huntsmen have their limitations and there is precious little luck involved. But sometimes, just occasionally, something can be made out of nothing and that is where the skill – nay the genius – of the man with the horn made the difference.

What looked set to be a dreary or blank day would suddenly burst into life. Suddenly, after hours of fruitless search, a hound would speak, then another, followed by Ernest's electrifying shriek ringing out across the combe. Immediately every horse would be *en garde!*, head up and alive, bodies quivering in anticipation. Frantically the reins would be taken up and the hat crammed down... the chase was on!

Notes

1. Hunting reports in the *West Somerset Free Press* archives, Williton.
2. Recollections of George Scoins.

East Hollowcombe Farm. Birthplace of Ernest Bawden (E.B.) 3 March 1878.

E.B.'s mother, the redoubtable Harriet Comer Bawden seen sitting on the left.

Hawkridge life as the young Ernest Bawden would have known it.
(Below and opposite)

Old Mr William Lock with his wife and grandchildren c.1890.

Above: *Jacob Adams shoeing at the forge c.1894.*

Right: *John Lock (bearded) working in his saw pit.*

Farrier Baker's animal surgery – the ramshackle hut behind the children.

Right: *Frankie Howard the village "Postie" c.1890.*

Below: *Hawkridge in mid-winter looking towards the church.*

Horsepower at Cloggs Farm, early twentieth century.

Officers of The Royal North Devon Hussars c.1898 showing Lt Col Shelley (standing centre right) who selected E.B., and Captain Bolitho (leaning far right) who won the D.S.O. in the same battle as E.B. was promoted.

No 3 Troop, 27 Squadron, VIIIth Bn The Imperial Yeomanry before leaving UK for South Africa. E.B. is third from right, second row, his great friend Harris Heywood is the right hand man, front row.

Four Exmoor soldiers of the R.N.D.H. at summer camp in 1902. Tpr Edgar Windsor (Exford), Cpl E.B. plus moustache (Hawkridge), Cpl Alan Marshal (Dulverton) and Tpr Harris Heywood (Winsford). Note the older and longer Lee-Metfords that were still in home service.

Senior N.C.O.'s of 'C' Sqn at camp in 1904. E.B. is third from left back row. Note the medals – only two others have the South Africa medal. E.B. was presented with his Long Service and Good Conduct medal later that year.

E.B.'s medals. Queen's South Africa Medal, L.S. and G.C. medal and the National Commemorative Medal.

Left: *The Caratacus Stone on Winsford Hill where E.B. and Elizabeth-Ann met and courted.*

Below: *One of the many magnificent views across the Devon and Somerset countryside from the Caratacus Stone.*

Elizabeth-Ann, E.B.'s "Missus" taken above Exford. The little girl is Lorna Slocombe, daughter of E.B's whipper-in.

Above: *E.B. begins his career as whipper-in to the great Sidney Tucker (left).*

Left: *Fifteen years on. E.B. (left) and his own whipper-in Gilbert Sloley. Note the immaculate cut of E.B.'s hunting coat compared to the previous picture.*

A moment's silence at the Froude Hancock memorial meet, E.B. mounted (centre). On the right is the Master, Colonel W.Wiggin, standing next to the Suffragan Bishop of Taunton.

A meet at Dunster in 1921. Just where did these vast crowds come from and how did they get there? Somewhere in the middle is the huntsman with the pack.

Another huge crowd at Cloutsham. Note the smart turnout of the foot followers.

A unique photo showing the hunt staff in white headgear during the great heatwave of August 1911. E.B. is the nearer, Sidney Tucker behind.

"The Big Three." E.B., centre, waiting for the pack with the tufters after the stag had gone away. Capt. "Ned" Lloyd (back turned) is on the left, Colonel Wiggin on the right.

The tufters doing their stuff and seeing the stag on its way.

"As pants the hart for cooling streams." The stag running down water.

"At Bay." Note how the hounds stand off, relaxed yet acutely aware of those antlers.

A rare photo showing the hounds pursuing the stag out to sea. After a while they would return leaving the boatmen to complete the chase.

Above: *The boatmen return and successfully so.*

Right: *The end. The head of a fine stag.*

Right: *The trophy room at the D. and S. Kennels showing two fine E.B. heads. Between them are two much older heads dated 1778 and 1793.*

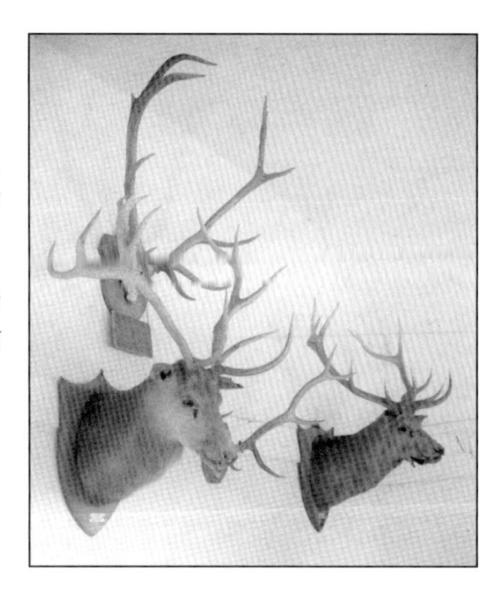

Below: *E.B. with a couple of his hounds in the kennels. It is here that the hunting begins and the kills are made.*

A striking photo of Elizabeth-Ann Bawden late in life. "Missus" was the only one who really controlled E.B.

Heads taken during the 2003–4 season. Note the magnificent head in the centre.

A study of E.B. examining the strange head of a stag that gave him the greatest run he ever undertook on 18 April 1931. Hounds ran for 37 miles in a little over three hours and the total climb was more than 5000 feet.

Potential officers of the King's Own Second Staffordshire Light Infantry Militia in 1879. W.W.Wiggin (later Master of the D. and S.) is standing on the right.

"The perfect combination." E.B. and his Master – Colonel Walter Wiggin – at a meet on the Exford village green in 1926 close to the kennels.

Huntsman Supreme. E.B. in 1937.

Harvesting at Hinam Farm. E.B.'s son, Percy, believes this to be the haywain that ran over and killed his father.

E.B.'s grave at Hawkridge. Such was his fame that this photo was made into a postcard, both here and in France where he had many admirers.

Chapter 11

1918 AND THE NEW PARTNERSHIP

The modern world has shown little sympathy towards hunting.

First came the railways with their impassable barriers of embankments and cuttings which sliced up the countryside – followed almost at once by the plague of urban sprawl around which horse and hound did their level best for as long as they could. Modern agricultural machinery, bigger and more voracious by the year, replaced the farm horse, thus enabling the farmer to plough ever more land, ever deeper. Headlands, thickets and coppices vanished in their thousands, hedgerows mile after mile. The ancient deciduous woodlands disappeared, succeeded by dark and impenetrable conifer forests in which little lives or grows.

Hunting survived because it had to, but the freedom and the great unrestricted runs of the pre-war years became more and more of a rarity, sometimes no more than a distant memory. Exmoor, it has to be said, escaped the worst of it all and those who hunt there are luckier than most. For instance, were today's members of the Dulverton Farmers or the Devon and Somerset to complain about their lot to fellow sportsmen from the Old Surrey and Burstow or the West Kent or the Garth and South Berks they would be laughed out of court. Exmoor has remained more or less the same because of its remoteness, but it has by no means got clean away with it.

* *

The damage began way back in 1822, shortly after John Knight bought the ancient Royal Forest from the Crown, together with as much of the surrounding countryside as he could manage. Part of the deal for him was to build a 31 mile long wall around his estate. It became a circular barrier 6 feet high and 6 feet deep topped with a beech hedge and with only a few entrance points. Furthermore, it sat right in the middle of the ancient Forest. Once this had been completed, Knight set about draining and ploughing the land within, before creating a network of roads and building farms (more than a dozen in all). Before Knight it was possible for a pack of hounds to run uninterrupted from Anstey in the south right up to Woody Bay on the north coast or from Filleigh in the west to Porlock Bay in the east, both runs points of just under 20 miles.

Nothing much more happened until after the Second World War, when generous grants encouraged farmers to reclaim the moorland. Almost immediately, thousands of acres went under the plough, a maze of wire fencing was put down to separate one piece of land from another, while miles of fir plantations spread upwards and outwards from the valley bottoms.

Were it not for the arrival of the National Park Authority in the fifties, Exmoor would have gone under, the landscape changed forever. The deer would have been restricted as never before and the unique nature of hunting the moors would have been lost. Such erosion of the open moorland was devastating but it was caught just in time and Exmoor lives on, the *status quo* of the fifties more or less maintained to this day.

Hunting continues; the farmers, landowners and the Park authorities for the most part living and working in harmony with the various packs of hounds. That said, staghunting no longer enjoys the freedom and space it did when Ernest Bawden carried the horn. As the open countryside has contracted over the years, so the size of the hunting field – and, in particular, the numbers of car and foot followers – has grown.

Today the huntsman and whips must remain constantly on their guard lest hounds follow the deer to where hunting is either impossible or to where it is unwelcome. It is more of a challenge today than hitherto but the hunt staff still manage to produce outstanding runs, the out of bound areas seemingly little more than a minor irritant to the thousands who follow the fortunes of the D and S.

There is nothing new about those who protest against hunting or who buy parcels of land to frustrate the hunt. Ernest first mentions protestors at Tiverton in April 1919, then again at Minehead and Porlock a year or so later, then at Barnstaple, then at Lynton. How much more of a force the protestors must have been then in order to make their presence felt in the days when mobility was so restricted, when telephones were unheard of and the media totally ambivalent to their business. Yet the hunt has always been alert to criticism, the potential trouble in those days was identified well in advance and great care always taken to avoid senseless confrontation.

* *

Life in the field may, in some ways, have been easier for Ernest, a fact due principally to a greater sense of freedom that prevailed, but the daily routine of the hunt staff was more taxing and time-consuming by far. There were no time or labour-saving devices available to ease the daily physical grind. Take away motor vehicles, electricity, hot and cold running water, the telephone and modern veterinary practices. Add to the list such luxuries as fuel oil, central heating, waterproof clothing and modern feed for the animals, and a picture begins to emerge of the hard and austere lifestyle of those involved.

Hounds met three or four times a week at the stated time no matter how long the preparation took; what went on between times was of no concern to the field and followers. It is the same today, and to meet such an exacting timetable is not easy, the hours of work in stables and kennels often going on way beyond any set routine.

Although indeed similar to 1917, everything in those days took much longer and required more physical effort. Just getting to and from the meet is an example. Cuzzicombe Post is more than 8 miles from Exford, Yarde Down almost 10 and North Molton nearly 12, yet there was no transport; each hack took two hours or more in fair weather or foul (the first use of transport was in 1933 and that was a lift *back* to the kennels after a hunt of more than 20 miles).

Today the pack and hunt staff arrive fresh and dry, and then, if they are lucky, return in comfort at the end of the day. No such good fortune for Ernest and his team – the diaries tell of frequent homecomings at ten or eleven at night after mile upon mile of slow progress through driving rain or sleet, riders often leading their mounts. Hounds by then must have covered sixty miles or more, horses and hunt staff close to exhaustion, and that was before the night's work began.

These days carcasses are collected from farms by truck with the aid of a winch, then it was done by horse and cart with just the smaller tow-horse in attendance.[1] The timely passage of information about the days ahead was another problem. The hunt staff needed to know what lay in store for them but such facts as were available would be brought in by post or courier with no hope of discussion or confirmation with the harbourer or landowners. Much had to be left to guesswork or chance.

Daily changes of hunting clothes (heavy cord breeches included) were washed by hand and somehow dried. Come dusk and the whole place was in darkness save where the oil lamps hung or were carried. Treatment of sick and ailing animals was undertaken by the hunt servants and their families, there being no way of summoning a vet in an emergency. Food and fodder for the many mouths had to be brought in and stored in advance.

Each one of these tasks, taken in isolation, might seem inconsequential – sometimes barely more time consuming or physically demanding than today – but the cumulative effect bore heavily. It was a mighty tough world back in 1917 where hunt servants, like so many other manual workers, worked harder and for longer to cover the same ground.

Ernest survived his first season and survived well; the succession to Sidney Tucker had gone smoothly. His Master, Mr William Badco, appreciated this, for there had been some excellent hunting in spite of the difficulties. As early as August that year Ernest produced a great run of over two and a half hours from Larkbarrow, then a cracker from Dunster the following month and another from Ralegh's Cross a short time later, when huntsman and hounds reached kennels after eight o'clock.

Conditions had not been favourable that year, on occasions they were downright hostile, but he was proving to be the man they had hoped he would be. Anything less and he would not have been retained. By now the Devon and Somerset Staghounds was a prestigious pack, many coming down to Exmoor for their sport before and after their own foxhunting season, and Badco was a proud man – one for whom only the best was acceptable.

The committee had asked William Badco to fill in for a season only while they searched for a permanent successor. In the event he served on for a second, seeing the war through to its end and leaving the following summer. The man approached to succeed him was Colonel Walter Wiggin from Worcestershire. Well-known to Exmoor having hunted there for more than twenty years, he was but a month short of his sixty-third birthday when he accepted the post.

"Too old to last," cried some. "And a *fox*hunting man to boot," muttered others darkly. In the event he was to hold the appointment for no less eighteen seasons, during which time his stewardship brought the Devon and Somerset to the very pinnacle of excellence; widely regarded as the finest pack of hounds in England.[2]

That he was quite so old, that he was renowned for a bucolic temperament which sometimes exploded into incandescent fury, and that he was already suffering from severe arthritis, only added to the mystery surrounding his success. But it was here, with his new Master, that lay Ernest Bawden's way ahead. The two men were to forge one of the great partnerships in hunting history. Colonel Walter Wiggin, "The Colonel", was a man after the huntsman's own heart. In return, Wiggin saw immediately the unique qualities of his right hand man. Ernest Bawden's talents were about to be given free rein.

Walter Wiggin hailed from a line of Staffordshire farmers but it was his father, Sir Henry Wiggin Bt, who founded the family fortune in Birmingham. There he came into a business, eventually succeeding the founder, which had perfected the extraction of sulphur from nickel ore. Henry Wiggin educated his sons at Clifton where early photographs of his second boy, Walter, show a truculent, devil-may-care youngster. It was not without good reason that somebody had penned "Tread warily!" underneath one of the pictures.

The direct, uncompromising look and strongly jutting jaw portrayed a strength of character in a man who began a life-long love affair with horses and hunting at an early age. It was, however, with the infantry that he began his military service when he and a number of friends joined the Staffordshire Volunteers; first with the King's Own Second Battalion (see photo) then, later, with the Third.

His wild ways and the devil in him may not have endeared him to the infantry, and in 1888, on hearing that he had not been recommended for further promotion, he decided to switch allegiance to the Yeomanry. So began an attachment of thirty years with the Queen's Own Worcestershire Hussars, where he finished as Colonel, having commanded the Second Battalion at home during the war.

Being restricted by age to home service during both the Boer War and the First World War was simply not good enough for him. He felt certain he had something more to offer and by judicious networking found himself as Horse Master in France in 1917 shortly before his sixty-first birthday, service for which he was to be twice mentioned in despatches.[3]

Colonel Walter Wiggin, charming, wealthy and a man of his own mind, had always taken life by the scruff of its neck. He played hard, sometimes allowing his mercurial temperament to get the better of him, mayhem and uproar occasionally resulting. There was the time when a poor hand of cards (perhaps not played with sufficient guile) caused him to erupt from the table in mock fury. Rushing across the room he leapt high at the curtains where he swung freely until he and they, pelmet and all, crashed to the floor.

Years later the staff at Gleneagles remembered the infamous missed putt on the eighteenth green. Wiggin went wild, a red mist descending as club after hickory club was broken over his knee, before they repaired to the bar and drank their sorrows away. How famously he and those heroes in Chapter 1 would have got on; one can just imagine the scene if he and John Mytton of the old Shropshire and Shifnal had ever got together!

He had hunted since childhood with the packs in Warwickshire and with The Worcestershire, yet came frequently to ride out with the Devon and Somerset. He loved the life and was determined that one day he would have for himself a fine pack of hounds and, when the offer came from the Hunt Committee, he did not hesitate. His first move was to acquire Stockleigh Lodge in Exford, just a short walk from the kennels, leaving empty Forehill, his Birmingham home, save when family business took him north. He and his wife, Edith, moved in immediately, busying themselves with their new home in preparation for the start of the 1918 season.

Taking up the Mastership was one thing, becoming successful and making a name for the pack was quite something else. It would take time, it would take money and it required patience. He knew this and set about the task with a single-minded determination, channelling all his enormous wealth and energies into achieving his aim. He needed many things but, most of all (and highest on his list), was a huntsman who could produce for him the quality of hunting that was so essential. More than that he needed someone in the post with whom he, the dynamic, forceful and unpredictable character that he was, could see eye to eye. They would have to get on.

* *

The relationship did not take long to establish, and there are a number of reasons. First, Ernest, the proud soldier that he ever was, saw much that he admired in Walter Wiggin. Both had been in the Yeomanry and both had gone off to war. Furthermore he would have remembered the Colonel well from his earliest days as whip fourteen years earlier.

In return, Wiggin would have appreciated Ernest's military background and the disciplined, vigorous approach to his job. He, the new Master, was later to demand an even higher standard of turnout from his staff, just as he was a stickler for courtesy, manners and discipline in the hunting field. His huntsman would have appreciated that, their relationship becoming something akin to that between a Commanding Officer and his R.S.M.

Everybody had their place but it was the new Master who reigned supreme. George Scoins remembers clearly how such courtesies were respected at the meet when Lord Fortescue, Sir Thomas Acland and others would come up to the Master and doff their caps. The Colonel, by this time, would have been moving among the followers, mounted and dismounted, welcoming warmly the newcomers as well as chatting to old friends. "Good morning, Master," rang out the salutation, then, turning to the huntsman, "Good morning Ernest." Back would came the formal reply "Good morning, my lord." A fine example set and one that the Colonel expected everyone to follow.

It was his ability as a huntsman that would have endeared Ernest most to his new Master. Here was the man who could do the job for him. Furthermore Wiggin was determined to breed his own line of hounds – he, too, being less than satisfied with the drafts from elsewhere. Ernest, he knew, was insistent on what was required, and Walter Wiggin was able to provide whatever was necessary for him to get it right. He took his huntsman to the hound sales at Rugby and the Peterborough Hound Show (staghounds are ineligible to be shown) where they identified what was needed and made arrangements for stallion hounds to be borrowed or the progeny of certain bitches to be reserved for them.

A forceful character and hard rider himself, Wiggin's money helped bring excellent horses to the stables. Ernest's drive and ruthlessness in the field would have appealed to him and he got the horses he wanted without question because Wiggin knew it was necessary. Each season he bought new dress and equipment for the hunt staff, bringing down his own tailor – Allports of Birmingham – to ensure the cut and style was just so.[4] Once, when Ernest complained that the man had not got it right, the tailor was ordered back again; a round trip of 250 miles to check on the cut of the cloth.

Having hunted over Exmoor for so long, Walter Wiggin realised the great debt the hunt owed to the farmers and landowners whose support was so critical. He ensured that grievances were addressed immediately and compensation paid where it was due. In his first season alone he paid out £1700 (almost fifty thousand pounds today), each payment accompanied by a note penned in his own hand.

Every year he showed his gratitude when, on the day of the Exford horseshow, an enormous marquee was erected on the showground and up to four hundred farmers entertained to a banquet laid on by a Dulverton hotelier.[5] At the end, the Master would rise to thank them all and propose the loyal toast after which they would sing the National Anthem before the toasting "Prosperity to Staghunting." While he was in the marquee with his farmers, his wife, Edith, entertained the farmers' wives elsewhere. They loved him for it, every one of them, and none more so than Ernest Bawden, the farmer's son from Hawkridge.

There was a third, and perhaps more significant, reason why the two men became so close. Walter and Edith had two sons; the second, Christopher, dying when just four years old leaving Robert, or Bob as he was known, as their only child. Bob Wiggin followed his father into the Yeomanry and volunteered for service as soon as war broke out. He quickly rose to captain but was killed in action, fighting against the Turks in Egypt on Easter Day 1916 – an engagement in which his cousin, Bill, was present. It is well-known in the family that the loss affected Walter deeply, something with which he was never able to come to terms.

Ernest could never have replaced the boy in Walter's eyes for their backgrounds were too different, but he was a younger man, young enough to be his son and one who loved the same things Bob had loved so much. The Colonel would have talked to him, chatted informally, as any father might on matters that were dear to them both. Those meetings in Ernest's parlour on the nights before hunting that went on for hours would have covered many subjects.

Ernest would have responded as any younger man would have done. He had just the one son himself and would have appreciated how the older man felt; certainly he would have known about Bob's time in the Yeomanry and the manner of his death. Furthermore, he would have seen in the Master the guidance and protection he had missed from his own father when he was a child. This strange, deep relationship went some way to filling the voids in both their lives, adding greatly to those other bonds which had already tied them so closely.

There came now to the staghounds a period of stability they had not known before. Although the country was still in a state of shock as communities learned to live with the horrors of war, the awful uncertainty was behind them at last. Everyone who was coming home was back and the dread of waiting for more bad news and further casualties had gone. Gradually, life improved. People began to smile and little luxuries appeared. Horseracing, cricket and football began again. Motorcars were seen (even on Exmoor) and people were talking about having a wireless in their homes. The cinema had arrived, theatres and ballrooms opened their doors once more.

* *

Colonel Wiggin and Ernest first set out together at North Molton on 29 July 1919. It was a great hunt, lasting for over three hours before they killed at the Hoar Oak Tree, way beyond Simonsbath. Only twenty or so of the large field completed the course as Master and huntsman left behind a third of the pack in their desire to run the stag to bay.

It boded well for the future. The herd of deer had been poached mercilessly during the war and there was a danger that the hunting days might have to be limited. A survey carried out by the hunt revealed that there were only two hundred and fifty or so head of deer left on the whole of Exmoor and but sixty more on the Quantock Hills.[6] Harbouring was going to be an exacting business; the herd would have to be treated with care and hinds taken only sparingly.

New hounds began to appear, but hounds that were selected by Master and huntsman rather than ones offloaded by others. They were brought in especially for their physique as well as their hunting prowess. The pack still ran too quietly, and too few of them knew how to work water, but Ernest, supported by his Master, persevered – both appreciating that success must begin in the kennels. It was not until 1925 that he was able to talk about his young bitch pack hunting splendidly at Heathpoult or the big dog pack running so well from Hawkridge *"Plenty of pace and plenty of tongue. Music at last,"* he wrote.

Slowly it was all coming together and the fame of the pack was spreading. Visitors came from France and Denmark, then from Spain, Italy and America. Walter Wiggin had provided the drive and the wherewithal but it was the huntsman that they had come to see: Ernest Bawden was the name on everyone's lips. Colonel Walter Wiggin was happy enough for that; he stood back and let his huntsman get on with it as he knew best. It was, indeed, the start of a new era.

Notes

1. A sturdy yet humble animal known as the "Cock" horse. Hence the nursery rhyme *Ride a Cock horse to Banbury Cross.*
2. *"A pack second to none… which attracted the best judges in the country." The Fairest Hunting.* Hewett.
3. Mentioned in Despatches or MID, awarded for gallantry or outstanding service on active service.
4. Recollections of Percy Bawden.
5. The hotelier was Mr F.W. Dullingham of The Lion Hotel. Recollections of Mr Edwin Thorne who, as a young farmer, attended the last such occasion.
6. Deer census conducted on 11 March 1918 by *"Messers Thornton, Colonel Amory, P.F. Hancock and Fred Goss in consultation together."*

Chapter 12

THE HORN TUCKED WELL INTO HIS COAT

The byword for the new partnership was organisation. Success in the hunting field was dependant upon so many factors beyond their control that the new Master and his huntsman set out determined to bring into line whatever they could. If Colonel Wiggin did not actually regard the pack as his own, he most certainly looked upon it as his responsibility.

He sought and secured the backing of the Hunt Committee to make whatever changes he considered necessary, funding a number of the initiatives from his own pocket. Here he was fortunate in that Lord Fortescue, who had been Chairman since 1899 and was to remain so until his death in 1932, provided the ideal continuity. It would have been through his chairmanship that Wiggin would have been approached in the first place and few men knew the ways of Exmoor better. He and others such as Froude Hancock would have given Wiggin the support and encouragement he needed.

The post of Secretary, another key committee member, was about to pass to Captain E.C. "Ned" Lloyd, himself an Exford man and a friend of Colonel Wiggin. During the last ten years the post had alternated four times but it was now to settle. In order to be successful, the Secretary of a hunt needs time. He needs to know exactly what is going on and the only way to do this is to hunt regularly himself, his mind taking in all he sees and hears. He must have a firm grasp of the hunt's finances and he must have a fair knowledge of agriculture, for it is he who will decide what compensation for damage should be paid. But, above all else, he must know the multitude of personalities involved in the hunt, be they followers or the large number of farmers and landowners across whose land the hunt will go.

Ned Lloyd, who had been severely wounded in 1916 when he lost an arm, was an ideal choice, thus the last piece in the hierarchal jigsaw was about to slot into place. Later, as Colonel Wiggin became more crippled with arthritis, Lloyd took on the role of Field Master, serving in all from 1923 to 1934. Fields grew ever bigger, often numbering several hundreds, and it was his task to maintain control over what would have otherwise become a wild and noisy cavalcade surging about in every direction.

Among the worst offenders were local farmers. An independent and determined breed by nature who saw the countryside as their own domain and who preferred to answer to no man, they required careful handling. Wiggin needed their continued support, yet it was the good Captain Lloyd's task to bring the field to order. That he managed to do so says much for his tact and diplomacy, as well, no doubt, as an occasional well-directed blast.

Finally, and of critical importance to the performance of the hunt, were the whippers-in. Here too, the committee had selected well and found two men, followed later by a third, who did the job admirably. When Ernest became huntsman he was succeeded as whipper-in by Gilbert Sloley, the new man joined later by Alfie Lenthall. Both were outstanding, Sloley going on to become huntsman of the Quantock Staghounds and Lenthall eventually taking the horn from Ernest in 1937. Ralph Slocombe, initially a second horseman, took up the vacant post before leaving to become harbourer when Lenthall was huntsman. It was a very strong team and one that was to remain together for years.

* *

Ernest settled easily, his own life in the semi-detached cottage nearest the hounds becoming totally bound up with the day-to-day business of the hunt. Every day before the meet, Colonel Wiggin would walk the short distance through the grounds of Stockleigh to Ernest's front parlour where the two of them would sit and discuss what lay ahead. Percy, by now an ebullient schoolboy, had either to remain quiet in his room or leave the premises with the firm reminder that there was to be no noise on his return. "Lights-out" at the kennels was at nine-thirty sharp by order of the huntsman and woe betide any who chose to disregard the rule.

The meetings took place in the afternoon, when Missus would serve tea and cakes while the two talked together. First on the agenda was always the meet the following day. While Wiggin had come down to hunt regularly before the war, he would have had little idea of the different character the location of each meet presented or the lie of the land, let alone the likely reaction of the deer. He would have known few personalities well – indeed, most of the locals would have been little more than nodding acquaintances.

In 1918 Walter Wiggin was sixty-two while Ernest, now in his fourteenth season with the hunt, was forty. The huntsman had known Exmoor intimately since he could walk and by now would have recognised every face in the hunting field, in particular those upon whom the hunt had to rely – where best to kennel the pack and with whom, who best to employ as extra eyes and ears, and so on.

The harbourer would be in tomorrow's area already but, by this stage, Ernest would have a shrewd idea as to what deer were in the locality and what Fred Goss or, later, Ned Lang had in mind for them. The harbourers would have been watching the deer for weeks and word would have passed to the huntsman. Decisions on where the field should be held, how the second and third horses should be handled and where the pack might best be kennelled, would be talked through over the map. The meetings, often lasting for an hour or more, went on until both were happy that everything possible had been thought through.

Talk would then move on to other matters – the state of the pack always a favourite topic. Ernest knew the genealogy of every hound as well as the capabilities and limitations of each individual. Both knew exactly what they were looking for and discussions about breeding would have been frequent. They were happy to import blood with which to improve their own stock, but both were determined to make the staghound line their own as soon as possible.

Ernest knew he had to be ruthless about putting down old hounds but he loathed having to make the fateful decision, the actual identification of those that had to be put down often reducing him to tears. He would be inconsolable, sitting in the parlour and crying bitterly as he reflected on the awful decisions he had just made.

The task itself was the only one he could not bear to carry out, delegating the final act to one of the whips while he escaped on some spurious excuse that took him well away from kennels until it was all over. The deep, almost childish, love for his hounds was never more apparent than on such occasions, mirrored only by his rapturous delight when the first of the next generation arrived.

Once the Colonel had departed, Ernest would brief the hunt staff on the routine for the following day. The hounds had been selected already and would have been separated from the remainder of the pack. Next morning they would be forced to forgo their daily meal, empty stomachs encouraging them to hunt fast and urgently.

While Missus saw to his hunting clothes, Ernest cleaned and honed his boots, the two of them ensuring that everything was ready before his last tour of the kennels prior to "Lights-out". Years later, when electricity was powered by a generator Ernest used to cut the power himself at a time of his own choosing (usually about nine o'clock) ignoring the howls of protest from the other inhabitants.

Reveille, and he was always to use the military term, was early. There was no alarm clock or early call from the staff, Ernest waking automatically at whatever time was necessary. Bearing in mind that the hack to the meet might take them over two hours, lamps were invariably lit well before dawn, sometimes before five o'clock. Ernest would do his rounds while his wife laid out his hunting clothes. He never breakfasted on hunt mornings, taking no more than a glass of milk and a biscuit to settle his stomach. Some claimed he did so out of sympathy for his hounds but a far more likely explanation was to minimise the chances of a sudden attack of diverticulitis during the day.

He took his time dressing. Every fold and crease in his stock had to be just right, the set of the pin just so. Every button on his waistcoat and jacket had to be gleaming, his cap brushed again and again. Missus carried out the final inspection by the back door, making any tiny adjustment she saw necessary before handing him a small glass of port, a tonic that steadied the nerves before he went outside, where he met the stable lad at the back door. It was a tense moment for he stubbornly refused to ride either anything he considered too big or whose turnout was not up to scratch.

"Get that bloody great donkey away from here and at the double, damn you, or we'll be late." All the wretched lad could do was to turn and run back down the road to the stables with the horse, knowing full well there would be worse to come if a more suitable mount could not be found immediately. The kennel staff used to plead with Walter Griffith, the stud groom, to get it right or it would be they, rather than the stable lads, who would feel the rough edge of the huntsman's tongue. No sooner had the fresh horse arrived than they were off.

* *

Homecoming was likely to be just as much a test of nerves for those waiting; the swings in his mood dependant almost entirely upon how the day had gone, or, more to the point, how Ernest considered his own performance had been. He was a hard taskmaster, demanding nothing but the best from those in his charge but nothing less than perfection from himself. He always felt that he had been on parade and in the public gaze where his performance would have been commented upon, his actions, as well as those of his hounds, judged severely. There was, he asserted, no room for error, none at all.

Percy remembers how he and his mother used to wait anxiously for a stable lad to come running with the warning that his father was on the way. "You could tell immediately," he recalls. "If he stood in the doorway, took off his hunting cap and made to throw it across the parlour then it had been a bad day... and I would be off." However, were he to stride into the room smiling, cap still on, then all would be well.

If it were not so then the evening was likely to be a grim affair – Ernest unable to shake from his mind the twists and turns of the day's events, sometimes brooding late into the night over what had gone wrong and whether or not he might have been able to have done better. Elizabeth-Ann handled such occasions in her quiet and resolute way while Percy slunk off into the night, seeking an evening with his friends rather than the gloomy atmosphere in the cottage.

Whatever the outcome it was up to Missus to soothe and placate, then listen and nod understandingly and finally to hush any outpourings of emotion. She would have the bathwater and dry clothes ready, together with the evening meal. Where everyone else might have failed, it was up to her to calm the anger or frustration. Usually she managed but not always. There were times when he would be late – the kitchen clock long since gone ten or eleven, sometimes later still – before they heard the horses. That would get him as far as the kennels when, by light of the lamps, he would begin his work, checking each hound through the footbaths and personally inspecting any mark that required attention.

By this time the hounds were ravenous, waiting desperately to get at the flesh and oatmeal that had been boiled in the coppers and stirred throughout the day. Even as the pack fed, his eyes never left them; he would stand by quietly, occasionally pointing out to the others some minor wound or ailment that had escaped attention earlier.

The distances covered by those animals during the day were, and remain, quite remarkable. A sheepdog works hard for its living but works in short bursts, rarely for more than two or three hours at a time. A gun dog will have done well if it covers 10 miles at a leisurely pace during the day, there being plenty of time to recover between drives, and a nice warm vehicle to take it home.

A staghound might cover that distance just *getting to the meet*, the tufters then work another 5 or 6 miles rousing the deer and then there is the chase itself. Time and again Ernest wrote of 10, 12 or 14 mile points (measured as the crow flies) in which the hounds ran double that at least, sometimes three times the length of the point. And how they ran!

Each one line astern yet in close proximity to the ones in front, every one of them head down in touch with the scent. Like this the pack would gallop for mile after mile over, through and across fields, coverts and the high moors; across bogs and sedge, through woodland and into water then on again, climbing out of one steep combe after another before descending once more. Each hound spoke as it ran, every cry, yelp, whimper, bark, whoop or shout adding to the voices around him making up the wonderful, spine-tingling symphony of hound music. And then, after the kill, the long, slow journey home – 10 miles, perhaps? 15, even 20 or more… thus 40, 50 or 60 miles for the average day.

On occasions when they got home it would be obvious that medical attention was necessary. Were a vet required, then somebody had to ride the 12 miles to South Molton and, even then, there was no guarantee that help would be forthcoming. By the time help did get there, the animal would either have died or begun to improve, so they did it themselves. Missus would be summoned with her dressing pot.

Her famous concoction looked and smelled lethal but its curative powers knew no bounds. The mixture of sulphur, train (engine) oil, spirit of tar and turpentine was applied liberally to all skin ailments, the recipient by this time being too tired and hungry to care. Wounds were washed and sutured before being bathed in iodine solution, while sore feet were bathed in Condie's crystals (potassium permanganate) or salt.[1] Torn pads were treated with neat iodine, loose claws either dressed or removed there and then.

Time and again Missus took over running the dispensary, often bringing the sorely wounded into her house. A farm girl herself, she had her own way with the animals and, in any case, there was no one else to whom they could turn. The next meet for which everyone was required was barely thirty-six hours away and the show had to go on.

Sometimes homecoming resembled a battlefield, such as on 5 October 1934 when the Culbone Stag plunged a hundred feet over the cliffs and on to the beach at Glenthorne, followed by half the pack. Eight hounds were killed instantly and several others injured in the fall. In spite of all their efforts at the kennels, two more died later. It proved a torrid week for Ernest, whose love for his hounds was a byword. Only a few days later when they met at Larkbarrow, the stag at bay fought heroically, killing two and wounding several more.

It was (and still is) the Autumn stags which inflict most damage, such as on 16 October 1918 when three couple were gored. Less than a year later Ernest wrote of "Finisher" and "Ruler" being gored to death. In 1926 an Autumn stag from Hawkridge killed one hound and gored several more, and a year after that, when hunting from Cuzzicombe Post no less than five couple were gored, several badly.

There is a reason for this. October is the time of the annual rut when the finest and largest stags challenge each other for possession of the hinds. The beasts are in their prime; sleek and muscular from the spoils of summer with their blood fired up for the battles that lie ahead. Some are not even bothered by the tufters when roused, either remaining seemingly indifferent to the disturbance,[2] or turning and charging, scattering the hounds in all directions. And it was the same when they were cornered or at bay.

* *

Only when he was completely satisfied with the evening's work would Ernest allow himself to relax. By this time, his filthy, mud-caked and often sodden clothes would have half-dried on his body but the body itself may well have suffered. Cuts, bruises and knocks were commonplace, but on St Valentine's Day 1923, his horse fell back into the Porlock road, trapping him and injuring his back. He managed to limp home but the damage necessitated a three-week lay off.

Two years later, he was gored badly himself when the stag at bay charged. The points of bone-hard antlers are sharp and mighty dangerous too, coming as they do at the business end of more than 350 pounds of desperate stag. Ernest refused medical attention but was again laid off for several weeks.

The worst accident of all was in March 1933 when he was crossing the swollen River Barle near Ashway Hams. They had just killed and the hind was being swept downstream by the current when it brushed against his horse. The animal reared up in the deep water *"and fell right back over in the water, giving me a severe ducking. On regaining his feet my horse knocked me about with his hooves giving me a blow on the head and a few other bruises... I got washed downstream a little way."* Fortunately he was saved by Captain Stephen Cox who leapt from his horse and into the river, holding him steady until he had recovered enough to get back on his feet.

His cap and, far worse for him, his horn had been washed away and his head was cut yet he remounted. Once again refusing assistance and with his clothes heavy and boots full of icy, spring river water he led the hounds on their 10-mile hack home. Hard as iron by any standards but the fifty-five year old body had taken a terrible pounding.

It was the loss of his precious horn that caused him untold misery and it was ages before another one of similar lightness and tone could be found. Years later, the original was recovered under extraordinary circumstances. Ernest was sitting in his garden one summer evening when he heard a horn – his horn, nonetheless. "That's mine," he cried ecstatically. "That's my bloody horn." An evacuee boy had picked it out of the shingle on the riverbank more than a mile from where the huntsman had lost it years earlier. The lad, a bugler, blew the instrument just once but it was enough for Ernest to stake his rightful claim. The full story, recounted by his great-nephew, is at Annex C.

But in spite of these various setbacks, Ernest usually arrived home triumphant after an excellent day in the field. Whip and cap would go onto a rack in the hall followed by the horn to its pride of place on the mantelpiece. And it was then, after getting into the parlour and stripping that an unusual and significant bonus was brought in for the household.

Those of means who had come from afar for their sport rewarded the huntsman generously with "boot" money. As they came up to thank him for the day, one hand would take his warmly while the other would slip sovereigns into the top of one of his boots. Percy recalls his father struggling out of his boots then watching, fascinated, as he turned them upside down releasing a stream of gold coins that clattered rolling and spinning onto the floor.

Each one would have represented two months wages in 1917, and there were occasions when the youngster collected handfuls before stacking them on the table. Such moments helped to draw what sting remained in the huntsman's ire and the day would end on a far happier note than might have been the case. Ernest had learned his lesson with money long ago and what he made now was banked carefully, with just enough kept back to supplement his wages and whatever he managed to make from selling the skins of the hunted deer – the huntsman's traditional perk. Saving their pennies (and sovereigns) was an expedient move.

They lived frugally and saved hard but wanted for nothing; indeed, Ernest made a point of watching his weight as closely as any clerk of the scales would scrutinize his jockeys. He was determined always to ride as light as possible and as soon as the scales approached his self-imposed limit of nine stones he would hire a car and driver then hasten over to Minehead where he would purge himself in the steam baths of the old Metropole Hotel. Every extra ounce of flesh meant precious yards lost in the hunting field and, for him, that was unacceptable. Year after year he submitted himself to his own austere, almost Spartan, regime. It was that same uncompromising, ruthless dedication emerging yet again.

He was as fussy and particular over his food as he was with everything else, but whatever hackles remained raised after an eventful day were smoothed by Elizabeth-Ann's culinary skills. Game was his favourite, especially venison, although he had a weakness for pheasant, hare and even the humble rabbit, all of which would have been hung for exactly the right length of time then marinated or garnished to his taste. A few of his choice recipes together with a number of Exmoor favourites are at Annex F.

Missus knew her man and there were rarely any complaints; Ernest was far too wise and the hunting supper became a family ritual washed down with warm beer or mulled wine. Only then, warm, replete and content, would he finally relax before retiring exhausted.

* *

The one remaining task in this endless cycle was for Ernest to write up his diaries and here, too, there was a strict routine. Invariably he would be up early the following morning doing his rounds of the kennels with the whips and overseeing the selection and separation of hounds for the next meet (no food for them that day) then checking over yesterday's casualties. By ten o'clock, though, he was sitting at his writing desk by the window in the front parlour, first answering the mail – for he was a prodigious writer – then pouring over the maps with a magnifying glass and small measuring wheel.

Carefully, field by field, feature by feature, he would go over the previous day's hunt. His knowledge of the ground was quite exceptional, the diaries showing that he had a name for every lane, piece of cover and farm, indeed most individual houses across the huge Devon and Somerset country as well. If he did not know the actual name of the house or piece of ground he referred to it by the owner's name. Many of the lines taken by the deer and hounds that he described would not be possible today such have been the changes and additions to the landscape. However, by following the natural features on the map, it is possible to see almost exactly how the hunt would have progressed.

He methodically recorded every detail of the day, commencing with a remark about the weather and what the harbourer had in store for them before dealing with the draw. He would conclude his report with a description of who was with him at the kill (seldom very many and sometimes no more than a handful) and it is interesting to see the same names appearing time and again. Those valiant, hard-riding few would have endeared themselves to him but he remembered special visitors as well such as in 1925 when the Prince and Princess Viggo of Denmark hunted with them – Ernest taking enormous pleasure in presenting Her Royal Highness with a slot.

Then the following year the Las Casas family were out (perhaps bringing the story of his deeds in the Boer war to Exford) and Frank Freeman, the famous huntsman of the Pytchley. On another occasion he recorded the presence of four young officers of the 11th Hussars, an event which pleased him no end especially as all four were among the twenty or so in at the kill that day. Finally, he would always record the distances ran and time taken, together with details of the stag's head.

The eight diaries, totalling almost seventeen hundred pages of closely packed, neat handwriting, are nothing less that a remarkable record of his time as huntsman. Not a single day was missed; even when he was unable to hunt himself he recorded what the whipper-in who carried the horn that day had to say.

The principal difficulty for the reader is his humility. Passages often have to be studied again and again (with the aid of the map) in order to determine exactly how difficult a particular task must have been or to read between the lines in order to catch a glimpse of his skill at work out on the moors. Others he praised – not too often – but about himself he had little to say, mostly writing in the third person... *"The huntsman lifted hounds,"* or *"The huntsman cast up the water"*. Fascinating reading, yet infuriating to be denied so much about the man!

It used to take him at least an hour, every phrase thought through carefully before the pen dipped into the double inkwell and he began to write.[3] Again the household would be committed to silence. Missus would have plenty to do for there were the hunting clothes to get ready and the Colonel would be coming for afternoon tea as usual. Amazingly, in the few spare hours remaining, Ernest made himself available to visitors.

* *

They came from every quarter: from Stockleigh where the Wiggins entertained lavishly there might appear the Duke of Beaufort, the Duke of Buccleuch or Lord Knutsford to talk about hound breeding. Local dignitaries would visit also such as Lord Fortescue who would call both in his capacity as Hunt Chairman as well as privately.

Once Sir Herbert Austin, a family friend of the Wiggins, came down bringing one of his tiny motorcars which he parked in the drive, sandwiching it between the Colonel's two enormous Rolls-Royces. Sir Herbert encouraged the Colonel, a burly man and, by now, badly arthritic, to climb in and go for a spin. There followed a struggle and much rocking of springs before the Colonel's big feet revved the engine madly. But he missed the other pedals, causing the little car to shoot across the drive and crash headlong into a stationary lorry – Exford's first motor accident.

Later, a young teenager called Ronnie Wallace would call during the latter part of his summer holidays from Eton, when he was riding to hounds on "Ginger" or "Cadet". Finally there would be the local folk who came sometimes on business and sometimes to pay their respects to the man who had already become a legend. Somehow he found time for them all.

As the seasons went by so his name spread. A typical example was an article in *The Times* of 3 March 1933 when the hunting correspondent wrote about him. *"In our opinion the greatest living artist is not a foxhunter at all, but Ernest Bawden, huntsman to the Devon and Somerset staghounds. Bawden,"* he continued, *"crosses that country at full gallop for hours together without apparent effort, always in touch with his hounds and usually with the deer as well. As the possessor of an eye for the country he is in a class by himself."*

Just one more of the many tributes was made by H.P. Hewett, the author and hunting correspondent, when he visited the kennels. *"If ever there was a contented orderly family, it was Ernest Bawden's hounds, and a visit to them was a revelation for the novice. When the kennel, where the hounds were on their benches, was entered, the huntsman merely held up his hand, and, save for thumping sterns, nothing moved. A hound was called out by name and discussed on the flags, and then in a conversational way told. 'Go back, old boy,' and another was summoned. At the end perhaps one came out unbidden and fawned upon the huntsman, who remarked half apologetically: 'Chorister, sir, an old favourite,' and back he went. One realised then why they worked for him as they did, and why, in the field he had them under such amazing control. To see them fly to Ernest's ecstatic screech was a revelation in utter faith and trust."*

Breeding such a pack was not something that happened over night. It is generally agreed that the best quality will emerge only in the second or third generation of selected hounds, each generation taking three years to come into their prime. Usually the bitches whelp in early Spring, the whelps remaining in the kennels until about the third or fourth month when they go out, either in couples or singly, to farmers or landowners to be walked [4] for a further six months or so before returning early the following year.

They are then entered for the Summer Puppy Show, after which they take up their rightful place in the pack. It is only then that the true merits and limitations of the latest additions can be properly identified – and it may take the huntsman a complete season before he is satisfied one way or the other. If all has gone well and the litter lives up to expectations, the hunt has the basis of a new line. If not then the process has to begin all over again.

This much over-simplified scenario is the most extreme case but it goes to show that several seasons are required before a new line can be established. It is not surprising, therefore, that Ernest was unable to write about the virtues and speed of his bitches or the music of the pack as a whole until 1925. It was on 1 August that he first mentioned the bitch pack hunting so well and a month later wrote about *"The big dog pack hunting splendidly – plenty of pace and music."* It had taken him more than six seasons.

The first mention of the Devon and Somerset Puppy Show and the puppy-walkers being entertained to lunch at the Crown Hotel in Exford was in 1908.[5] Captain Stanley and Sidney Tucker had made a start but, for one reason or another, never managed to continue. When Ernest took over towards the end of the Great War he found that there were but thirty couple of dog hounds in the kennels.

It was a dire situation but he had the foresight to realise that, after the war, hounds would be all but unobtainable – everyone would want to hang on to whatever they had. Nonetheless, he managed to acquire an excellent bitch called "Harmless" from the Garth who was put to the outstanding Heythrop "Comus". Harmless was used again the following year and it was her progeny that formed the foundation of the great staghound pack.

Walter Wiggin used all his considerable influence to improve matters further, which included obtaining the services of Brocklesby "Dragon" who sired many great D and S hounds: the immortal "Dragoon" among others. Tiverton "Actor" and Lord Poltimore's "Guardsman" were two more famous sires. Puppy shows now became a regular feature of the D and S calendar, more and more people realising that the hunt was now not only breeding their own but producing a very fine line and one ideally suited to the Exmoor conditions.

In his book *A Huntsman's Log*, (1925) Mr Isaac Bell wrote as follows: *"I was unaware that the D and S were now home bred, instead of being a collection of drafts, until, one day, on passing the kennels, I called in to see Ernest Bawden. I could hardly believe my eyes when couple after couple of these magnificent hounds danced before my eyes on the flags… Most other visitors agreed that if these hounds had been eligible for the Peterborough Show they were potential winners of a number of classes, and we all agreed that we had never seen such a handsome kennel of such size, and yet such symmetry and quality."*

The famous pack had well and truly arrived but it had taken a number of years and much hard work.

* *

However perfect the situation now appeared to be, Ernest still had his battles in the hunting field. Nothing could ever be taken for granted. On 29 August 1922, after the meet at Hawkridge, hounds ran well – too well in fact – and pressed the deer so hard that it ended up in North Molton *"jumping a high wall into a little garden and from there into the doorway of a dwelling house finally coming to a standstill in the front sitting room… hounds* (followed but eventually)… *were taken away."* Imagine the panic and drama in the cottage that afternoon!

Then again on 3 March the following year in Porlock when *"she got on the roof of a thatch dwelling house at the back and climbed over the roof and ran along the front side…..several couple of hounds followed her and all fell off."*

Four months later they met at Cloutsham. A single hind *"ran back to Webbers Post, to water near East Water foot. There she ran by a man lying dead in the water where they* (everybody) *ran by without taking the slightest notice."* Nobody, least of all the huntsman, stopped to enquire further. It was a case of "Kick on, kick on" to the kill between Poole Bridge and Stoke Combe.

Admittedly these were exceptional cases, his most persistent adversary, as always, was the weather – occasionally pure magic, more often difficult and changeable, sometimes very hell itself. Such as on 19 Sept 1922. Haddon: *"Could not lay on the pack because of fog… went home soon after 3 p.m. the fog was bad on the high ground and it rained in torrents the whole day."* Just two days later at Dunkery Hill Gate: *"This was a blazing hot day and no scent."* Yet they killed.

24 Jan 1928. *"The Barle was overflowing its banks in many places and unfordable."* Yet they killed. Two days later *"It poured with rain and hail all afternoon and the wind was blowing a proper gale."* Again they killed. Two days later from

Cuzzicombe Post: *"It poured with rain again the whole day and by three o'clock the Barle was unfordable."* That day the deer got away but the next day, when *"besides the fog, it again rained in torrents the whole day and the wind blowed a full gale,"* he accounted for two hinds… and so it went on.

Stories of where he managed to make something out of nothing are legion. Time and again his brilliance saved the day, giving the followers a hunt to remember. Days such as 15 February 1923 when hind hunting from Hawkridge. The clever hind began by leading him a merry dance, continually joining up with others, yet Ernest doggedly stuck with her, casting forward each time until she was on her own and eventually ran to water.

Here he *"cast up the Barle and laid on to the hind out of the water by Brewer's Castle… hounds hunting well in and out of the Danesbrook. Later she was fresh found once more in water until hounds accounted for her in the stream at Chilcott Bottom."* An extremely difficult day yet he kept the pack at it until four o'clock – giving the field a fine hunt of no less than four hours.

A year later at Cuzzicombe Post, Ernest put his faith in two couple of trusted tufters thereby securing another remarkable hunt. He laid the pack on early and they ran fast to the Barle where fog descended. Most got onto the quarry and hunted her until she joined up with some stags, at which point he called them off and returned to the water where, earlier, he had noticed that two couple of tufters had split (and had gone off at a 90 degree tangent).

They had *"taken their hind on all alone by Sandyway and Heasley Mill almost to South Molton."* It was a tremendous hunt and according to Ernest *"a very hard day for horses and hounds. They did not reach kennels until long after dark. Carmen, Charity, Harold and Flagman were the heroes that long day."*

The point about all these anecdotes is that while any huntsman worth his salt might achieve such feats as these from time to time (and would be applauded deservedly for his skill), Ernest did so regularly, almost as a matter of course. Day after day, season after season, the supposedly simple hunts were interspersed with demonstrations of amazing skill. Such was his prowess that visitors came from afar safe in the knowledge that their hopes and expectations would be fulfilled, they could almost bank on a great day… there lay the difference between Ernest and his peers and his successors.

George Scoins recalls a time at Exford when the meet was on the green. Two visitors from Kentucky, U.S.A. approached him holding open an American hunting magazine. "Excuse me," one said, "But is *that* him over there?" The title of the double page spread was *"The most famous hunt in England and the most famous huntsman – Ernest Bawden"*. "Yes," Scoins replied. "That's him." It was clear that they had come all the way down to Exford to see one man and he watched as they made their acquaintance, Ernest shyly doffing his cap.

* *

Percy Bawden left Exford school, and home, in 1925 moving to Barnstaple where he studied mechanics and electrical engineering before becoming apprenticed to a garage. His father was shocked at this sudden change, Percy remembering a change coming over him. "As the time came for me to leave home, so he seemed to mellow towards me. For the first time he started to take an interest in what I was doing and it was as though neither he nor mother wanted me to leave." Life, for Ernest, had come a full circle. There, mirrored in his own son, was nothing less than his own burning desire to escape to a life different to that which was on offer, and at exactly the same age. It was a bitter irony.

Perhaps he had seen it coming, or perhaps it came as a surprise, but Ernest had to accept that his son was never going to show an interest in country pursuits and most certainly wanted nothing to do with life in the kennels. The boy had done well at school and knew what he was after, but it meant leaving home and it was his parents who felt the separation more, his mother in particular. Barnstaple was a considerable distance from Exford and the lad was barely seventeen. Ernest moved swiftly, buying him a Norton 18 motorcycle,[6] something he was able to afford with his boot money.

Riding the Exmoor roads on a motorbike in all weathers was rarely a pleasant experience, even when kitted out in a First World War Royal Flying Corps leather helmet and goggles. Two years later the machine was uprated to a motorcar,[7] a luxury almost unheard of for a village boy in those days. One suspects that the calm and persuasive manner of an anxious mother lay behind the decision, nonetheless Ernest was happy enough to provide once more, his son now becoming quite the young man about town.

However, there was another reason for changing the machines: Percy loved speed and drove with a wild and desperate abandon. His record for covering the 25 miles from door to door was just thirty-one minutes, the speedometer nudging 100 miles an hour on the appalling Exmoor roads – and on a winter's night at that. It was the ominous "Hawkridge wild streak" reappearing with a vengeance and his parents were aghast.

Ernest missed his son and did what he could to make life more amenable for him whenever he was home, later building for him the first garage in the village. He was rightly proud of him, forever amazed at his grasp of the mysterious new mechanical world, and they were to remain close for the rest of his life.

By now he was approaching fifty, and while all the fire and dynamism remained with him in the hunting field (indeed many were convinced that the older he got the harder he drove himself) he was indeed beginning to mellow. Although the tongue remained as sharp as ever and the fuse dangerously short, some of the hardness had gone. He was never easy, the nervous pent-up energy in his strangely withdrawn character remaining volatile, but the departure of his son had had its effect and a gap appeared in his life. Extraordinary as it may seem, he missed the company of the young.

Dick Lloyd remembers Ernest riding out to Pitsworthy to see his father, Ned, about hunting matters. He and his twin brother, Pat, would wait for him, hoping he might spend some time playing with them. He always did and the boys loved it. Lorna, Ralph Slocombe's daughter, remembers him well when she, as a young girl, had no fear at all of the man with the awesome reputation. And there was Jean, the youngest daughter of his younger and favourite sister, who remembers his kindly smile and strong hands as he helped her scramble onto his lap. All of them spoke warmly of him, but it was Jean's eldest sister, Dolly, who finally melted his heart.

Ernestine – for that was Dolly's name – had developed into an attractive young woman who had her admirers, yet was badly jilted in a love affair. Ernest hated the man, Percy too, and they had warned her about his ways but love prevailed until it was too late and the girl was left in the lurch. It was Ernest who took command, stepping in and arranging for her to come and stay at the kennels until she had regained her composure.

He never learned to drive (maintaining his deep mistrust of anything mechanical until the end) yet picnics and outings to the seaside were arranged, the transport provided by Fred Newton from the village who would drive them out for the day. The huntsman would navigate – his small, lean face peering anxiously over the top of the high dashboard of the huge American "Overland". With Dolly and Missus in the back, they would grind their way slowly over the Exmoor hills to some particular spot he had selected.

Modern life crept slowly into the village, in particular electricity and it was not until 1930 that the kennels had even a generator of their own – the machine whose timings Ernest controlled with such fiendish delight. A wireless, however, came earlier. It was a cumbersome affair built in Barnstaple and powered by two wet batteries that Percy changed each time he came home. Fred Lock, the blacksmith, was summoned to erect the aerial on the outside wall and the machine was installed in the cottage with a great flourish. Ernest was fascinated, arranging what little spare time he had around his favourite programmes as keenly as any TV addict today.

Albert Sandler and the Palm Court Orchestra on Sunday evenings was a must, later it was Flanagan and Allen, then Gracie Fields. Sporting contests, whenever England was involved, took on an importance all of their own, Ernest sometimes being caught out by the clock as he sat crouched listening to the ball-by-ball commentary of a Test match. A great moment at the kennels was a visit by Sir Walter Hammond. The famous batsman had been ill for some time and came down to Exford to recuperate. Being a keen follower of hounds, he had heard all about the D and S and the huntsman in particular. An introduction was arranged when the two of them enjoyed a memorable afternoon together.

* *

However much softer or easier life might have become at home, Ernest remained totally committed to his hunting. Records show that as time went on so he became ever more successful in the field, the runs recorded by hunting correspondents becoming more remarkable by the year and word of his deeds spread throughout the hunting world.

Richard Stapledon writes of him in *Exmoor – Elegance and Rhythm*: *"He was a great artist and complete master of his professional craft... In some respects he was almost a deer himself – the deer's mind and his working on the same lines."*[8]

Lionel Edwards, the artist, spoke of him as *"a most remarkable personality – a man of indomitable spirit pluck and perseverance....he galloped over wet ground and down the steepest hillsides at an astonishing pace.....flapping like a curlew o'er the moor, and with as great ease".* His page-long tribute in *Country Life* was illustrated with sketches of Ernest with his hounds.

G.G.Collyns sums it up perfectly with one line in his book, *Exmoor Staghunting*: *"It need only be remarked that the general opinion is that he can never have had a peer in his profession."*

One wonders what it was that drove him so relentlessly when there was nothing left to achieve. Of his many outstanding qualities there were three that stood out in his later years, the first of which was his pride. Ever since he was a small boy he had demonstrated an almost fanatical determination to succeed: later winning numerous pony races, prizes for marksmanship, athletic prizes for middle distance running and trophies for his performance in the Royal North Devon Hussars. His competitive spirit to remain the best – his pride – was deeply engrained in his makeup.

Secondly, he demonstrated an intense loyalty and sense of duty. He could be relied upon always to give of his very best, no matter what the circumstances or how high the odds stacked against him might have been. He was devoted to the hunt and to his Master in particular. Nothing but nothing was going to sully their names – he would see to that.

Then finally, and deep down inside, there lurked that cruel and totally ruthless streak (the dark, sinister third personality). Every hunt was a challenge; a duel to the bitter end and nothing was to stand in his way. Even his very last hunt of all on 20 April 1937 was a day to remember.

* *

But enough has been said – indeed there is little more to say – and it is time to pull it all together. As the 1920s turned into the 1930s, so The Devon and Somerset Staghounds were at the very peak of their fame. The hunt had entered its golden era, something Ernest himself will describe in the next chapter.

Notes

1. Potions and concoctions confirmed by David Randall (now retired) huntsman to the Albrighton, Holderness and Badsworth hounds.
2. Captain E.R.Lloyd.
3. Writing desk and inkstand now with his grandson, Mr Gerald Bawden.

4. Looking after the puppies i.e feeding, exercising and caring for them as outside dogs but never as indoor pets. The walkers became very attached to "their" puppies, following their progress with the hunt throughout their career.
5. *A Short History of the Devon and Somerset Staghounds.* Ralph Greaves.
6. A fearsome beast of 500 cc which, in 1924, cost £90 new.
7. A Morris Cowley "Occasional Four."
8. Richard Stapledon, as headmaster, taught at "Kestrels", a nearby preparatory school to which he would invite Ernest to lecture the boys on hunting and wild life.

Chapter 13

THE GOLDEN YEARS

There can be no better way of describing the hunting during Ernest's era other than to get the man himself to do the talking, directly from his diaries. However, selecting the very best of the hunts has *not* been easy. He hunted hounds well over two thousand three hundred times in all, providing outstanding sport on literally scores of occasions, five or six of which almost beggar belief. It was not so much a question of what to include, rather which of so many brilliant runs had to be omitted. In the end I decided to cover just nine, together with the greatest hunt of them all.

I chose three for the Autumn stags, three for hinds and three for the Spring stags, picked from the whole of his twenty years as huntsman and it is interesting to note that all but one fall within the relatively short period between 1924–1932. They were all great hunts which I selected from every corner of the moor yet, even here, one or two did not always go according to plan such as when he switched deer. Very occasionally it was the deer that won the day – after all, the man was only human. Even so the reader should be able to get a feel for what it must have been like to ride to hounds when Ernest carried the horn.

Before the great man takes over, a number of points need to be stressed. First, and it is not possible to escape from it, the weather. There seems to be little doubt that the pattern of our climate is changing and doing so far more rapidly than we might suppose. Currently it appears to be far less extreme than seventy-five years ago. Ernest never exaggerated – he never had to – and, time after time, he wrote of appalling weather, when the frost was iron hard for weeks on end, when snow drifted up to the top of hedgerows and filled the gateways or when even the upper reaches of the rivers were unfordable. When a mere stream in flood was unfordable to a fearless horseman in a hurry, the countryside must have been very wet indeed.

Then there is Exmoor. While not particularly high in comparison with other National Parks – Dartmoor is several hundred feet higher – the ground is often steep and the climb from the bottom of the deep combes to the top of the high plateaux long and hard. For instance, the route out of the little village of Oare (Lorna Doone) to Larkbarrow rises 700 feet, from Tarr Steps to the top of Winsford Hill it is 750, and from the coverts beneath Yarde Down to the top of Fyldon Ridge it is a long haul of nothing less than 1000 feet. It was, and remains, mighty tough on the horses when, on even an average day, the hunt will climb and descend many times.

The bogs, while not lethal, can set a horse floundering up to its girth in the space of a few strides. The sedge can be every bit as exhausting to cross as plough, while galloping through heather and bracken (where the ground underneath is blind to horse and rider) can tax the strongest of nerves. Rivers can be deep, the woodland coverts thick and the tracks through them narrow and twisting.

Finally, there is the chase itself. Remember that it is Ernest who is hunting so, once underway, the business will be fast and furious. There may be a check or two but you must get yourself there in time for a blow before they pick up the line and are off again. There will be no formal jumping but there will be mad scrambles across open ditches or low banks, and the odd wild leap across the bottom of rock-strewn and waterlogged gullies.

The further you get down the slopes the steeper they become so you must set your own pace and not get carried away by the rush of those around you. On the flat open moorland it is a case of "devil take the hindmost" and riders will be taking their own line in an attempt to make up for lost time. How very different the countryside here to the neat, chequer-board country of the gently undulating Shires.

But you will get there in the end – if you are lucky. Ernest will have already killed the deer and be hovering over the carcass, jacket off and sleeves rolled up. Horses will be standing with legs apart and heads lowered, steaming and blowing hard. Their riders, by now dismounted, will be swapping hip flasks and adventures of the chase. Above and behind you in the woods you will hear others hurrying down to the scene.

Ernest will have cut off the slots to be awarded to those who have done especially well.[1] If he had noticed you riding hard and "kicking on", then one could be for you. His final task will be to clean out the carcass, the paunch going to the hounds. As the pack takes its reward so he will blow the long plaintive "Mort" on the horn when caps will be raised in salute to a gallant stag and a fine run.

Later the carcass will be skinned and cut up, the venison distributed to those over whose land the deer had been feeding, and the offal reserved for those who had given special assistance. The dressed carcass of a good stag can weigh upwards of 100 kilos so there will be plenty of venison to go round. It will be up to the Master to decide who, if anyone, should have the head. Most likely it will go to a farmer or landowner, or perhaps to the village hall close to where the deer was found or even the public house where they met that day. On the other hand he may decide to keep it for himself (Colonel Wiggin often did), or it might be destined to hang in the kennels.

* *

The following runs have been taken straight from Ernest's diaries and have been cross-checked with the *West Somerset Free Press* archives from which I have taken their initial captions such as "A glorious gallop ensues". I spent hours picking and choosing but am more than satisfied that they were all wonderful runs and worthy of inclusion. I have edited his words as sparingly as possible leaving you, the reader, to wonder how a man with no formal education could write as he did. Whenever I have seen fit to comment I have done so in italics. Finally, it is worth wondering how he unfailingly found the time in his busy schedule to sit quietly and write up such meticulous accounts.

Now then... it's time to check your girth and gather up the reins. Hounds are about to move off.

Autumn Staghunting

1. Dulverton. 16 August 1927. "A glorious gallop ensues."

The Master (Col Wiggin) arranged this meet in connection with the opening of the new Town Hall by him at Dulverton on this date. To celebrate the occasion further, for the first time in the history of the D and S hunt the pack consisted of all bitches (twenty and a half couple). Hounds were taken to

Highnam Farm[2] and kennelled. Lang had a good stag harboured in Buckminster Wood and the tufters roused him at once. He broke away up through lower Durhams then across the Danesbrook, running up the south side of Hawkridge Ridge then over to Three Waters Cleeve. Back again… to Church Wood, turning down to White Rocks then away towards Five Crossways. Being headed here he right turned-down through Shircombe Slade and on across Windball where the tufters were stopped and the pack laid on.

They ran into Burridge Wood where our stag joined another fine deer. After many turns around the covert most of the pack became settled on to the hunted stag again. They hunted him beautifully up across Windball again, across the Barle at Draydon Ford. No one could follow owing to the Barle being in flood, however hounds hunted up the Ashwick covers to Dipper Copse where part of the pack broke away on a hind with the remainder getting back on to our hunted stag at Castle Bridge. After a while we quite unknowingly changed to a young four year old stag.

Hounds went up the Danesbrook, over Anstey Common (at a great pace) away over Molland Moor to lower Willingford Bridge. Here two hinds caused complications, however, hounds were got together and laid back on to the stag now away onto Lords and then left handed over Worth Hill and Withypool Common to the Barle above Landacre Bridge. Up stream a little way then up over Bradymoor to Ashott Farm. Here he turned sharp left handed and from there across Gipsy Lane and on by Honeymead, across the Simonsbath road to the Prayway wall. This he followed for a mile before turning down into the Exe, which he beat up a little then turned to Warren Meads before crossing Trout Hill into Buscombe. Hounds checked here for sometime but they were cast downstream and owned the line once more before running to Badgery Water just below the Cott.

There they hit off the line on the Deerpark side and hunted nicely up into the heather near the top of Woodcock Combe, working right up to the stag where he was lying up in the tall heather. He just managed to get away from them down to water and was taken just at the bottom of the Waterslide at 4.15p.m. He was a four year old and carried a small head.

Note. Interesting for several reasons. First, Ernest switched stags. Very unusual but the likely reasons were the wet, flooded ground and thick cover. It was the middle of August yet the Barle was in flood! They had been messing about in the Barle Valley for some time and he wanted to get on with it. Secondly, note his descriptions of the checks. One has to imagine how he handled things to get them going again. Thirdly, he must have been right up with the pack and in sight of the stag at the end of this very fine hunt.

Once Ernest had got the stag away the run was a 12½ mile point – a little over 20 as hounds ran but, before that, they had had a 13 mile hack out to the meet that morning. The tufters worked hard for a couple of hours before the chase and, at the end of the day, they had a 6 mile ride home.

* *

2. Brendon Two Gates. 17 August 1929. "A chase of over three hours."

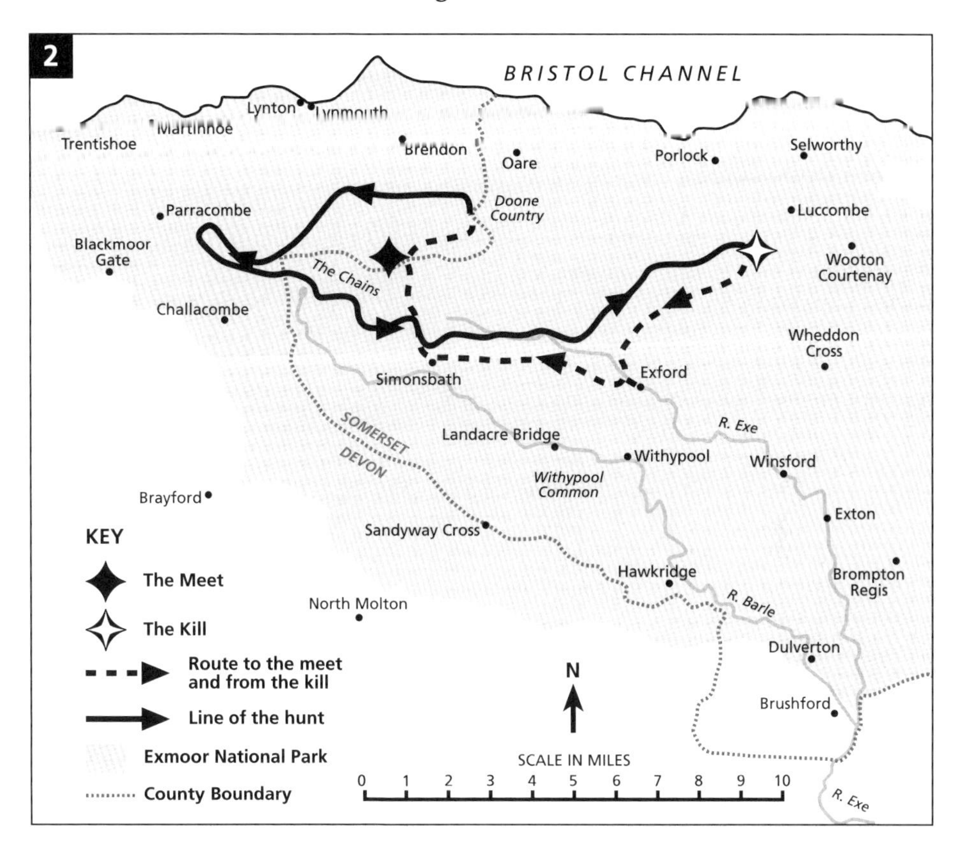

Kennelled at Badgery Cott. Lang had six stags of various sizes harboured in Badgery Wood. On our way to the draw a stag was observed lazing in the bracken in Badgery Cleeve and it was decided to hunt him *(Ernest's eye caught just the tip of the antlers in the bracken).* On being roused, however, two more stags got up, the best of them a fair stag. They broke up over Badgery Lees so the pack was laid on.

They ran very fast up by Withybush across the Brendon road at Dry Bridges then on over Farley Water before going away left handed across Cheriton Ridge. They then ran over the Chains leaving Saddler's Gate on the right, hounds crossed Woodbarrow Arms on to Longstone bog where the two stags divided. Hounds very fortunately stuck to the better of the two and hunted down Butterhill into Woolhanger plantations where all the pack got on to some hinds.

They were stopped and on being cast back fresh found their stag close by Mr Slater's house. However, after doubling once around the ponds he turned back over Butterhill (low down) then went right up the valley, away at the top along Stone Barrows before swinging left handed on North Regis Common close by Pinkery Pond. Then all along the Chains wall which he crossed before reaching Exe Head. After running down Tang's Bottom he went on over Ridds

Hill to Prayway Gate. Being headed there by motor cars, he doubled right handed down into Limecombe. From the bottom of this he broke away left handed by Barton Farm across the Simonsbath road. Then on across Ashcombe, leaving Cloven Rocks on the right and on to Honeymead where he sunk down to the Exe under Ware Ball.

From there he beat downstream to Western Mill Farm, then up by Castle Farm to the Wellshead road for some distance before crossing it and dropping into Allcombe Water. He then beat downstream again before breaking out above Pitsworthy. Hounds hunted nicely up over Pitsworthy Common, over Almsworthy then down by Chetsford Bridge and so on downstream. He left the water just above the new water works and climbed over Poole Plain then over Wilmersham Common into the gorse and bracken near the farm. Here hounds fresh found him and raced him down the valley where they finally accounted for him above the footbridge at the bottom of Redway at 3.20p.m. *(Phew!)*

Three hours twenty from lay on. A light bodied forest stag of two atop either side. A very fine moorland hunt. From the find to Woolhanger is 6 miles across the map. Woolhanger to Simonsbath is 6 more and from Simonsbath to the kill under Cloutsham Ball is 8. This makes a total point to point of 20 miles exactly. A big pack of twenty-two and a half couple out; all up at the kill except for one and a half, one couple of which were puppies.

Note. A massive hunt by any account. Interesting to see that they did not go for the harbourer's stag but took a gamble on what they saw on their way in (very risky – all or nothing, no less). Staghunters often hunt two or more deer together, waiting for the one they want to break away, and this was a classic example of the practice. Notice how cars were already getting in the way – much to Ernest's disgust!

Ernest's reckoning of 20 miles is simply straight lines joined together. Twenty five, at least, would be more like it, added to which the stag climbed and descended for all of 2000 feet before he got to the top of the Chains and would have done the same again over the next 12 miles or so. How, might one ask, would your horse look at the end of this run and that's before the hour and a half hack back to Exford?

* *

3. Hawkcombe Head. 10 October 1929.
"A brilliant run of nearly four hours."

Lang had heard two or three stags belling in Culbone plantation where, after a little trouble with some hinds, one of them was found near Twitchen combe. Hounds settled to him well and hunted him about the plantation for nearly half an hour before he went away… over the main road and away down over North Common. Tufters were stopped and the pack brought from Lillycombe House. After giving the field a chance to come up, the pack was let go and they started to run at a tremendous pace right down to Oare Ford then up on to Mill Hill.

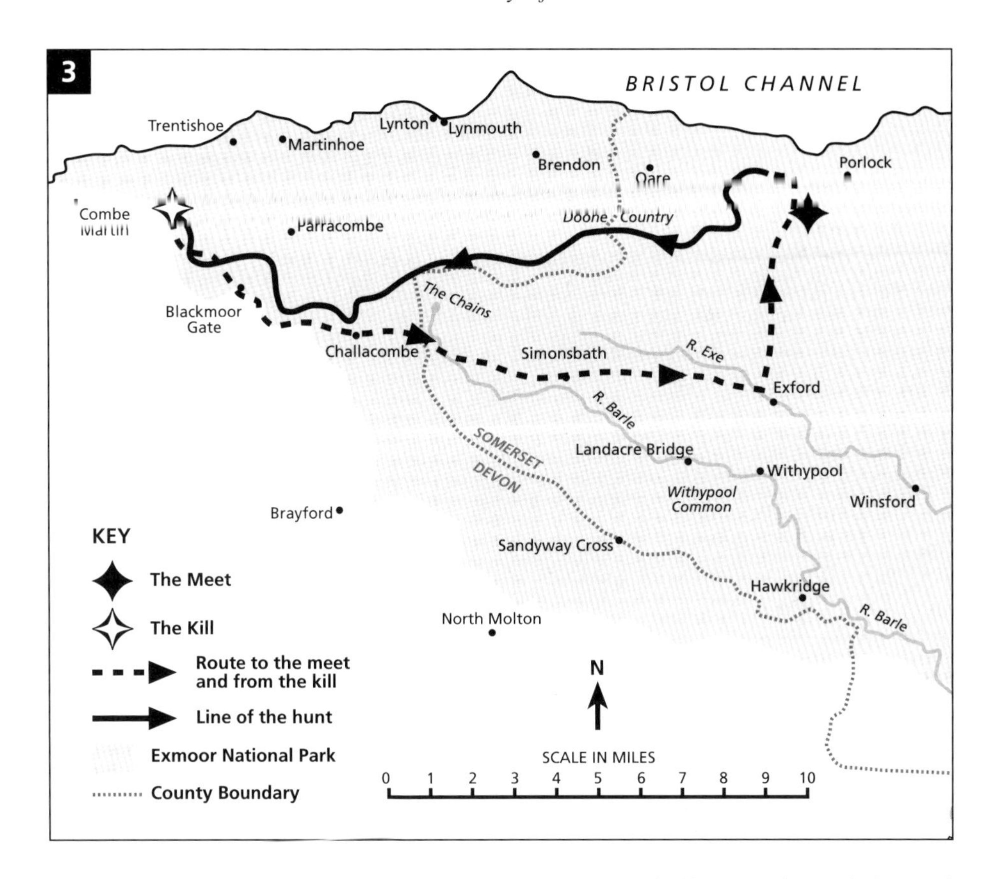

Swinging right handed down Alscott combe into Chalk Water, hounds hunted beautifully up to Stoford crossing and then hit the line out of the water and away over Oare Common. They were here held up for a few minutes to allow the field to get up. On being let go again they ran down Clannacombe then along the bottom of Deerpark, crossing Badgery Water then away to Withybush where they were again held by the huntsman to allow the field a chance.

When let go again they veered left handed along Brendon Common crossing the road near Brendon Two Gates before sinking down to Farley Water. Hounds were cast upstream without result but, on being tried downstream, soon hit off the line and drove on over Cheriton Ridge crossing Hoar Oak by the Oak Tree. Away streamed hounds right over the Chains and away thence above Saddler's Gate into Woodbarrow Arms. On reaching Longstone bog, the stag turned left handed down over Swincombe. Only the huntsman and Bert Lang had been anywhere near the flying pack and, on overtaking them, they were checked among sheep at the bottom of Swincombe.

The line was soon recovered and hounds hunted down to the Challacombe Inn. After casting hounds soon recovered the line but this check had enabled the field to catch up. Hounds then hunted in a delightful manner away above Swincombe towards the Friendship Inn but swung right handed across

Westlands and Rowley Down, crossing the main road and railway above Rowley Barton before sinking down under Cowley Wood. The stag doubled back on his own line but hounds soon hit it off and then broke away towards Kentisbury Down. Hounds were fast gaining on him now and, getting to close quarters, raced him across Higher Cowley farm and accounted for him finally in the lane near Dean at 3.30p.m.

Three hours forty minutes from rouse in Culbone. He was a good stag with three atop both sides. The farthest points touched during this hunt was over 12 miles, mostly all on the moor. A great many of the field got to the end of this fine hunt and all hounds were up at the finish (Twenty and a half couple of bitches).

Note. 25 miles again. The sheer pace of the run shines through his account – "Tremendous," he wrote. "Hounds running beautifully" and "the flying pack" can only mean one thing – even he was hard pressed to stay with them. He rarely stopped for the field to catch up yet here he felt obliged to do so on three occasions, which allowed so many of them to get in at the end. The stag ran across several of the steepest and deepest combes on the northern side of the moor and it is remarkable that every single hound kept with it to the end. What a hunt it must have been! One final point… kennels were all but 20 miles from where they killed.

* *

Hind Hunting

4. Winsford Hill. 20 December 1924. "Best hind hunt of the season."

Found a few hinds in Burrow Wood that ran down the Allotments, Edbrooke and Week woods over Hollam Knapp into Redcleve and Broford Wood. A single hind went on through Sale Wood across Stockholm Park. Stopped tufters here and laid on the pack.

Ran to water at Anthony's Weir then downstream to Lower Baronsdown Lodge, hitting off the line where she kept the water, then up into Helebridge Wood where hounds fresh found their hind. She broke away across Jury Hill through Rookwood and Pezzlecombe Wood to water against Perry Meadows. Hounds caught a view here and raced their hind towards the chemical works then up over Burston Farm and along by the railway past Keens and Morebath Station to the River Batherm at Petton.

She beat upstream to the mills and then broke away up over Potters Farm into Raddington Valley. Turning up here past Chubworthy Farm and on to the River Tone just below Waterrow, she beat downstream under the viaduct to Hagley Farm. Leaving water again here she went on down the valley to Stawley where hounds killed at 1.55p.m. about three hours from find to finish. Except when waiting about ten minutes for the pack at Chilly Bridge, there was no check at all. The big dog hounds hunted beautifully all the way

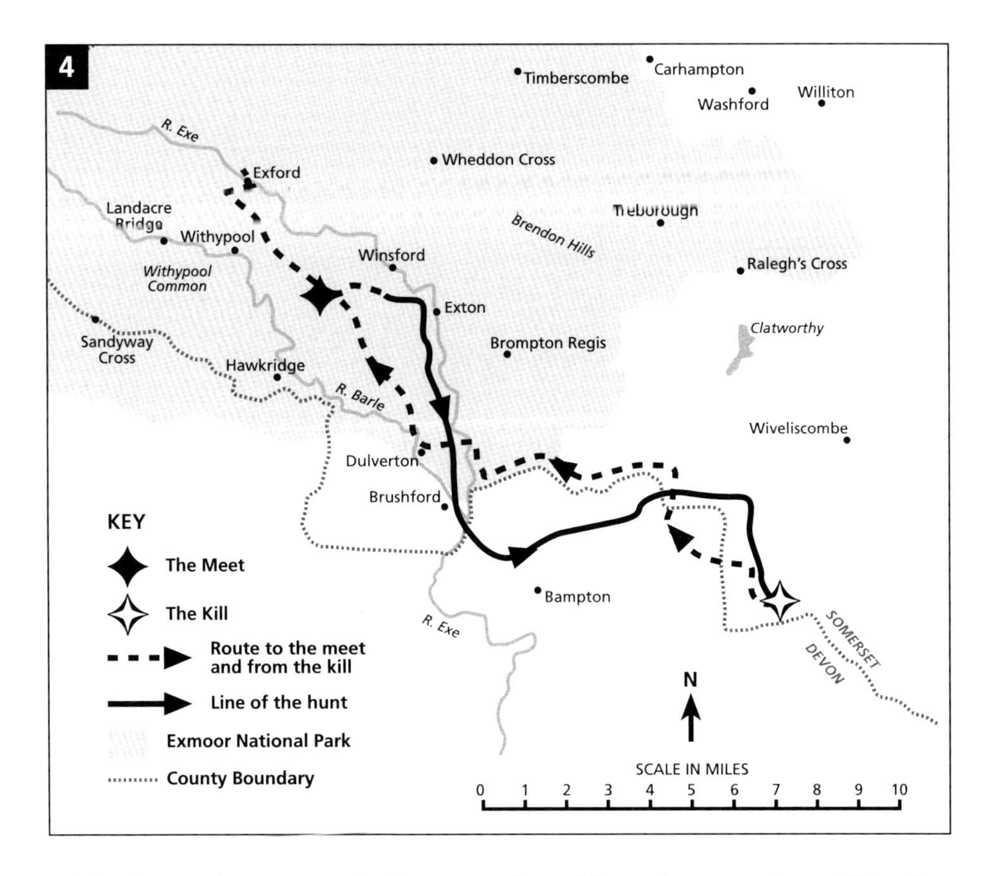

with plenty of tongue and all up together. The point was about 13½ miles but as hounds ran it was much more than twenty. The best hind hunt so far this season.

Note. A classic hind hunt where the quarry twisted and turned in and out of the coverts before breaking away. The big dog hounds were more likely to be used in the tougher going of woodland and farm lands (leaving the faster and lighter bitches for the open moorland). Here Ernest writes about "plenty of tongue" something he and the master had been trying to breed into the pack. It paid off for he was able to keep in touch throughout this cracking hunt.

5. Larkbarrow. 10 January 1925. "Two brilliant hunts."

(A lovely wild and desolate moorland farmhouse vacated during Second World War and used by the Americans as target practise. Very little now remains).

Laid tufters on to a few hinds low down in Lankcombe at 11.15a.m. They ran up Tippacott Ridge then left handed by Withybush to the top of

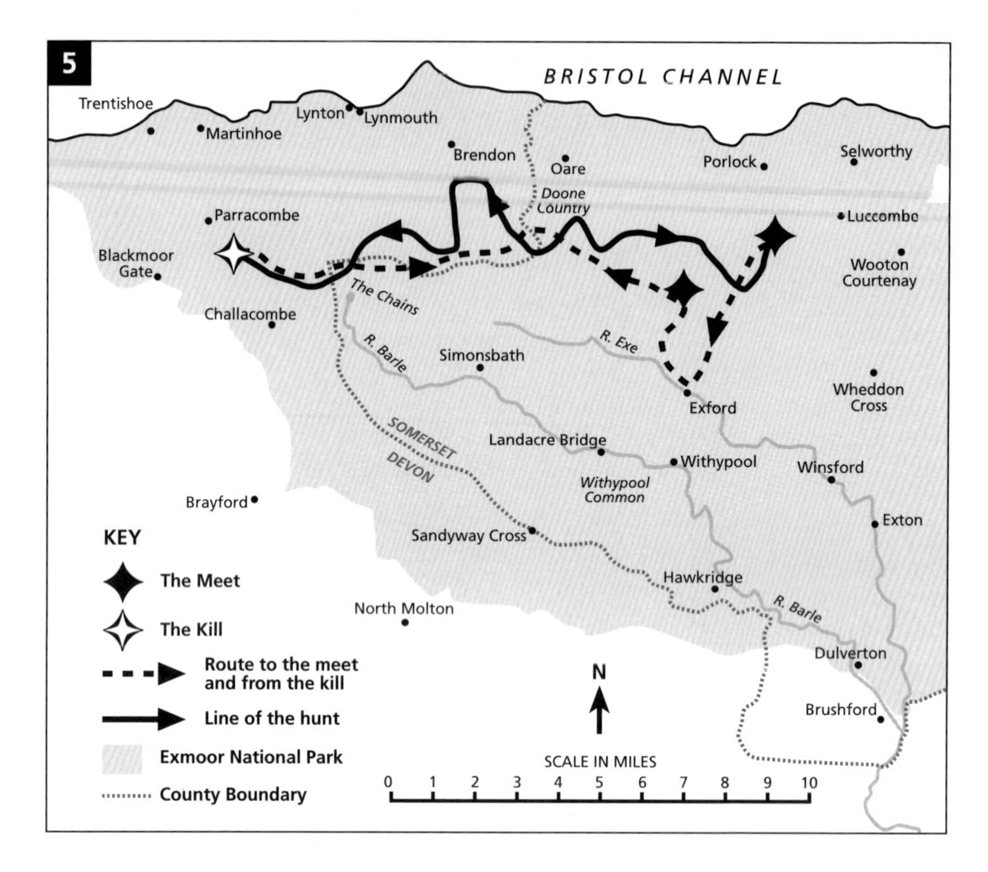

Brendon Common where they joined another small herd of hinds. They all went over the Brendon road into Farley Water where the tufters settled on to a single hind.

They went away over Cheriton Ridge and on by Hoar Oak Cott, across the top of Ruckham Combe, leaving Saddler's Gate just to their right. On again across Woodbarrow Arms, Longstone Bog, Chapman's Barrow to the top of Swincombe, turning sharp right handed from here they ran down to the right of Tennerley Combe and killed by Holworthy Farm at 12.30p.m, one hour and ten minutes from the start. Captain Le Bas and myself were the only ones in this hunt as all the field stayed in the Brendon road.

It took just over an hour to get back to Badgery Cott where the tufters were laid on to a few hinds in the Doone Valley at 1.35p.m. They went into Hoccombe Water and back again over Hoccombe Hill and Badgery Lees into Landcombe and turning up to Withybush. Four and a half couple turned back on a single hind and, from here, went down Lankcombe across Badgery Water up Woodcock combe and Deerpark where the pack was laid on.

They went away at a tremendous pace across Oldhay Heath, Chalk Water, Mill Hill and Black Barrows into Weir Water then right up this and away left handed over Luccott Moor to the hill fence above Luccott. They then turned sharp right handed down Luccott Brake into Nutscale Water close by New Mill, before turning up stream. Hounds raced up to their hind under Nutscale Brake but she got away and climbed up over Poole Plain on to Stoke Ridge as if for Sweetery but then turned right down by the Cloutsham road some distance before again turning left handed down by Stoke Pero. Here she ran to water at the bottom of Prickslade then on down stream to Eastwater Foot where hounds got up to their hind and killed just below at 2.45p.m.

One hour and ten minutes from lay on in the Doone Valley. These two extraordinary fast hunts were done in exactly two hours and twenty-five minutes. The point from where we killed the first hind to Eastwater Foot is 14 miles as the crow flies. All those who know the country will understand what a tremendous pace hounds ran to do it in this time. A good many of a large field much enjoyed the second hunt. The moor was very wet.

Note. Two for the price of one! As so many missed the first hunt (why, we don't know), the Colonel would have given Ernest the nod to have a second go and he needed no second bidding.[3] *The speed over the deeply rolling countryside was quite tremendous and by 2.45p.m most, if not everybody, would have had enough. Sadly he does not tell us which pack was hunting – my guess is that it would have been the bitches.*

* *

6. Cuzzicombe Post. 12 February 1924.
"Hounds beaten by the weather."

Fog was very thick on all of the high ground so the Master decided to draw down Gourte Wood way where it was a little clearer. Found three deer there which went away up on the moor where hounds got on to another herd which they rattled around Molland Moor and Cuzzicombe. They went back towards Gourte Wood and away at the top of Coombe Wood where the pack was laid on.

They, however, could not settle on to the line for sometime but hunted on to Woodlands and Twitchen, before passing Five Cross Ways and going on to the Barle at Castle Bridge. Here she turned back up to Whiterocks where a lot of fresh deer got in the way. Hounds turned right handed near Venford and went on to Church Wood before going into the valley and on almost to Castle Bridge.

Here they went up the Barle and away up to Mounsey Hill Gate. Most of the pack was lost in the fog from here but were recovered again under Oxenhams Brake where they had come in from Winsford Hill. Here the hind was fresh found after a cast upstream to Batsom. She went away by Bradley Quarry, over Winsford Hill and down by Bradley Bog to water under Oxenhams Brake again.

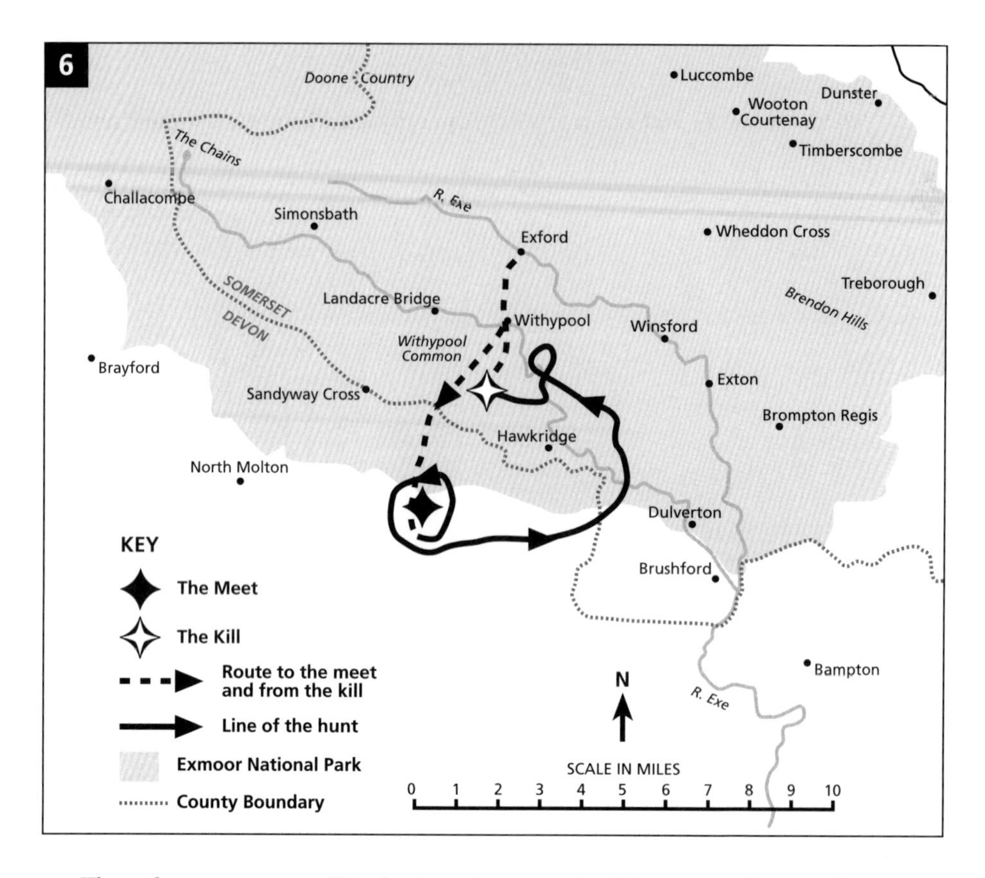

Then downstream to Hindspit and on up the Westwater Stream just short of the farm she left the water and made for Lords. The fog was, however, so thick, that by now the hounds had to be stopped at 4.30p.m. The hind was only just in front and dead beat. This was one of the hardest days of the season as hounds were running for nearly five hours.

Note. This hunt is included not because of the sport it gave (which was excellent) but for the sheer audacity of hunting in such thick fog. The Master must have known his man for Ernest got away with it – just – having lost the pack near Mounsey Hill Gate. Yet still they went on. The hind, which must have been a seasoned campaigner, won the day even when Ernest was snapping at her heels and he would have been the first to raise his cap to her.

The reader needs to read Ernest's account again and again in order to see just how much skill he put into the day's work – his patience, perseverance and hound work were all quite exceptional. But such boldness sometimes paid off, for the next day it froze hard then snowed, causing all hunting to be cancelled for three weeks. This is a report when we would have loved to have learnt more about his skill in working hounds.

* *

SPRING STAGHUNTING

7. North Molton. 26 March 1932. "A great hunt through ten parishes."

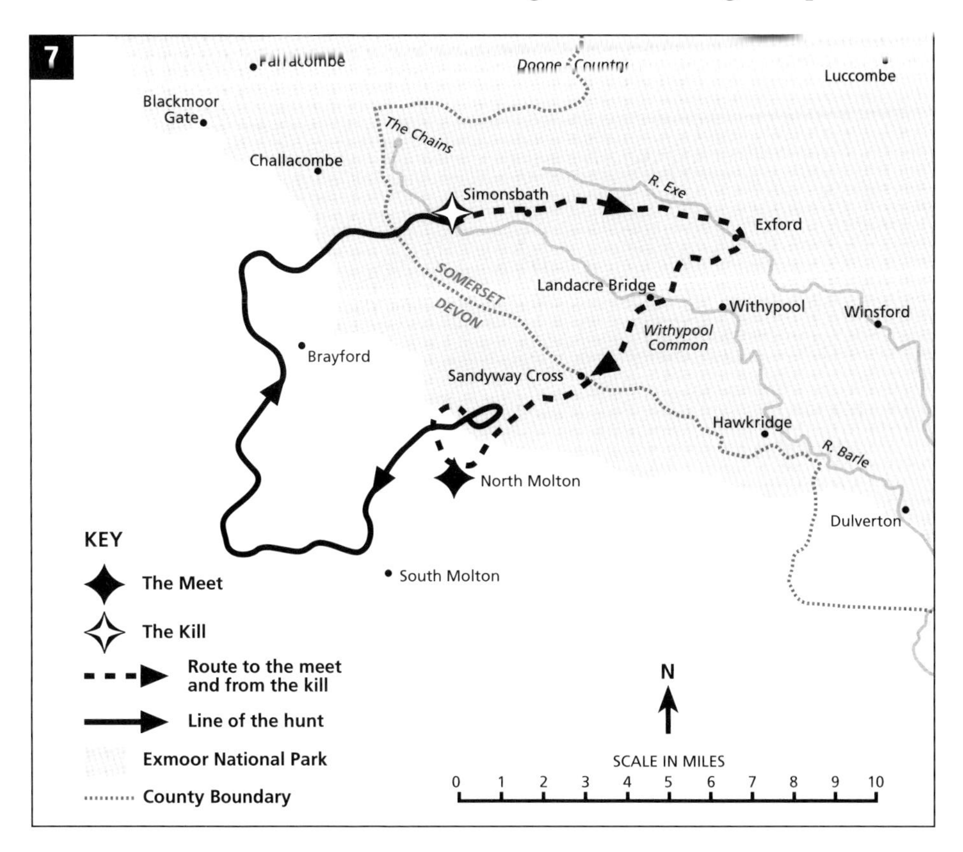

Heavy rain had fallen during the night, making the very hard state of the ground a little better for horses and hounds. There was thick fog on the hills but the stag of the day took us down country and by the late afternoon all the fog had cleared. There was a large field out which followed the pack to Heasley Mill to kennel. Lang had five stags harboured on Barcombe Heath, three of them big deer, one a four year old and one a three year old. By the time the tufters got to Barcombe Heath the deer had moved into the thick gorse above Brinsworthy Farm.

On being roused the small stag parted out at once and went up towards North Molton common. However he doubled left handed down Barkham Heath, went through the "Isle of Dogs" plantation and South Wood, crossed thence into Home Park and then broke away at the top across the Yarde Down-North Molton road towards Combeshead. The tufters could not be stopped so the pack was fetched and laid on by the huntsman some fifteen minutes behind.

They went at a great pace via Oakford, Westpark, North and South Lee farms thence through Hacche Wood to the railway at the bottom of Hacche Moors. He crossed over and away by South Molton town swinging right handed from there to Kingsland Barton and Hill, on by Townhouse and into the Bray River where he turned upstream for some way before going on towards Filleigh. Before there however hounds turned left handed by Bradbury and Langston before running almost into the village of Chittlehampton from which place four and a half couple of tufters were got up to.

The deer had turned back from the village and had gone on fifteen minutes ahead by Heywood into the Hawkridge Brook and ran up this a little way before going on over Tower Moor towards Swimbridge. However he turned right handed by Kerscott through High Down to the railway under Brights Leary. By this time the sun had got quite hot *(imagine the state of the horses!)* and scent was beginning to fail.

After a slight check the line was hit off over the railway and carried on at a good pace towards West Buckland. Just short of here, however, the stag turned by Gubbs and Taddiport into the Stoodleigh Bottom, thence over Stoodleigh Down. On reaching Barnacott a lot of sheep and cattle caused a long check before the line was again recovered and hounds hunted steadily on by Beara and on to Little Bray Cross to the Cape of Good Hope.

Swinging sharp right handed down Leworthy Farm and into the River Bray hounds soon owned the line down stream but unfortunately overshot the point where the stag had left water into Ovis Wood. He had been viewed by Mr Robins passing Gratton Farm while the pack were being cast down the Bray and it took some time for the information to reach the hunt. The stag was now forty-five minutes ahead but hounds picked up the line and ran on by Five Cross Ways before sinking down under Natsley then climbing up between Muxworthy and Kedworthy on to Bray Common.

Up to this point and for more than an hour hounds had great difficulty in carrying the line at all but, by degrees, they worked it out to the top of Sherracombe and on to Ricksey Ball where they threw up on account of this being burnt ground. They were picked up and cast forward to the Barle under Smallacombe and very soon owned the line where the stag had left the water for a little way before entering it again upstream.

It was now 5.30p.m. and the stag was an hour ahead. All horses were dead beat so hounds went down the Barle Valley to Simonsbath and home. This wonderful, tough stag was found at twelve o'clock. He had been hunted for five and a half hours, more than half the time at a great pace. From the farthest point he touched on Barkham Heath to Chittlehampton is 8½ miles across the map and from Chittlehampton to the Barle under Driver Cott is 11, making a total of 19 in all. Only a few got to the end. Nineteen and a half couple of bitches out and all were up except one at the end.

Note. Ernest was the first to salute this incredible young stag, however his map reading was wrong. Covering the ground from point to point as he described it, the distance was almost exactly 30 miles and a total climb across the country of nearly 3500 feet. No wonder the horses were dead beat and what about the hounds who would have covered far more ground?

But, here again, one can see it was marvellous hunting. Very early on they must have decided to settle for the youngest stag and, once on to it, could not stop the tufters. Then everything got in the way – railway lines are the very devil and there was the heat of the day, the burnt ground, and over half of this great run was across low lying farmland – with all the fences and hedges and other obstacles to contend with. Yet still they pressed on, most likely having to do without their change of horses. A remarkable day. It might be worth considering how you would have played it were you riding second or third horse on these enormous hunts. How and where would you have covered the ground in order to meet up with the huntsman?

* *

8. Hawkridge. 19 April 1930. "A brilliant run."

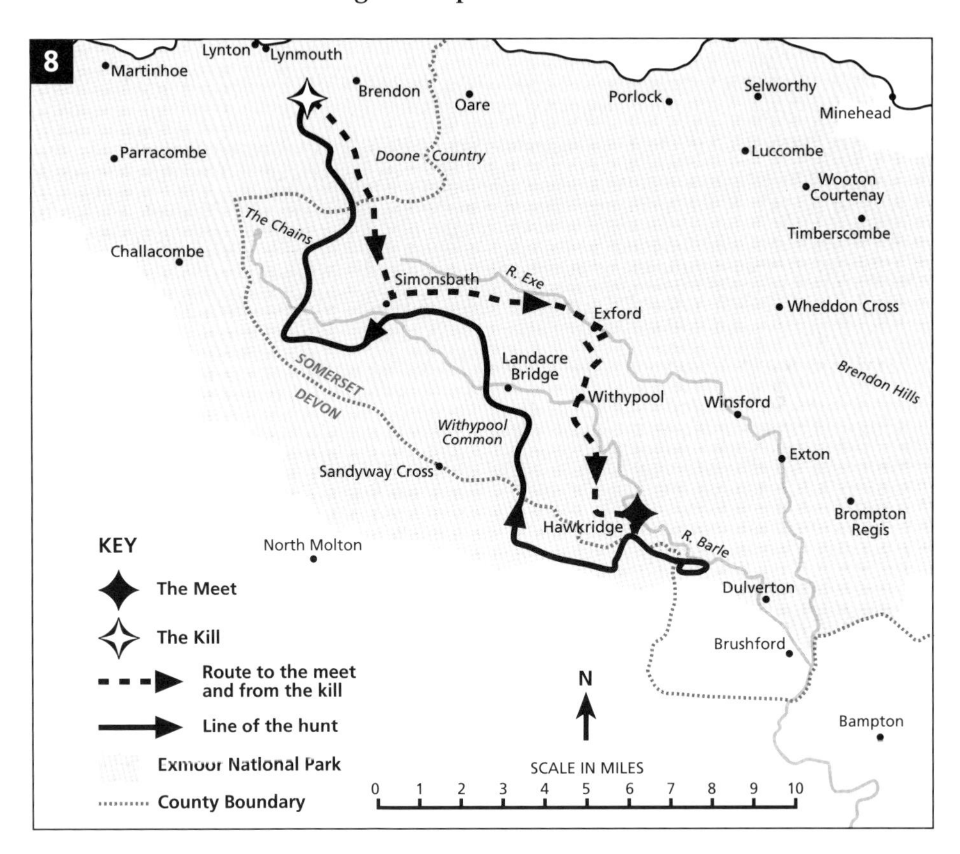

Weather was bitterly cold with a gale blowing from the N.W. accompanied by showers of hail and sleet. Lang had some stags harboured in

Shircombeslade and three more along with a herd of hinds in Yamson fields. It was decided to draw for the latter but, after running them around the covers for a while, it was decided to leave them as we could not get a stag away from the herd.

Tufters were then collected and taken down under Highnam where they immediately got on to six stags. They ran through Shircombeslade and away over Northmoor Common[4] where, just short of Windball Hill they doubled back to Shircombeslade and there divided. Most of the tufters stuck to a stag that went across the Barle at Highnam meadows and continued up the Ashwick Woods, crossing the Barle under Slade Wood before climbing over Hawkridge Ridge to the Danesbrook beating up this to Drucombe Gate.

Hounds got up to him in the water and then went up the commons opposite Church Wood at such a pace that they could not be stopped until reaching Anstey Barrows when the pack was signalled for and laid on. They ran along the south side of Anstey Common on to Molland Moor, turning right handed over the top road and on up Redford bottom away by Soggy Moor. Two stags and a park deer were now in front of the pack and they all went on to Higher Willingford Bridge, up Sloley's Allotment before turning across Halscombe road and Westcott's Allotment. Here they went on by Brightworthy Barrows across Dillacombe and the Barle just below Sherdon Hutch, up over Brady Moor and into the head of Shutcombe bottom where the deer divided.

Most of the hounds stuck with the stag that turned left handed across Gypsy road and then dropped into Whitewater above Picket Stones. Hounds hunted up to Cloven Rocks and then hit off the line and carried on by Winstitchen farm and across the Barle just below Simonsbath before turning away above Halscombe Plantation and all up beside the Yarde Down-Simonsbath road to Bluegate where they crossed.

Hounds now drove on across Burcombe, Horcombe and Squallacombe then crossed the Barle and turned up over Hearlake and on to Titchcombe. Here they turned sharp right handed across by Exe Head bridge, inclining them across Exe Plain and into the head of Farley Water. (*And it was about here, according to newspaper reports, that he dismounted and ran for almost a mile. He would have jogged steadily through the heather, bog and sedge, in full hunting rig, leading his horse and carrying his cap, whip and horn – and in all that foul weather. The man was fifty-two years old!*)

Hounds hunted all down this to Holcombe Barrows where the stag had left the right hand of the water for a little way before dropping into it again just above Pighill Ford where he continued on downstream. Just before reaching Farley Wood hounds hit off the line out of the left side of the stream and hunted up over the cover opposite Farley Farm as if for Cheriton Ridge.

However, fresh finding the stag under the top fence of the cover, they now raced him down to Bridge Ball where, after a few turns up and down, he was accounted for at 2.50p.m. after one of the finest moorland hunts one could wish for. Hounds ran at a great pace from lay on to Farley Water and except for a few brief intervals were running right into the teeth of the gale that was blowing. Hail storms at times made it impossible for one to see against it but, in spite of these unfavourable conditions, and the great pace at which hounds ran a very large portion of the field got up to the end.

The furthest points touched ie from Northmoor to kill was 15 miles but, as hounds ran, it must have been quite 26½. The stag was a four year old with two atop each side.

Note. A wild Exmoor day yet still a marvellous hunt. Here we have a very good example of where Ernest let tufters hunt a group of stags together (a common practice today) while waiting for the one he wanted to break away. The problem of doing this is that, if he has to wait too long, there is likely to be a long ride to fetch the pack, and therefore a long wait. Should this happen then there is a danger that the deer might get clean away.

Here he foresaw this and sent for the pack before the group of deer got too far from where the pack was kennelled. It was a wise decision because the deer ran on together for a further 10 miles. In doing what he did he kept the momentum going and the large field was treated to a marvellous hunt right across Exmoor. He wrote of the distance being 'at least 26 miles'. In fact it was a shade over 30 (as confirmed by E.T. MacDermot) with, once again, a huge total climb of over 3500 feet – and all of it right into that wild and bitter northerly gale

9. Sandyway. 2 April 1935. "The huntsman on side saddle."

A cold biting east wind for several days had dried up the ground considerably. *(Sandyway lies at over 1300 ft.)* This, of course, greatly affected hunting conditions and scent as well. Lang had five young stags harboured in Darlick Cleeve just opposite the top end of Long Wood so the pack was left at The Sportsman's Inn to await events.

On being roused by tufters, the deer broke up Shortacombe Brake but, on reaching the top of this, they ran up against some of the field whereupon they doubled back down to Long Wood again. Hounds eventually settled on to two that broke across the fields towards North Radworthy. However, something headed them right back into the wood where they divided. One of them, a one-horned stag, went up the cover and broke out against Longstone Wells and Tabor Hill then on to Barkham Heath. All the tufters except one were on this deer and they ran fast down over Little Barkham and the Isle of Dogs into the River Mole under Home Park Wood. Here they turned upstream a little way before going through the wood to Bulled's Brake.

As the tufters broke out of this they were held and the pack signalled for, they having, in the mean time, been moved down to Longstone Wells. The stag had exactly thirty minutes law *(start)* before they could be laid on and this was a great handicap under such bad scenting conditions. It took a further ten minutes before they settled on to the line properly, leaving Bamfyldes Clump

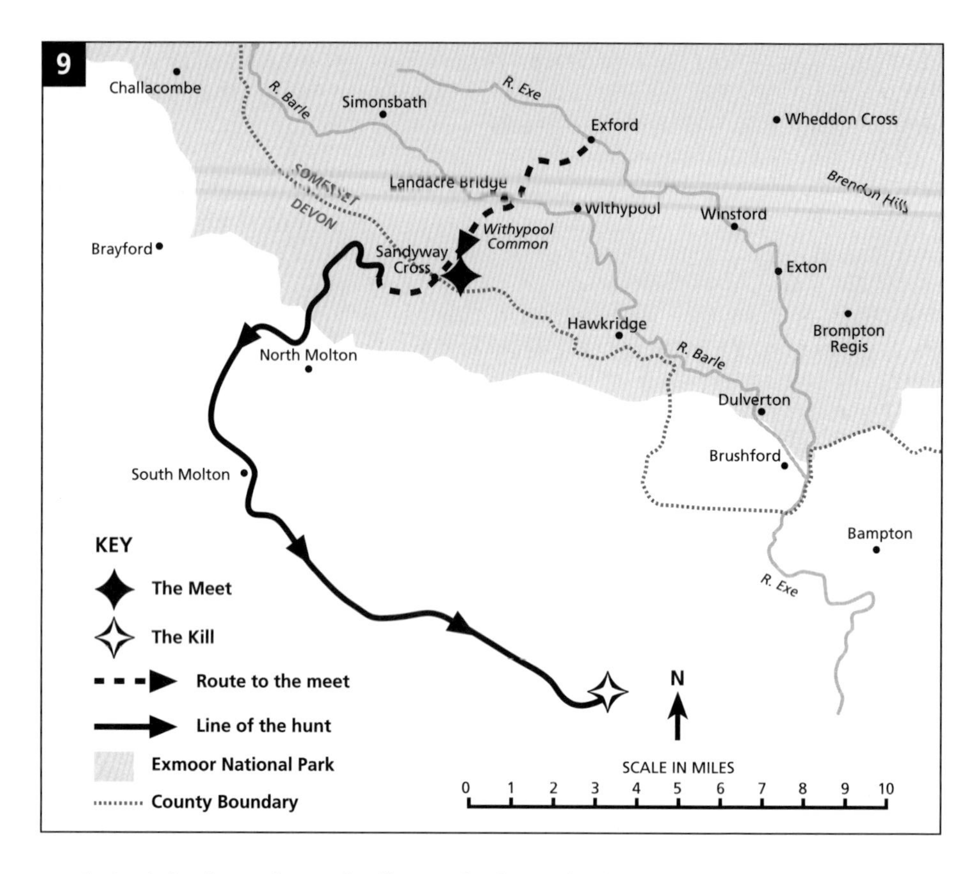

on their right, hounds gradually worked out the line by Combshead into Venn wood. Here they turned up the little stream towards Flitton Barton then away across Nadrid, North and South Lee Farms and into Hacche Wood.

Hounds soon fresh found their deer and, after running one circle in cover, he broke away by Hacche Farm House and then crossed the railway line by South Cockerham as if for Whitehills, having been headed on the main road. However he turned sharp left handed and passed through the grounds of South Molton vicarage and workhouse then over the station road. Keeping close to the eastern outskirts of the town he went away across Great and Little Hele Farms to the River Mole. Without beating the water at all the stag went on by Radley into Crooked Oak stream and up this a little way before reaching the village of Mariansleigh where he turned down to the little stream at Meshaw Mills.

After a slight check here hounds carried on with Rose Ash on their left before crossing the Beaples Hill-Gidley Arms road by Ash Moor chapel. Here the deer dropped into Sturcombe River under Creacombe where hounds first tried upstream but without result. On being taken back and cast down water they quickly owned their line and after about a quarter of a mile of water work, hounds got close to their deer. As he broke away over Wilson

Moor he was viewed by Mrs Harry Amory, the huntsman being on foot at this moment. She kindly let him have her horse for a while to keep in touch with hounds.

Scent across this dried-up country with so many flocks of ewes and lambs kept on causing hounds to check but being now closer to their deer they ran at a good pace to Northcombe. At Bradford Mill, a little way down stream he was fresh found but immediately broke away from hounds and went on across the moors for a mile or two into a cover named Newland Brake. Hounds hunted beautifully around this and presently set the stag at bay but he made one more effort by doubling back around one of the moors and then laid fast in a ditch until hounds came up to him.

He was killed at 5.05p.m. about 2 miles south from Rackenford village after a hunt of five hours and twenty-five minutes. The deer were found in Darlick Cleeve at 11.40a.m. and the pack laid on at 1.13p.m. The farthest points touched on this great run was exactly 12 miles and quite a good few of the field were out to the end. The hunt horses and hounds went back to Rackenford and then home by motor van. This took a long time and hounds did not get to kennels until 11.10p.m.

The stag was a well grown three year old in extraordinary good condition for the time of the year. He only carried one horn and this was broken off by the tray point. There was no sign of a horn on the other side nor did it seem that ever one would have grown there.

Note. There is a lot here – not the least of which is the fact that the huntsman was on his feet again, only to finish the day riding side saddle. Just how he coped is not recorded! The draw was a classic case of having to work hard to get the stags going. Strangely, young stags with odd heads seem to run well – see the next and last hunt. This hunt developed very much into a lowland affair and although not geared for mile after mile through close, low-lying farming country (especially at lambing time) the staghounds and their huntsman managed admirably.

Ernest had been running for over a mile (now aged fifty-seven) when he was lent a horse. Although spared the merciless climbs of moorland hunts, the distance hounds ran was almost 35 miles – a very good hunt indeed. And what a treat to be taken home by a 'motor van' for, had they been forced to hack home, it would have been another 20 miles.

* *

10. Yarde Down. 18 April 1931. "The Great Staghunt."

Widely regarded as the greatest hunt in modern times and acknowledged by Ernest Bawden as the toughest he ever undertook.

Weather was bitterly cold with showers of hail and sleet. A large field was out. The pack was taken by Molland Cross to kennel at Rocks Head (Mr

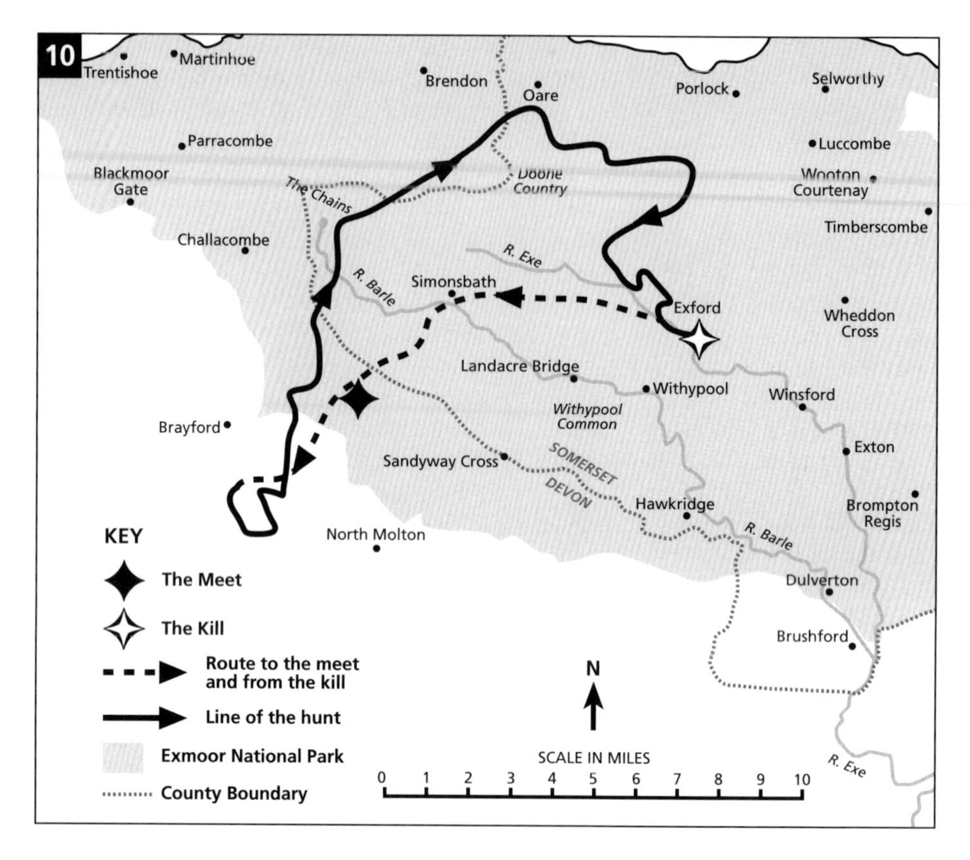

Slader's), a jog of 3 miles. Lang had six stags harboured in Reapham Wood and seven others in Lower Molland wood. It was decided to draw for the Reapham deer among which was a switch-horn stag *(deformed antlers)*, all the remainder having cast theirs.

They were found at once and hunted down to the lower end of the covert. Two hornless stags *(stags had, by now, shed their antlers)* and the switch-horn broke away towards Brayley Bridge with a couple and a half of tufters in pursuit. They were stopped by Lang for it was decided to lay on the pack. In the meantime the remainder of tufters had been stopped from hunting a big stag going towards East Buckland. With forces all reunited the pack was let go and in a little spinney on the left bank of the Bray just above Brayley Bridge, the three stags were fresh found.

They all broke back up the Bray valley under Lions Rump and crossed the main road thence into Huntstone Wood and ran right up it to Popham. Here it was discovered that hounds were on to the two big hornless stags but they could not be stopped until reaching Lower Molland Farm. A cast was then made back into Hunstone Wood for the switch-horn stag and he was very prettily fresh found by hounds at 1.15p.m. where he was lazing under the cover fence just under Walscott.

They now raced him up by Popham into Lower Molland Wood where, unfortunately, he joined up with other deer Lang knew to be there. Ten couple of hounds however stuck to the hunted deer in a remarkable manner and forced him away across Withygate and Beara Farms into Beara Wood. He went up through this, turning up Sherracombe near the top of which hounds turned left handed and were held for a few minutes to allow the field to come up.

On being let go they raced away towards Moles Chamber, crossed the western edge of Great Vintcombe leaving Roostitchen just on their left. They crossed the Barle by Goat Hill then away over the hill and Hundred Acres common on to the Chains. The stag was, by now, scarcely out of sight of hounds and they completely outdistanced the field and huntsman, racing away over the Chains and Hoar Oak Water (near the Oak Tree) then on over Cheriton Ridge, Farley Water and the Brendon road a little on the north side of Brendon Two Gates. From this point the line was carried across Brendon Common, Lankcombe and Malmsmead Hill into Badgery Water just below Cloud Farm.

Hounds recovered the line early down to Malmsmead on the right bank of the water (all on their own). They crossed the fields towards Oare Manor where the huntsman got in touch again. A short check ensued but the line was soon recovered just above Oare Manor and hunted thence upwards over Withycombe Allotment, leaving Prince's Bog just to the right. They then crossed Oldhay Heath but, somewhere near Chalk Water, our hunted stag joined fresh deer. Hounds carried on over Mill Hill towards Weir Wood near where several, unfortunately, broke away on another stag. Just at this moment the hunted stag was viewed by the huntsman leaving Weir Water just above the wood.

Five couple were all that could be stopped to put on his line however, they ran splendidly up over Porlock Common, passed by Hawkcombe Head and then over Bromham Plain into the top of Bury Castle. The stag had, however, doubled right out of this again and went on to the head of Blackford Combe before sinking down over Babe Hill into Nutscale Water. He turned upstream to the reservoir then turned away from there up over Nutscale Brake where he crossed the top of Great Hill and on over Goddard's Allotment. Leaving Alderman's Barrow just on the right, hounds now turned right down over Wellshead Allotment where four fresh stags were encountered but hounds stuck to their deer. They ran right down by Pitsworthy House to the bungalows at the bottom of the meadows where they turned left handed up Swincombe to the bottom of Downscombe bog.

The line was now hunted into Mill Lane just below Hillhead Cross. Here the stag was turned in the road by a motor car and ran down to Downscombe Farm before crossing to Higher Mill and the hairpin bend in Mill Lane. In the corner of a field close by Edgecott, a couple of hounds (Crystal and Gaylass) had got him at bay. On the arrival of the huntsman and four other couple he immediately broke away down over Luckesses and went on over the Exford showground, passing just by the D and S kennels before carrying on by Mr Hoare's house (Monkham) and soiled in his pond under Court Wood.

He just left this before hounds arrived. They, however, got to close quarters under Court Wood and ran down to the Exe at Hantons. After several turns up and downstream he was accounted for soon after 4.30p.m. The pack was laid on just after 12.30p.m. He was a four year old and in wonderful condition for the time of year. One of his horns, about a foot long, grew straight out in front of his face, the other was only an upright but long and grew straight out from the head just like a bullock.

The farthest points touched on this great run ie from Brayley Bridge to Bury Castle is 14 miles and only a few besides the huntsman who rode the whole chase ever got to the end. The remainder of the pack that broke away on fresh deer in Lower Molland wood were stopped by Lang somewhere on Fyldon Ridge and he took them home to kennels whilst the whips got the others that broke away on Mill Hill.

MacDermot wrote: "Allowing for the numerous valleys crossed, he had run about 35 miles in three hours and ten minutes and, in the huntsman's opinion, was the stoutest deer he had ever hunted. Not a single horse completed the course, the huntsman had to leave his near Downscombe and run for some distance before a lady member of the field lent him hers." (In fact, Ernest recorded the time as four hours).

Note. How on earth does one begin to describe this hunt? It was a truly enormous effort. During Spring staghunting it was policy to go for sick, injured or deformed deer (culling and cleaning the herd). However, if they considered that the one they had found today was in anyway a weakling and needed to be put out of its misery, they were about to get the shock of their lives.

A careful analysis of the map, allowing a little for the diagonal of the steep ground, makes the distance from where the tufters began the chase to the kill, a distance of over 37 miles. Before that they had had a 10 mile hack out from kennels at Exford, then a further ride to kennel the pack and the tufters had to work hard before the pack were laid on. Another gallant lady gave up her horse for the huntsman – bringing his total to four that day. Just reading about it makes one breathless.

Let us finish by getting the day into perspective. The run was slightly longer than from Junction 27 on the M5 near Tiverton to a point some way beyond Barnstaple but with a total climb of almost 5000 feet (Ben Nevis is barely 4500). For those in the Shires it is the equivalent of running from the outskirts of Leicester along the A607 to Melton Mowbray, then turning south onto the A606 and riding hard through Oakham to Corby on the A6003, and then on for a bit. All that but without the climb.

Notes

1. Today it is the Secretary who asks people if they would like a slot: if he has not made it in to the kill then it is the Master. Those asked are often youngsters, visitors or people of distinction.

2. I have kept to his spelling; however, the more usual spelling is Hinam.
3. In those days they were nurturing the numbers of the herd (which had fallen dangerously after the First World War. Today, as part of the annual cull, more than one hind is often taken and there is little or no discussion about it.
4. Northmoor Common is now a fir plantation a typical example of how the topography has changed over the years

Chapter 14

SUNSET

For a while it seemed as though the high reputation of the Devon and Somerset would live for ever. Season after season, the hounds hunted as never before. They, the hunt staff and those administering them seemed impervious to events occurring around them – to the American slump and Wall Street crash in 1929, to Amy Johnson flying to Australia a year later, or to such political turmoil as the arrival of Oswald Moseley. Even with all this going on, Exmoor seemed capable of hiding itself away.

It was as though nothing could change the way things were or had been – but no, every era must run its full distance at some time or other and the D and S were no exception. As the hunt moved smoothly from one season to the next amidst this apparent tranquillity the first changes were beginning to take effect – not necessarily for the worse, but changes nonetheless. And they were changes that would ultimately affect the life of the huntsman.

The hunt had enjoyed a period of stability since the early twenties when a team of outstanding individuals had been brought together. Both those working in the kennels and stables and those controlling the hunt were men of exceptional ability and dedication but many, especially the elders or grandees who wielded such influence behind the scenes, were getting on in years. In 1932 Ernest was fifty-four. Colonel Wiggin, however, was seventy-six while Lord Fortescue – the Hunt Chairman who had been Master way back in 1882 – was in his seventy-eighth year, and Froude Hancock – the great mentor of the Hunt – approaching seventy.

These men, most of whom had selected Ernest, were happy to let him have his way in both kennels and the field. Why tinker with such success? They knew the full worth of the man and how best to handle him, while he admired and respected them all in return. It was a system that worked (as results showed) but, in standing back like this, there was a danger of them granting too much autonomy to the man around whom they had created a protective shield with their own personalities. Had the huntsman been affable and easy-going or receptive to ideas then all might have been well but he was not. Ernest's brittle temperament and ruthless drive took him down his own narrow path; he neither sought advice nor would he have welcomed a guiding hand.

There was never anything to suggest that he abused such freedom or that his authority or fame went to his head, as so often happens today when sporting or media celebrities are quite incapable of living on their exposed pedestal. Ernest never became pleased with himself or what others said about him. He was never arrogant, never flamboyant and never boastful of his achievements. In fact, it was quite the reverse. Right to the end, he remained deeply suspicious of his own standards and was constantly his own most severe critic. He avoided the limelight whenever he was able, becoming more and more introspective and wary of too much contact with his admirers.

Those in charge knew how to handle him and they had his respect but his authoritarian manner and ever-shorter fuse hardly endeared him to those with whom he had to work and those under his command. He fought change, usually successfully, with those suggesting it happy enough to bow to his persuasion. He demanded the continuance of his rigid and autocratic routine, occasionally taking matters to extreme and unreasonable lengths, such as demanding to ride the same horse throughout a long day's hunting, in particular his favourite, "Pineapple". The stables rebelled. Not only was this unreasonable but it was an impossible demand to be made from any horse.

But whatever might have been the situation "at home" the standard of hunting continued to be of the very highest order. Visitors descended in ever increasing numbers, knowing that their time on Exmoor would be well-spent. Local hunting correspondents continued to write about one fine run after another, such as in September 1932 when Ernest hunted brilliantly from Dunkery Hill Gate before killing *"after one of the most difficult day's hunting one can possibly imagine."* Or a few months later from Willingford Bridge when *"a large field met in weather that was ideal for hunting... hounds hunted in a most delightful way producing one of the best hind hunts of the season before killing at Bridgetown."* Perhaps such quality of hunting might have blinded those in authority to what was potentially a difficult situation or perhaps they were happy to shrug it off and let things be.

One day, however, there would have to be a new regime – "Anno Domini" would see to that – and how would Ernest react to younger men with new and bright ideas who would want to do things their own way? Lord Fortescue died in October 1932 while still Chairman of the hunt. Ernest had known Lord Fortescue since he was a small boy at Hawkridge and this sudden loss affected him deeply; he was stunned. *"He was with us only a week ago,"* he wrote despairingly. *"His Lordship was right up with me practically the whole way and going as well as ever I had seen him."*

He went on to write about the funeral then continued emotionally. *"I cannot close without mentioning how deeply grateful I am to him for the great kindness and consideration that he has always shown towards me ever since the first day I started with the staghounds... a great sportsman has disappeared whom it will be very hard and difficult to replace".*

Less than a year later, Froude Hancock died. Ernest mourned this second loss, writing an even longer eulogy. Hancock had been Field Master way back in March 1907 and the two men would have known each other very well. *"In my humble opinion he was the greatest authority on staghunting ever, his great knowledge of the country enabling him invariably to get in at the end, no matter how long or difficult the day might be. He always took a great interest in the staff no matter whether on or off the hunting field and rarely, if ever, did he fail with a cheery word if the staff had had a hard and unsuccessful day.*

"Most people are loud enough in their praise when a great triumph has been scored but few ever remember that it is the cases of disappointment when hounds and servants need sympathy and encouragement most. His kindly manner and complete understanding of Westcountry people had endeared him to all... He will assuredly go down in history as the greatest Staghunter of all time."

Strong words and emotional indeed, the more so as they were written in his private diary. There is no doubt that he felt their loss keenly, both personally and as men for whose hunting ability he had the highest regard. A closer look reveals that there may have been more to his words. It was as though he knew they had been his guardians and whose departure had left him feeling vulnerable. Their passing appeared to have rekindled his deep-rooted insecurity of old, something that he had never quite been able to overcome and there was a hint of uneasiness in his writing.

* *

Walter Wiggin's health began to fail at about this time yet he continued to drive himself hard, winning the admiration of Ernest and all who rode with him. Barely able to walk without two sticks, he had to be helped (heaved almost) into the saddle and would have lain quite helpless on the ground had he taken a fall. Ernest became worried and his diaries showed this concern. Here, too, it is possible to read between the lines and detect a note of anxiousness. On 28 September 1935, a huge gathering assembled at Sandyway when the new Lord Fortescue, himself now Chairman, made a presentation to the Master. It was to be the Colonel's final meet and Ernest wrote warmly about him.

"He was beloved not only by all his hunting friends but all his business associates as well. His generosity to the Staghounds is too well known for me to say more here his name will assuredly be a household one as long as there is staghunting." A touching tribute yet prophetic for his name – together with the likes of Lord Fortescue and Froude Hancock – does, indeed, live on today.

The new regime moved in and, barely six months later, Walter Wiggin was dead; preceded a few weeks earlier by Ned Lloyd who died suddenly aged forty-eight. Lloyd, a great servant of the hunt, was another much admired by Ernest, the two had enjoyed a firm friendship for many years. Now there would no more tea and cakes in the kennels in the afternoons before hunting, and no more riding out to Pitsworthy to discuss matters with the Secretary or the light banter with his boys.

Suddenly everything had changed and, if this was not enough, Ernest's diverticulitis was worsening, causing him more and more discomfort. The old guard had gone and the new team, headed by the Master, took control. Tommy Hancock, a man still in his thirties, was a relative of the much-lamented Froude and a member of Arnold and Hancock, the Westcountry brewers. He, at once, set about making his mark and stamping his authority on his domain, the result of which was inevitable – a bitter clash with his huntsman.

Looking back on the situation it is plain that there was fault on both sides. It is also easy to see that it was time for a change anyway. Ernest's position, his authority and his particular way of doing things were now exposed. He would have found it difficult to transfer his allegiance to anyone and was quite incapable of doing so to Hancock who was very different to the Colonel. For a start, the easygoing relationship and mutual respect that the huntsman had enjoyed with the late Master had gone. The new man had his own ideas and never sought Ernest's opinion. He was a foxhunter and, although local, had done rather less staghunting prior to taking up his appointment.

It was not long before he had upset Ernest, initially by his behaviour in the field. It is obvious that opinions differed on how the day should be played but the huntsman bridled, complaining that his new Master *"had no experience of staghunting and did not understand."* On another occasion Hancock, so the huntsman wrote, insisted on taking certain measures that did not work. The day *"proved to be a useless and unnecessary effort."*

If he had little regard for his new Master then he had no time at all for the new Secretary. Percy, Ernest's son, recalls several occasions when angry voices were raised, something that would have been inconceivable with Ned Lloyd. Philip Greig, son of the late Master Morland Greig when Ernest was whip (a man who he admired greatly and who was killed at Gallipoli) had a reputation for drinking – often appearing the worse for wear when his feelings would get the better of him. Ernest, ever alive to the effects of drink, recoiled sharply.

Then, in January 1937, distemper struck causing twenty couple of the younger hounds to be laid up, of whom five and a half couple died in spite of Ernest and Elizabeth-Ann's best efforts. The weather was terrible throughout this unhappy period, a matter that could only add to the general air of despondency. Pressure after pressure was building and something had to give.

After the hunt on 23 March, Ernest handed in his resignation, asking that it should take effect from the end of the season. His troubles came tumbling into his diary where he complained bitterly that, among other things, his second whip had been removed and that he was now having trouble with his horses. All that may have been so but these grievances have to be seen as nothing more than excuses he was making for his disenchantment with the general state of affairs. Underneath it all he was simply unable to adjust to the new order yet, astonishingly, hunting continued as successfully as ever. For his part, Ernest had now crossed his Rubicon, and there could be no going back.

As if to hammer home the final sharp nail, a bitter row broke out just four days later when five shots were needed to kill the stag at bay.[1] Ernest was horrified, writing quite openly of his disgust. For him it was a point of honour that, once the chase had been run, the deer had to be despatched quickly and humanely. Blasting off like this, and in front of the field, was more than the huntsman could bear. The situation was now beyond redemption.

Could such a dreadfully sad predicament have been avoided? Probably not; but for certain it could have been handled better by all concerned. Ernest's intransigence had got him into a tight corner, one from which a man with such pride was never going to back down or compromise. It was partly his own fault but this attitude, even his approach to the newcomers was beyond his control. It was the very nature of the man himself but he could have done more and ought to have done. He should have kept his counsel then made clear his feelings in a more orderly fashion.

Tommy Hancock and Philip Greig, whatever truth there may have been in Ernest's allegations, saw need for change. The way was open for them to do things as they saw best and history recalls that the new team coped far better than the situation backstage suggested. However, for his part, Hancock should have read his man better and handled matters more subtly. He should have assessed Ernest's prickly and proud character, then given this outstanding and loyal hunt servant a chance to have his say and allow him some room for manoeuvre. Furthermore, the behaviour in the hunting field could only tarnish the name of the hunt. Diplomacy, tact and patience were lacking.

There was an excellent man in the wings – Alfred Lenthall. The much younger first whip had proved himself already and, if they wanted Ernest out of the way, then it should have been done properly. It would have taken courage, for hands would have been raised in horror across the hunting community and they would have had to live with their decision, but that is the price to be paid for firm and decisive leadership.

Instead, both men stood their ground and relations soured until Ernest could take no more. Inevitably word got out and there was a huge groundswell of support for the huntsman, as his testimonial later showed. But, and it is important when a popular figure such as this retires, he left the hunt when he was right at the very top of his profession. He was a huntsman first and last and would one day be judged against all others on that alone.

Better to depart like this rather than to hang on until age took its inexorable toll, when standards would begin to slip and tongues wag. Fifty-nine was by no means old for a huntsman to retire, yet the demands of the long staghunting season and the effects of diverticulitis had taken their toll, and it was the great Nimrod himself who stated that, after sixty, a huntsman begins to slow.

And so, on 20 April 1937, he tucked his horn into his jacket for the last time. He had given thirty-three years to the hunt, twenty as huntsman. No less than 4318 deer had fallen to him, 1859 as whipper-in and 2459 when he carried the horn.

* *

Ernest's last day in the kennels, although sad, proved to be something of an anti-climax. By the time he came to leave hunt service, his son, Percy, had returned to live in Exford after qualifying as a mechanical engineer. Some years earlier Ernest had built an extensive garage for him, from which he was now running a successful business. He, Percy, together with his own wife and child lived in the accommodation above and it was here, for the last few days of their time at the kennels, that Elizabeth-Ann lodged while Ernest stayed on alone to see business through.

Once the removal men had completed their task, Ernest turned to the two whippers-in, wished them luck and bade farewell. Rather than climb aboard the vehicle and drive away, he chose to walk but not through the village. After one final glance at his beloved hounds, the huntsman walked down the drive and through the gate then on down to the river which he crossed by a small footbridge.

Skirting around the village, he climbed out of the valley to where he had asked the van to wait for him. His small frame, leaning forward into the climb must have cut a lonely figure, his emotions now hidden from the two who watched him go. Neither Master nor Secretary were to be seen; the gulf between them and their huntsman had become too wide. It was over.

Whatever the nature of the parting, Ernest was by no means out in the cold; in fact he was a man of considerable means. Not only had he built the garage in the village for his son but the previous year he had purchased Hinam Farm, near Dulverton, and then built a bungalow for himself and Elizabeth-Ann in the grounds. It was an amazing deployment of capital for a servant of the hunt. The salary of a huntsman, including even the traditional perk of selling deer skins and animal hides, would have allowed him and the family to live comfortably, perhaps putting a little aside, but no more.

The extent to which Ernest's hunting boots had been filled with money over the years, now becomes apparent for the garage alone would have cost a considerable amount, even in those days. It was well-constructed,[2] well-equipped with modern machinery and it was in a prime location in the village. Assuming that he had saved carefully – and assuming the boots had indeed been well-filled – the garage can just about be accounted for. What about the farm and bungalow, however, purchased at the beginning of his last season and long before any final gratuity came his way? There were no loans or mortgages [3] so how could a man in his position afford to become a landowner?

The only possible explanation is that Walter Wiggin had helped Ernest with his financial affairs. Ernest had filled a huge void in the Colonel's life, bringing to him and his wife a wonderfully happy period in their later years. They were extremely wealthy but had no children of their own. Not only did Walter Wiggin and Ernest get along famously but Edith Wiggin had high regard for Elizabeth-Ann, the two of them seeing more of each other than might have been usual in those days.

The timings for this theory were right, also. Although he had given up hunting a little earlier, Walter Wiggin died in April 1936, a few months before Ernest purchased Hinam Farm (Autumn that year) and began to build his retirement home. If this was indeed the case, then it was just reward for the nineteen years of devoted and unstinting service Ernest had given to the man he regarded so highly. Somehow, somebody had seen to it that the huntsman and his family would end their days comfortably, and the most likely benefactor was the late Master.

Almost immediately, the Bawdens moved into their bungalow and began to settle, but now there was a catch. The farmer at Hinam was a tenant. Sidney Heywood was his name, none other than Elizabeth-Ann's elder brother. To complicate matters further, Sidney's wife was Mary-Elizabeth, Ernest's younger sister, the one he had always adored. There was thus a double family connection and unless relationships all round were going to be cordial, the potential for discord was considerable. Sidney Heywood was, by now, over seventy and his second son, Hector, lived and worked there with them. Hector, Ernest's nephew, was hewn from the same tree as his uncle – the dreaded Hawkridge wild streak lurked close to the surface. It was going to be difficult.

The new landlord, as vigorous and as persistent as ever, not only lived on the site but he was out of a job as well. He was at a loose end, irritable and casting about looking for things with which to involve himself. Inevitably, he began to take a close interest in the way his new acquisition was being managed by the family and, as usual, was determined to have his say.

The net result was for hackles to rise all round and it was not long before Hector and Ernest, neither one a model of discretion nor prone to compromise, clashed. Percy claims it was love and hate at first sight. Sometimes, he stated, the atmosphere was as taut as piano wire, the two of them stalking around each other and staring each other down; on other occasions they would walk out together, arm in arm, laughing and joking like old friends.

It was at the Exford Show, later in the year of his retirement that Ernest received the official farewell from the hunt. Lord Fortescue, the son of the man Ernest admired so much, presented him with a cheque for over thirteen hundred pounds. It was, he told the large gathering, a true reflection of the high regard that so many who followed the Staghounds felt for their huntsman.

Indeed this was so: it was generosity of a truly extraordinary nature. The presentation was before hunting that season had begun thus many of the more prosperous hunt followers were absent, their homes being scores, if not hundreds, of miles away. Neither Devon nor Somerset were rich counties, neither were there any major centres of industry or commerce where wealthy subscribers lived in numbers, such as in the Midlands.

The bulk of the money was raised by local people, ably supported by those of means. The list of donors reads like a census for the villages around the edge of the moor, over one thousand names in all making their contribution.[4] In those days a pound represented a week's hard won wages, while even a few shillings were several days work for some.[5] Many gave more. Ernest was dumbfounded, shattered and quite unable to rise and reply to the tribute. Those present were on their feet applauding the man who had, for a generation and more, brightened their lives with the dash and excitement of the chase, yet who now sat staring about him, misty-eyed and lost. The occasion was too much.

* *

His final link with the hunt had now been severed. He, like others of his age, would be expected to bow out gracefully and enjoy a quiet and well-deserved retirement. But no, Ernest set about fighting retirement on three separate fronts, of which the first was his bungalow garden.

All his life he had been used to neatness and order but the builders had left an untidy wilderness behind them. For a year, nature had run riot around the new dwelling but now it was to be brought to order. He cursed the workmen roundly then, furiously, set about putting things straight. There had been little scope or time for gardening at the kennels but, here at Hinam, he threw himself at the task, determined to create something out of nothing.

The farm sat high on the south bank of the River Barle, overlooking a landscape full of memories for its new owner. It was here that the steep-sided, wooded valleys had offered sanctuary to the red deer since time immemorial, and it was here so often that either his tufters found their quarry or the pack ran the hunted deer to water. The crops and pastures at Hinam, like everywhere else in the valleys around the moor, had forever been subject to raids from herds of deer, either for the rich summer pickings or for sustenance during the long winter months.[6] Ernest, unlike most others who were more tolerant, refused to countenance such intrusion.

First, the high-banked hedges had to be repaired. This required weeks of back-breaking effort by man and boy who then had to cut and pare 8 foot high fencing posts which they set against the banks and on to which wire netting had to be fixed.[7] Ernest knew his deer, and knew well that they were persistent, but so was he: the determination he had shown earlier in the hunting field was directed against them once more. He saw it as his bounden duty to see that no deer were to trespass on his land.

No sooner had one point of entry been shored up than another breech was made further along the edge of the woods. He slaved and he sweated tirelessly. It exhausted him, but far better that than spending his time tormenting Sidney and Hector to distraction with his constant challenges and unwanted advice.

Sadly, though, whatever energy there was left was directed inevitably against the long-suffering Hector. Here, as so often before, Ernest simply could not help himself. It was as if he was deliberately spoiling for an argument or getting in the way, making mountains out of molehills and irritating those around him. On one occasion he confiscated the new tractor which, still hot from being used, had been deliberately left uncovered. He just had no idea! There were threats, the mutterings grew louder and feet were stamped. And yet, and yet… somehow the family seemed able to take it all. Gradually, no doubt coaxed by Elizabeth-Ann, they became impervious to Ernest's tireless attention.

Hunting, as ever, was the escape. The moment hounds were mentioned, Ernest, almost like a child, dropped everything. And it was here that Hector proved his worth as a true companion, for the two of them would walk for miles together in order to catch sight of the hunt.[8] One day, when the meet was too far away, temptation overcame them and Hector used his car. It was something Ernest swore he would never do.

Suddenly the mighty hunter of yesteryear had become *"one of they damned motor people."* He had always treated those who followed by car with contempt; in his eyes they were an inferior race. Now he was one of them – him, of all people. To his credit, when they challenged him about it and pulled his leg, his face puckered into a mischievous grin. "Ah, but it's different now. Things are different these days."[9]

If Ernest missed being able to visit the kennels, he never showed it. As with all hunts when huntsmen change, it was a case of "The King is dead, long live the King", the outgoing man staying well clear until the new boy had found his feet. His knowledge of hound breeding, however, was in demand and his presence as a judge at puppy shows or as an adviser on kennel matters, was sought both locally and across the country. Many of those who had visited him at Exford now sought his advice, the Dukes of Beaufort and Buccleuch and Lord Knutsford among them. He was often away.

In 1939 Tommy Hancock left, first to join the army, then altogether. His place was taken by Miss B.K. "Biddy" Abbot, another long-standing and popular member of the hunt, who knew Ernest well. By this time Alfie Lenthall was his own man. The two had remained friends throughout the difficult period of transition and Ernest was told he would be welcome back at the kennels whenever he wished.

It was a generous offer from the new Master and huntsman and one that he never abused, appearing only occasionally and at the puppy shows where he was invariably invited to judge. For a time it seemed as though even he had found enough to keep himself happy and that his tireless energy might be satisfied at last. Those closest to him must have prayed for this to be the case, but it was not. In September that year, just after the new hunting season had got underway, war with Germany was declared.

For those at home, the Second World War began slowly. The Battle of Britain was almost a year away and, during that first winter as the British Expeditionary Force (B.E.F.) deployed hurriedly to France and Belgium there was no fighting. But the conflict had to come and the "Phoney War" ended the following spring. On 10 May 1940, Hitler's Panzers blitzkrieged their way through the Low Countries and France. The B.E.F. was thrown back, just managing to scramble clear from the beaches at Dunkirk with little more than the clothes they stood up in and the weapons in their hands.

France was occupied. Britain now stood alone and Hitler turned his attention towards what he saw as the biggest prize of all. For a time the country lay defenceless, exposed and vulnerable. Then the cry went out for volunteers; a new army was required – the Local Defence Volunteers (Home Guard) – one that would defend the country by fighting *"on the beaches and landing places.....and in the hills."*

Ernest heard the call and became a man inspired. Dulverton Town Hall, to where recruits were told to report, was but a few miles ride away and he was among the first there. His presence must have startled those behind the desk; they were looking for young men to fill the ranks, not sixty-five year old Boer War veterans. The man confronting them had been rejected on account of age and health at the beginning of the *last* war, twenty-five years earlier and now here he was again. It was ridiculous, he was far too old, they told him. He should go back home and look after his wife and family.

Ernest stood his ground, insisting that he still had much to offer and for a while there was stalemate. Having tried in vain to get rid of this tiresome old man, they must have wondered what on earth they could do with him. It must have been an extraordinary encounter, those responsible for recruiting now forced into urgent and whispered consultation at the back of the hall. Eventually somebody had an idea.

The Dulverton Home Guard was to be responsible not only for the town and surrounding area but for a considerable part of south eastern Exmoor. The countryside up there would have to be covered somehow, for enemy aircraft might crash land or saboteurs and infiltrators might be parachuted in. Worse still, there was talk of invasion and it would be their duty to defend every corner of the land. The only way this enormous expanse of wild country could be patrolled properly would be on horseback.

What the Home Guard needed was a mounted detachment. A number of volunteers had stepped forward already, but nobody with any military background and, for certain, nobody with any idea of mounted operations. They looked at him again, and then at his military record. Perhaps there was a job here after all. Would he be interested?

The Mounsey Hill (Mounted) Detachment of the Dulverton Company of the L.D.V. was to be based where its name suggested, at a bleak spot 1200 feet up on the moors where two roads and a track met. There was nothing else there. Eventually a caravan was towed on to the spot then, three months later, a wooden hut was erected.

For a while there were no uniforms (they made do with arm bands). There were no helmets, so they wore their cloth caps. Weapons were restricted initially to one rifle between ten men; everybody else brought their shotguns for which they were issued S.S.G. (the same type of ammunition as was, and still is, used to kill the deer). An assorted group of farmers, estate workers and foresters were ordered to assemble at the point where the roads met. There they would meet their new commander who would give them their instructions.

If those at H.Q. were worried about what might be going on at Mounsey Hill, they need not have been. Staff Sergeant Bawden took complete charge. No weapons or uniform might have been the case initially but the detachment could at least – and from now on most certainly would – get themselves on parade properly turned out, with a decent hair cut and with their boots polished. Their mounts would be well-groomed, hooves oiled and the tack clean. They would parade with whatever their commander ordered, everything packed neatly into satchels or back packs. Punctuality became the bye-word; excuses were not accepted. Training began immediately, a duty roster was drawn up and, within days, the first patrols were sent out.

If that was not enough, Ernest's Lee-Enfield rifle reappeared, as well-oiled and lethal as the day it had dealt with the Boer sniper. Somehow he managed to acquire live ammunition, including tracer, and blank rounds with which he proceeded to inject an element of realism into training his recruits. Training for the Mounted Detachment was "battle inoculation" of the first order, unorthordox and unauthorised yet, stimulating and effective.[10]

By this stage, Percy Bawden was in the Exford detachment of the Porlock Company. He recalls word coming back to the village of anxious mothers who were fearful of the training to which their sons were being subjected and, now concerned for their safety, were seeking out his father. Ernest, so it appeared, was a greater threat to their offspring than the unknown. He, of course, was in his element and for nigh on a year ran the detachment with a steely grip, constantly badgering H.Q. and visitors for more and better equipment. As their efficiency improved, so their morale rose and the search for the enemy went on, night after night, week after week.

It is easy to look back and smile at such desperate and amateurish measures without considering the overall situation at the time. Our regular forces had all but been destroyed and it was while they were struggling to get themselves together once more that the Battle of Britain was raging overhead. Underneath, the defence of the homeland was left to the likes of Ernest Bawden, for that was all there was. Without him, and thousands more like him, there would have been nothing… nothing at all.

Of even greater irony was the role he was now playing. Forty years earlier he had landed in South Africa as part of the mightiest force on earth whose task it had been to secure the countryside and defeat the ill-equipped, rag-tag army of sullen farmers who stood in their way. Now it was his turn; now he was the farmer, armed with nothing more than a rifle or shotgun and mounted on a sure-footed pony, preparing to defend his homeland against the most powerful army in the world.

Like the Boers on the veldt, his command consisted of old men and boys who knew the countryside backwards and who were prepared to fight with whatever they had, defending their homes and families to the end. It was a serious business, just as it had been for the Afrikaners. The Mounted Detachment treated it as such and remained faithful to their task until the threat of invasion subsided.

In 1941, Ernest was assigned to other duties and left the Home Guard. Volunteers were required whose task it would be to carry sensitive and classified documents around the countryside when communications failed or when radio silence had been ordered. Over the last year, land defence measures had improved radically and many such contingency plans were now put into operation.

The couriers had to be reliable and trustworthy. They had to operate alone, by day or night and they should, at all times, steer clear of roads and habitation. They had to move quickly and surely, and for this they had to know the ground well. Ernest was a perfect choice. It was a task at which he excelled, and time and again he traversed the hills on horseback – covering the ground between one H.Q. and another at his own pace, choosing the routes he knew so well and riding hard.

* *

Life at Hinam was bleak, as it was everywhere else. The constant demands for higher and better food production were difficult to meet, rationing bit ever deeper and of life's little luxuries there was no sign. There was more than enough work for everybody. Fuel was in desperately short supply so they used horses as well. Every parcel of land on the farms was cultivated. Where there were no horses, they worked the land by hand, their labours sometimes reinforced by evacuees or by the Women's Land Army (Land Girls) and, later, by prisoners of war. Everybody had to do their bit – old and young together.

Just as they had done twenty years ago, hunt committees decided to keep going as best they could but, as before, it was a soulless and half-hearted business. Numbers of hounds were put down and horses surrendered for work elsewhere. Hounds met twice weekly if they could. There was the occasional whist drive or dance, but that was all. War, even for those at home, had little to commend it.

The harvest in 1943 was late but it was a good one and, on Exmoor, they began to gather it in during the first week in September. At Hinam, the stooks of corn had been collected together and lay drying in neat rows facing the sun. Tuesday 7th was hot and sultry. They thought it might turn to rain later – thunder even – so decided to get underway as soon as they could, once the corn was dry. By early afternoon, they were well into their second load, but the storm clouds had gathered and somebody had felt the first drop of rain. They pressed on.

Ernest was leading the carthorse, walking slowly backwards along the line of stooks so he could see what was happening behind. Every now and then he would stop and wait while the others tossed the stooks onto the cart with their pitchforks. He made as though to move again but this time he stumbled. Exactly what happened next is not clear for opinions differ widely – as is so often the case with witnesses to a severe accident, and it was the same here. Some say the horse turned sharply down the slope, others say it bolted and the cart turned over trapping him. Whatever happened, nobody was to blame.

As he led the horse, so the animal quickened its pace, causing Ernest first to stumble and then fall backwards. Now thoroughly alarmed, the horse pulled harder and, before he could move out of the way, one wheel of the heavily-laden cart ran over his chest. It was all over in a second. For a moment he lay still then; amazingly, he staggered to his feet before collapsing again. It was obvious that he had been badly hurt and needed help. Two of the soldiers billeted nearby ran to fetch a hurdle which they used as a stretcher to get him back to the house, where they found his injuries were far worse than they first thought.

A doctor and ambulance were summoned. The full extent of his injuries became apparent only when he reached Minehead Hospital where the surgeons could see that there was nothing to be done. The heavy, metal rimmed cartwheel had literally crushed his chest and he died three days later. As the autopsy report made clear, the injuries he received were terrible.

"After referring to the large exterior bruising, Dr McKinney, the doctor who first attended him continued his report. The chest was fractured in two places, five ribs on the right side and four on the left side were fractured, both lungs were very extensively lacerated, and there was a large tear across the liver. The cause of death was heart failure and internal haemorrhaging due to the injuries to the liver and the lungs."[11]

That anybody, let alone a man of his age, had struggled on for three long days before dying, was incredible. Dr McKinney later told the family that, apart from these injuries and his damaged intestine, his body was in remarkable shape. "Good for a hundred or so," was his verdict but it was not to be.

Ernest was buried at St Giles' church, Hawkridge, five days later – just a few hundred yards from East Hollowcombe Farm where he was born. The community was stunned. Mindful that there would be a considerable gathering at the funeral, it was decided to take the body from Minehead the day before and lay it at rest in the tiny church. It was a sensible precaution, but nobody could have imagined the reception that greeted the hearse.

It was Tuesday and hounds were about. As the bearers went to draw out the coffin they could hear them in the Danesbrook valley below them – the valley where Ernest first watched the deer as a child. Suddenly there was silence; hounds must have checked but, at that moment, three couple appeared on the road, having detached themselves from the pack. They came up to the small party gathered around the vehicle and watched silently as the coffin was lifted.

One at a time, they came forward and rose on their hind legs as if to see better then, one after the other they began to sing mournfully together – as they sometimes do in the kennels. A number followed the undertakers to the church door, where they stopped before going on their way once more. It was an uncanny moment, eerie, for there was no possible explanation to such behaviour.

It was indeed a huge gathering. St Giles' church can hold no more than a hundred and there were many times that number present, most having to wait patiently outside before they could pay their last respects. Ernest's fame lived on long after his death, when a visit to the simple grave became something of a pilgrimage for those who had come down to Exmoor for their hunting. A photograph of the flowers on his grave was made into a postcard, the description on the back written in both English and French.

Wherever there is hunting, his name lives on: one small incident being so typical. The year was 1987, more than forty years after Ernest's death, and it took place in Yorkshire at a lonely farmhouse just after a young man had knocked on the door. William Deakin, then only thirty and huntsman of the Holderness (now of the Warwickshire), had come on business. As he stood talking he stopped suddenly and pointed to a framed photograph hanging in the hallway. "Well I'll be *damned*!" he gasped. "That's Ernest Bawden. How on earth d'you know him?"

Such a reaction, half a century on – from a young man far too young to have known him, and born and bred at the other end of the country – surely says it all.

Notes

1. Once a gun had been introduced the responsibility became that of a member of the committee, usually the Secretary.
2. Percy, while working in the Midlands, had come across some off-cuts of the girders used to construct Sydney Harbour bridge. These were used – the garage was, and still is, very solid!
3. Percy Bawden.
4. Details held by Gerald Bawden.
5. In 1939, Ernest bought two cottages near the farm for £750, almost certainly with some of this money.
6. A red deer eats more than a sheep thus a herd of fifty can devastate a field of roots or corn in a single night.
7. Sheep or chicken netting was used but never barbed wire for Ernest had seen too much of the effects this had had on the deer over his years with the hunt.
8. Soon after the war, Hector Heywood became harbourer.
9. Percy Bawden.
10. When Ernest was killed three years later, the rifle was taken into safe custody by Percy. In 1975 it was handed in to an officer in the Territorial Army when it was de-activated and offered to Barnstaple Museum where it is today.
11. Obituary notice in the *West Somerset Free Press*. Saturday 18 September, 1943.

EPILOGUE

Ernest Bawden lived and worked in a different age. Life was harder and scant regard shown to the less fortunate. On the other hand, it was a more straightforward and less complicated world in which the more dubious benefits of modern technology and communications had yet to impose themselves. Hunting enjoyed certain advantages but there were difficulties, too.

Ernest had his moments of good fortune, for sure, and was blessed with the support and understanding of great men who shaped his destiny. However, not everything always went his way; not by any means. On numerous occasions, lesser men would have been brought to their knees by his misfortunes – the terrible accidents in the field, distemper in the kennels and the harsh, uncompromising environment; not to mention the thirty-three seasons in all, each one nine months long, or his adversaries with whom he clashed. His lot, looked at almost a century on, appears to have been finely balanced.

So, how great was he? Three factors must be taken into account – the sport he showed year in year out, the hounds he bred to do the job, and what was said about him both at the time and since. Three factors that, surely, need no further qualification. Taking everything into account, Ernest Bawden stands out as the greatest staghunter of all time (and a number of outstanding men have carried that illustrious horn). However, it is impossible – and invidious – to make comparisons with him against the great names in foxhunting. It is like trying to compare a great spin bowler of one cricket era with a great pace bowler of another. How can one possibly compare, say, Lance Gibbs of the West Indies with Harold Larwood of England? It is absurd to even consider such an exercise.

What is beyond any doubt at all is that Ernest Bawden will be up there somewhere now, sitting comfortably at hunting's high table alongside Tom Firr, Tom Goosey, Jack Musters, Thomas Assheton-Smith and one or two more. These ghosts from the past would have been watching his performance down here and nodded their approval before moving along the bench to make room for him as he stepped through the Pearly Gates. They would have clapped him on the back and filled his glass – then the arguing and the banter would have begun.

Ernest, as Ronnie Wallace and so many others affirmed, was a genius – one of the greatest huntsmen ever. But for me, a man of Exmoor myself, he has to be the greatest of them all.

Annex A

THE BAWDEN FAMILY TREE

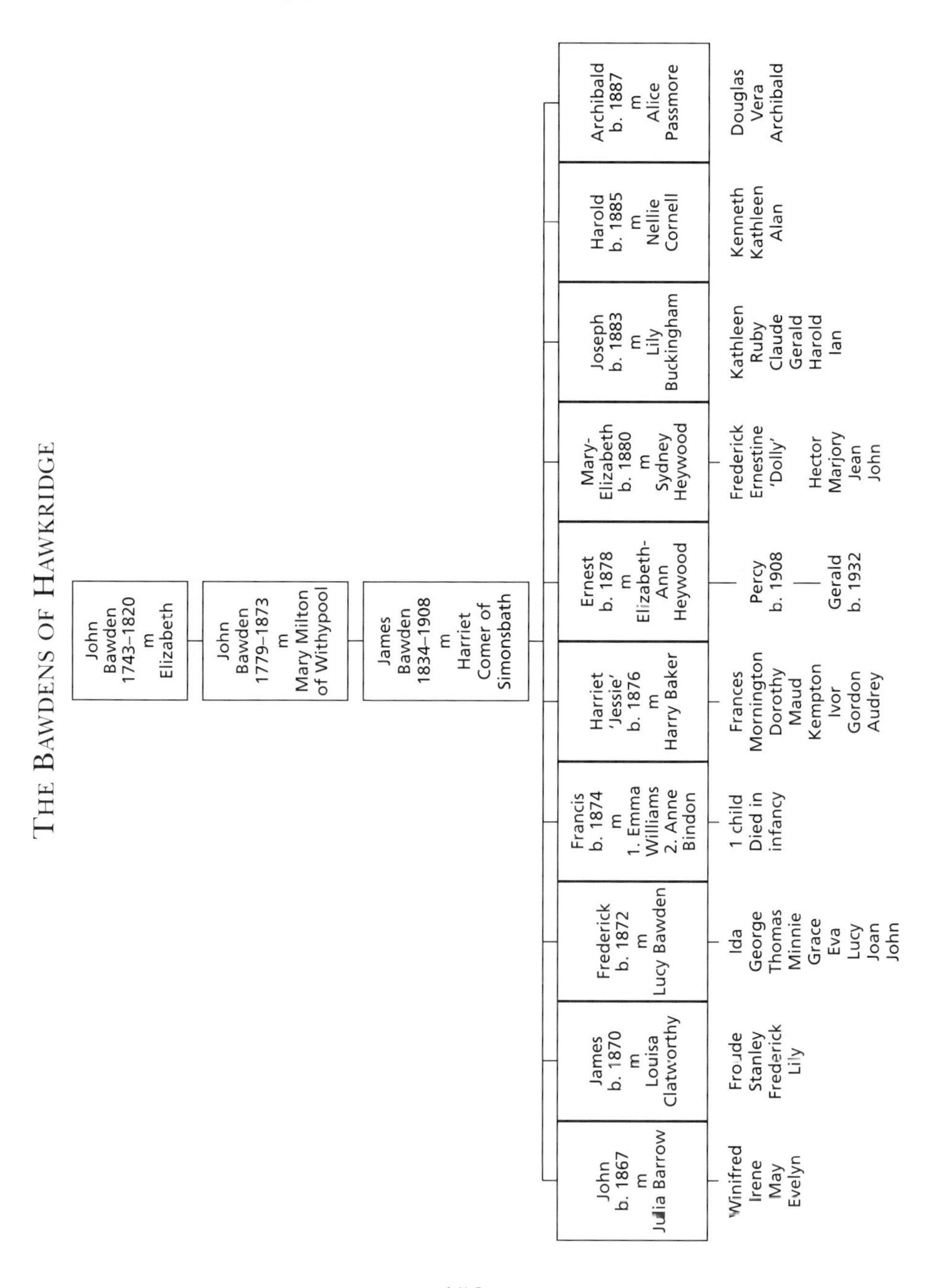

The Bawden and Heywood Families

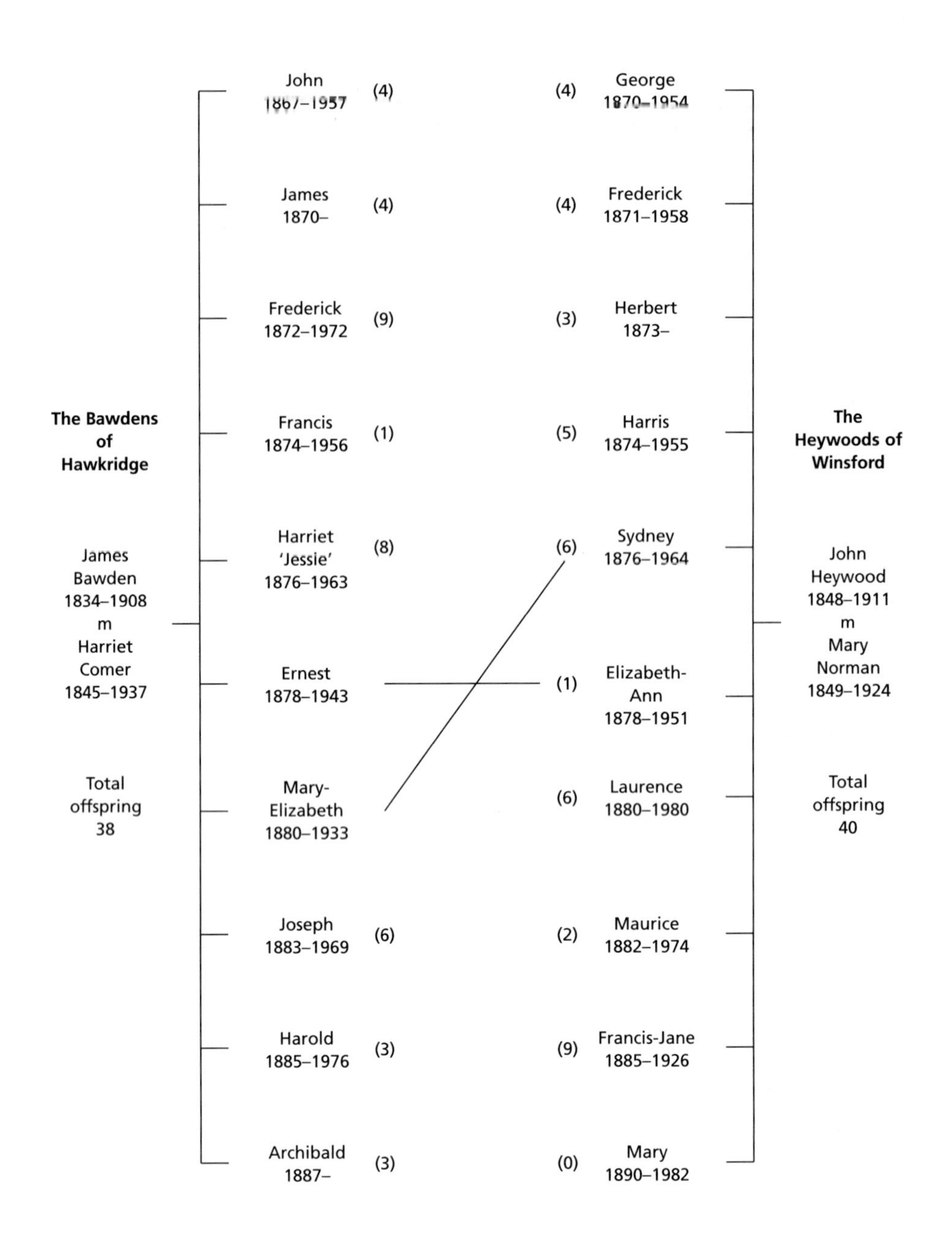

Note ( ) Denotes the number of children in the next generation.

Annex B

Chronology of Ernest Bawden's Life

3 March 1878.	Born at East Hollowcombe Farm, Hawkridge.
Autumn 1881.	First rode to hounds.
May to November 1883.	The sum total of his formal education.
Spring 1892.	Rode his first race on his father's pony "Reago."
Summer 1894.	Joined The Royal North Devon Hussars.
1 March 1900.	Sailed for South Africa on board the *Manchester Merchant*.
13 December 1900.	Battle of Nooitgedacht. Promoted to full Corporal.
25 June 1901.	Arrived home, docking at Southampton.
September 1901.	Reverted to part time soldiering and left home to work in Exford for his brother, James.
9 August 1902.	Rode in Guard of Honour at Coronation of King Edward VII.
1903.	Promoted Sergeant in R.N.D.H.
1904.	Awarded Long Service and Good Conduct medal.
21 June 1904.	Married Elizabeth-Ann Heywood.
30 July 1904.	*First rode as whipper-in to The Devon and Somerset Staghounds.*
July 1917.	*First rode as huntsman.*
1933.	Builds garage for his son in Exford.
1936.	Purchases Hinam Farm and builds bungalow.
20 April 1937.	*His final hunt.*
Autumn 1940 – February 1941.	Served with the Local Defence Volunteers "Home Guard."
February 1941 – September 1943.	Special Liaison duties for War Office (Army Dept).
7 September 1943	Fatal accident at Hinam Farm.
10 September 1943	Dies and is buried at St Giles' church, Hawkridge.

Annex C

His Favourite Hunting Horn

As told by his great-nephew – Bruce Heywood.

I am extremely fortunate to have been given my great uncle's favourite hunting horn which has been passed on to me by his son. He, Percy, was anxious for the horn to remain in the family – if possible with one who hunted with the staghounds. He decided upon me as I have hunted all my life and it is perhaps fitting, indeed an honour, to have been thus selected as guardian.

As soon as he became huntsman to the Devon and Somerset, Ernest was on the look out for a lightweight horn that would produce exactly the right tone. For years many attempts were made at thinning various horns with lathes or with emery paper, but without success. His elder brother, James, who (by this time) was farming in Wiltshire, visited Exmoor frequently in order to buy up quantities of Exmoor Horn sheep. He knew of his brother's quest and was determined to see if he could help.

A Wiltshire friend of his, one Colonel William Alexander, who hunted a pack of beagles near Upavon, was consulted. One day, word arrived at Exford. "I've got the very thing for you, Ernest. We'll have you fixed up, as soon as I'm next down." Alexander, a 6'9" and 20 stone giant of a man, was a keen huntsman and as good as Ernest on the horn. The instrument duly arrived – a small Cotswold type made by Kohler and Son of Piccadilly – bearing the inscription "E.B. from H.W.A."

Ernest tried it and was overjoyed. "Listen!" he cried. "Listen to this… all my life I've been looking for just this!" By this time he had tried literally scores in his search for the perfect tone, including one given by Captain Kinglake – Master of the Quarme Harriers – but to no avail. Now the drama begins.

Sometime in the early thirties, hounds were hunting in the Barle valley. The river was in flood. Anxious, as always, to be up with his hounds, and fearing nothing, Ernest attempted to ford the river but was swept from his horse. Both somehow escaped, but the horn was lost. *(The most likely location and scenario was on 16 March 1932, when his horse reared up after the dead hind brushed against it and Ernest was nearly drowned).* He was distraught, apparently more concerned for his horn than for either himself or his horse. When the floods had receded, search parties were sent out time and again but nothing was found. His treasured horn, so it seemed, had gone for good.

Ten years passed. Ernest, long since retired, was sitting in his garden at Hinam on a summer evening when he heard a horn – his horn. "That's mine... my bloody horn!" he cried excitedly to Elizabeth Ann. She, as calm as ever, was convinced he had taken leave of his senses, but no. It transpired that some evacuee children staying nearby had been playing at the water's edge and found the horn lodged in the pebbles and sand. One lad, a bugler, duly blew the instrument within earshot of its owner. Ernest's head shot up, he knew the sound at once.

The boys, hoping for a bit of pocket money, tried to do a deal with Arthur Court – a local antique dealer – whose shop was close to the Dulverton mill leat. But they were unlucky for the diligent and alert Arthur had spotted the initials E.B. on the now badly scored surface. "I think I've got your horn," Arthur announced on the telephone. Just so – huntsman and horn were together once more.

Later that season hounds were hunting hard near Dulverton and running under Hinam. It was all too much; temptation tore at the old huntsman. He snatched up the horn, ran outside and stopped for a moment before putting the horn to his lips. Silence. Hound music ceased; the pack slowed and stopped then came up to him. None could have known him, none had ever heard the horn but something deep down stirred and the pack responded just as their forefathers had done a decade earlier.

The Master galloped up. "Don't, Ernest," he cried urgently. "Don't do that, for God's sake or you'll ruin the hunt." Then, as an afterthought. "Why did you blow it?"

Ernest shrugged. "Oh, I don't know. Just to see... well, just to see if they'd respond." And they did, every one.

* *

By now it was 1956. Edward du Cann had just won the Taunton by-election. The following day he was due to drive through Exford on his victory tour. Dick Lloyd (now President of the hunt) hurried to Percy's cottage in the village to see if there was a hunting horn he could borrow to blow in salute. By a stroke of luck his wife was in and handed him the old favourite which Dick blew as he had never been able to blow before. He realised at once what an instrument it was and had to borrow it for the Horse and Hound ball in London where the national horn blowing competition was to take place.

He competed on four occasions. The first year he came second to Master and Huntsman of the Tiverton foxhounds but then he found his mark, winning each time subsequently and beating every professional in the process. Even the bookies' favourite – Albert Buckle of the Whaddon Chase – failed to beat the Exmoor man – and Ernest Bawden's horn.

Annex D

"The Day of all Days"

By Archie Pape

12 August. Hawkcombe Head.

Charlie and I met at the Devonshire Inn (Chard) at 5 a.m. then bicycled and met Dick and Miss Williams at Taunton. We put the bikes on the train and journeyed to Minehead. We then cycled to Porlock where we left the bikes and climbed up the very steep hill, 3 miles long and then on again until we reached the meet at Hawkcombe Head.

The hounds were taken to kennel at Culbone Stables and a good stag was harboured in Lillycombe. It was, however, over one and a half hours before Mr Sanders (who was hunting hounds that day) was able to put the pack on to his foil. When he did they gave us a lovely view of the run all round by Larkbarrow and the Deer Park then back again – about 8 or 9 miles I should say.

Then he crossed the Lynton road by Culbone Stables and beat about in Lord Lovelace's Plantation for some time. At last they drove him out at the far end and here my run commenced. I ran the Lynton road for about 4 miles in the awful heat until I found them baying him on the hillside. He, however, broke away and passed over the road close to me at County Gate and sank down into Glenthorne.

I now slid and fell down the treacherous hillside to the house and, by asking at the front door, got a path down to the beach where I met Mr Sanders and about five others who had left their horses and descended by foot. About half a mile on we came up to the hounds baying their stag up in the cliff. It was a glorious sight to see him keeping hounds off with his antlers.

At last he came down on to the beach. I and another chap collared him by the antlers and held on. But he upset the other chap *(tossed him!)* and then ripped my coat right up and tried to get to the sea. However, in the surf, he fell over a rock and a lot of chaps grabbed him, me among them. And then came the gladdest moment of my life. I was allowed to cut his throat with my own knife. This instrument now hangs up in my room as a hunting trophy. I was presented with a tush and then we had to climb 300 feet straight up the cliff to the nearest path, as we were cut off by the tide from the path we had come down.

On arriving at the path I found it was 5.15 p.m. and I was dead tired but managed to pull myself together. We ran or walked all the way to Porlock which was 8 miles away then biked the 6 miles into Minehead arriving on the platform at 7.15 p.m. to find the last was 7.25 p.m. Here I had to have a brandy as I had had nothing to eat but a crust of bread snatched at Porlock Weir since 4.30 a.m. when I had breakfast. Also I had cramp badly on getting to Minehead. Here I met the other three and related my experiences and heartily wish they had shared them with me.

On getting to Taunton, I had a really good dinner and a whisky and soda and then felt a bit better. We trained to Chard and Charlie and I bicycled home where I arrived at about 12.20 a.m. I was about as utterly done up as I think it was possible to be. It took me several days to get right again and, even now as I am writing this a month after, I can feel it in my legs a trifle. But, what does it matter, for I would most certainly do the same again if I could ever find such a glorious experience.

9 September.

Found a stag at Stockridge in some gorse and ran him well all down through Horner Woods and away to Balls Wood overlooking Porlock. Here we beat about for some time. When he came back into view of us at Borrow Farm he stood at bay in the yard, Bill got hold of him by an antler over a wall and hung on. We had to wait several minutes before a single horseman came into sight. It was (Sidney) Tucker.

Found again at Sweetery now all round by Dunkery and back by Bagley Combe to East Water Foot. Here he beat about the Horner Woods for upwards of an hour and then hounds brought him to bay just above Peasy Pool. He was a young deer about five years old but the first was a very old stag going back in his antlers. Tucker gave us some liver from each, which we truly enjoyed for dinner and breakfast next morning. Ernest Bawden also sent us the two tushes of each stag.

We had a lovely tramp home back through Horner Woods to the Mill. We had tea with Mrs Floyd and then went back to Allerford to stop the night. That evening we went over to the Anchor Hotel at Porlock Weir and saw Mr Goddard.

Note. The reader must appreciate that these events took place in 1905, soon after E.B had joined the Hunt. It was a brutal and savage world compared with today where such activities at the end of the hunt would never be tolerated. But look at the day as a whole. What fanatical enthusiasm and what energy! Archie Pape was a comrade of Ernest's in The Royal North Devon Hussars and the tushes are still with the family.

The first day was a formidable undertaking, not the least because Hawkcombe Head lies at almost 1400 feet and they would have started at virtually sea level. Their run (on foot, of course) took them miles across the moor followed by a 4-mile road run, and all in the August heat. After this they scrambled down to the beach – and then all the way back up again before beginning their long journey home. Wrestling with a stag at bay in the water is not for the faint-hearted either. In total it was a twenty-one hour day of perpetual motion and all for the thrill of the chase. Tough men and stout hearts; I wonder how many foot followers today would like to try it.

Annex E

Hunting Talk

"From Bratton to Porlock Bay"
By Sir Henry Newbolt

Chorus *So… hurry along the stag's afoot*
The Master is up and away.
Hullo! Hullo! We'll follow him through
From Bratton to Porlock Bay.

1.
The forest above and the combe below
On a bright September morn,
The sons of the sod give thanks to God
That ever his body was born.

Chorus

2.
With all his rights and seven atop
His eye like the eye of a King,
He'll beggar the pride of them that ride
Before he leaves the ling.

Chorus

3.
Hark to the tufters challenge true,
A note that the red deer knows,
His courage awakes as the covert he breaks
And away to the moor he goes.

Chorus

4.
Here comes Ernest bringing the pack,
He now is laying them on.
By the sound of the chime, we'll tell 'tis time
To harden our hearts and be gone.

Chorus

5.
Then Knightacott, Narracott and Horacott past
And straight for the north he raced
He's leading us straight for Blackmoor Gate
And he's setting a pounding pace.

Chorus

6.
We're running him now on a breast-high scent
There's many a left stood still.
When we're swinging around by Wistland Pound
He was far up Challacombe Hill.

Chorus

7.
The pack is a string of struggling ants,
Our quarry is a dancing midge,
We're trying reins on the edge of the Chains
While he's on Cheriton Ridge.

Chorus

8.
He's gone by Tippacott, Lucott Moor,
He's gone by Woodcocks Ley.
By the little white town he turned right down
And he sailed for the open sea.

Chorus

9.
So... hurry along, we'll both be in
The crowd is a parish away.
We're a field of two and we've followed him through
From Bratton to Porlock Bay.

Chorus *(Fortissimo!)*

Note. This hunt, if ever it took place, would have been a very good one indeed, covering 20 miles at least as hounds ran and taking the field over some of the wildest and most beautiful parts of north Exmoor. Weather permitting, the views would have been marvellous. No wonder they sang so heartily later.

* *

ERNEST – THE WAY HE WROTE ABOUT HUNTING

One of the most remarkable features of Ernest's hunting diaries is his prose. Time and again he brings some situation or a particular scene to life so vividly with a beautifully descriptive phrase. He writes as he must have spoken and one can almost hear his soft, rich Westcountry burr. It is as though we are out there with him and my pulse quickens each time I read these lines!

- They were racing her down the water.
- The old hind had been well run by tufters.
- Plenty of tongue, plenty of song.
- Pack was let go and settled on to a single hind.
- Gale, fog and blinding rain… difficult to tell what hounds were about.
- He doubled about like a hare.
- A proper hurricane of wind, hail and snow all day.
- They simply coursed her over Molland Moor.
- The small pack hunted in admirable fashion, running up together with a great cry all the time.
- She – Gambol – worked her way up to the stag and fresh found him.
- They hustled him out of the wood.
- As pretty a hunt as one would wish to see… a very capital chase.
- Hounds were racing her the whole time *(three hrs)*. The big dog hounds hunted merrily and threw their tongues in splendid style all the time and were well up together.
- They pressed him hard and got him well beat.
- Hounds spoke all at once and hunted most beautifully upstream… they hit it off into Stoke Wood and hunted him up with a great cry.
- The hind had had a good bustling.
- The deer had been viewed more than an hour before… but hounds could not carry the line further than the Punch Bowl and had to give up.
- The bitches stuck to their hind and ran with a rare cry all the time.
- The tufters rattled him up and down the coverts for full an hour or more.
- Much fog on top however a little clearer back down in under.
- All the field got lost except Tom Bawden, Dan Milton and myself.
- Fog still remained in possession of all the moorland until nearly eleven. It then lifted just enough.
- He sank down to water below Marsh Bridge and was quickly accounted for.
- Lang had heard a stag belling.
- Hounds were close in on his haunches going down over the meadows but he just about managed to get to sea and was not accounted for.
- Ground was still frozen hard on the blind side.
- They all went away with a great burst of music.
- A very hard and rough wild day.
- *(17 Feb)* As it was getting late hounds went home. The day had been bitterly

cold with a gale of wind blowing in from the east and visibility was poor. A good deal of frost was on the high ground as well as snow.

- The pack nipped in, then they drove on very fast up over Horner Valley.
- A beautiful bit of water hunting with old 'Sapper' showing the younger ones how to do it.
- Hounds opened on his line with a great cry.
- He was a nice forest stag in good galloping order and carried a fine head of two atop both sides.
- Hounds were just about able to hold their line and by clever hunting worked their way through the combe.
- The day was gloriously fine and sunny and with most excellent visibility… scent was first rate.
- The hunted hind was observed by the huntsman stealing back towards Whitstones.
- *(12 Sept 1933)* The ground was got as hard as iron and terribly burned up by the scorching heat which has lasted more or less since 16 March.
- Hounds had outdistanced everyone once more in this great hunt but they could be heard chiming merrily down Westwater stream and on into the Barle at Hind's Pit.
- Hounds simply raced her around the plantation on a screaming scent.
- A very fast hunt. Never did hounds leave him for a moment and the way they worked out his doubles and the pace at which they ran were remarkable. Their music, too, was a treat to hear.
- And so it proved a very long cast down to Heasley Mill *(over 2 miles)* which was not successful and we had to own defeat. Only Master, huntsman and the first whip saw anything of this hunt, the field got left well behind under such terrible weather conditions as ever I saw.

20 April 1937.

Huntsman quickly had hounds on his line… they raced upstream and killed him under Tarr Ball. Quite a large number of the huge field that was out got to the end of this very fast forest run. Had it not been for the dismal weather, what a day it would have been to end my career as huntsman to the Devon and Somerset Staghounds.

Annex F

Exmoor Game Recipes

Introduction

All these recipes are well-known to Exmoor. Many have been used by farmers and hunters down the ages, indeed most were probably in use long before King John grabbed the ancient Forest from its rightful owners all those centuries ago. They have been checked out with a well-known local chef who has replaced one or two ancient ingredients that are no longer available with a suitable modern equivalent.

An interesting point that Ernest and Missus would have well understood is that the venison of a well-hunted deer is generally more tender and ready to eat then that of a deer which has been shot standing or poached with the gun.

But be warned – this is *not* instant food! They will take a bit of time to prepare but it'll be well worth the patience and effort.

* *

Venison

1. The Staghunter.

Shoulder of venison with mustard and ale.

Best cooked long and slow so that the meat is melting off the bones. It is exactly what Missus would have had ready and waiting.

Ingredients for 6–8 portions.

4 lb shoulder (bone incl).
3–5 large spoons of mustard (English or continental).
Lard.
Salt, pepper and herbs.
2 small sliced onions.
2 carrots, peeled and sliced.
2–3 sticks of chopped celery.
1 pint of brown ale.
3 large spoonfuls of
Demerara sugar.

Cut deep incisions into the meat at one inch intervals then stuff amply first with mustard then with lard. Cover the shoulder with a paste of warmed lard and mustard, add seasoning. Place in a roasting dish and pour half the beer gently over the meat. Cover and roast in a hot oven at (Mk 8, 450F or 230C) for 15 mins then slow right down to (Mk 3, 325F, 170C) for a further two and a half to three hours. Check frequently and baste – not forgetting to add the beer. Take out thirty minutes from the end and paste with whatever's left of the mustard and beer then cover with a thick coating of sugar. If supper is not ready then reduce oven temperature further but remember to keep the meat moist. Serve with Queen Victoria's sauce (see 'Extras' below).

* *

2. Venison in Red Wine.

Very popular and there are countless variations but allow at least a couple of days for preparation.

Ingredients for 6–8 portions.
3 lb of shoulder.
Mixed herbs (dried will do but fresh is better – thyme, parsley and marjoram).
3–5 onions.
3–5 large carrots.
2 sticks of celery.
4 oz (100g) butter.
1 oz (25g) plain flour.
Rowan or redcurrant jelly.
3 cloves of garlic.
One bay leaf.
A generous slice of lemon.
10–12 crushed juniper berries.
12 crushed peppercorns.
Bottle and a half of decent red wine.
Seasoning as required.

Slice up the vegetables and spices and put them all into a large bowl with the venison then cover with the marinade (see below). The bowl should be as tight fitting as possible so the marinade covers the meat – then leave it to marinate for two days. Next remove the meat and pat dry before smearing well with half the butter. Place it in a large bowl (casserole). Boil the marinade in a pan down to half, adding herbs, seasoning and lemon juice then pour over the meat. Let the whole meal simmer gently for at least two and a half hours, stirring gently from time to time. Note – if the venison is tough then continue until it becomes tender. Take out the meat and keep it in a warm oven while you mix the flour and softened butter with half the remaining liquid. Whisk into a paste and add the remainder of the wine sauce. Allow it to cool and thicken. Check for seasoning. Can also be served with Queen Victoria's or Red Wine sauce (see below).

* *

3. Exmoor Roast.

Roast haunch of venison with onion and mustard sauce.

One of the best known hunt suppers.

Ingredients for 6–8 portions.
3–4 lbs of haunch.
2 large onions, peeled and well chopped.
4oz (100g) mushrooms finely chopped.
Small spoonful of grated nutmeg.
A few sprigs of fresh rosemary.
Large spoonful of plain flour.
Pint and a half of rich gamy stock
(probably kept over from the previous game meal).
2 crushed cloves of garlic.
Spoonful of olive oil.

Marinate the venison in the same way as above. Pre-heat the oven to (Mk5, 375F, 190C) then roast the meat under well-oiled foil for one and a half to two hours with the rosemary added, basting frequently. Traditionally, before the advent of foil, a paste of flour and water was spread over the joint to retain moisture. In the meantime make up a thick sauce in much the same way as above. This time fry the chopped onions until brown in the oil and add mushrooms for a further two minutes. Add the stock then mix in the flour, garlic, nutmeg and seasoning and stir well. Allow it to boil briefly before simmering gently. Carve the haunch then pour over the sauce before serving. Choose your sauce from below.

* *

Hare

4. Jugged Hare.

A much loved old favourite – perfect for a cold winter's day.

Ingredients for 5–6 portions.
1 hare. Skin, paunch and clean then cut into small neat pieces,
remembering to drain off and keep the blood.

3 oz butter.
Salt and pepper.
1 large onion.
2–3 carrots.
4–6 cloves.
1 glass of port or claret.
1 large spoon of lemon juice.
4 oz of streaky bacon cut into strips.
12 crushed peppercorns.
A sprig of fresh or dried herbs.
1½ pints of stock – the same as above.
1 oz of plain flour.
12 oz of sage and onion or veal stuffing. (See 'Extras' below).
Lard or cooking fat.
1 tablespoon of redcurrant jelly.

Prepare the hare. Heat 2 oz of butter and fry the pieces of hare until well browned, then fry bacon. Place the hare and bacon in a casserole with salt, the onion halved and stuck with cloves and the sliced carrots, half the wine, lemon juice, peppercorns, sprig of herbs and hot stock. Place a tight lid on the casserole, add red currant jelly and cook for about three hours, (Mk 4, 350F, 180C). Knead the flour and remaining butter together, stir into the stock about half an hour before serving. Add remaining wine and seasoning to taste. Make stuffing, form into small balls and fry. Gently heat the blood, stir into gravy and allow to thicken. Serve with redcurrant jelly.

5. Hare Casserole.

Another old favourite and one which can be kept simmering while waiting for the hunters or guns to return.

Ingredients.
1 hare. Prepare as above.
3 oz butter.
1 large onion.
2–3 sticks of celery.
3–5 cloves.
Bouquet of herbs (Rosemary, sage and thyme in particular).
1½ pints of stock, flavoured with dry cider
(about 1 pt of chicken stock, half pint of cider).
1 oz of flour.
12–16oz of sage and onion stuffing.
Seasoning.

Fry the pieces of meat in 2oz of butter until brown then pack closely into a casserole dish. Slice and fry the onion then add, cloves, herbs, seasoning and stock and the sliced celery. Stir well and pour over the hare. Cover well and allow it all to simmer for two and a half hours to three hours. Thirty minutes before ready knead butter and flour together, divide into small pieces and add. Then, five or ten minutes before ready, break stuffing into small balls, fry in hot fat and add. Flavour with herbs and add seasoning to taste.

* *

6. Roast Baron of Hare.

A wonderful dish that was once cooked on a spit over an open fire.

Ingredients.

1 hare. Prepare as above but use only the body (legs below the hock, neck etc used for soup or a future stock).
12 oz of sage and onion or veal stuffing.
6–8 oz fine bacon strips.
Lard or dripping.
1 pint of Boar's Head sauce. To be prepared beforehand. (See 'Extras' below).
1 glass of port.
Redcurrant jelly.

Partly boil the liver then chop finely before adding it to the stuffing and stuff the hare. Sew it up or tie securely with string. Lard it well then add the strips of bacon before wrapping it all in well-greased paper. Roast in a fairly hot oven (Mk5–6, 400F, 210C) for forty-five minutes, basting frequently with hot butter or dripping. Remove the paper when there is fifteen minutes to go. Add the port to the sauce then serve separately with the redcurrant jelly.

* *

Pheasant

7. Roast Pheasant with Mushrooms.

One of so many variations yet the mushrooms, lemon and herbs add that extra touch.

Ingredients for 4 helpings.

1 pheasant. Insert 2 or 3 slices of apple to help keep the flesh moist and to add flavour.

5–6 slices of fat bacon.
12 largish mushrooms.
2 oz of butter.
Salt and cayenne pepper.
Lemon juice.
3–4 sprigs of rosemary.
1 Apple.

Prepare and clean the bird. Peel and chop the mushrooms, mix with butter, season well and add juice of half the lemon. Stuff the bird with this mixture and slices of the apple then lay the bacon across the body of the bird and surround with rosemary. Pre-heat the oven to Mk4, 350F, 180C and cook for forty-five to fifty minutes, checking and basting along the way.

* *

8. Slow-roast Pheasant with Mustard and Beer.

A delicious recipe that can be prepared some time before the meal and kept warm until ready.

Ingredients for 4.
1 pheasant.
2 oz of lard.
2 heaped tablespoonfuls of continental mustard.
Seasoning.
Mixed herbs.
1 pint of a rich, dark ale.
1 tablespoonful of brown sugar.
Juice of 1 lemon.

Ease the skin away from the bird and grease the body well with a mixture of half the lard and mustard. This is messy and tricky so take care! Replace the skin as best you can and lay the remaining lard over the body before placing it in a roasting tin with most of the ale. Sprinkle on the dry herbs liberally. Roast at Mk5, 375F, 190C for half an hour, basting two or three times then turn down to Mk2, 300F, 150C for another hour. Keep basting. Remove and spread the remaining mustard on to the bird then sprinkle on the brown sugar. Grill or roast well for ten minutes then baste again. Keep warm until ready, basting with the gravy and the rest of the beer if necessary. Pour lemon juice over pheasant just before you're ready.

* *

Pigeon

9. Roast Pigeon.

Nothing wrong with the humble pigeon it's delicious and a very old recipe from the days when they used to have doves in the dovecotes.

Ingredients for 6 modest helpings but some will be able
to manage one on their own.
3 Pigeons.
3 oz butter.
Seasoning.
Lemon juice.
3 small rashers of lean bacon.
3 pieces of well fried bread.
Sprigs of rosemary.
Water cress.

Clean and wipe down the birds then insert into each, 1 oz butter, a good squirt of lemon juice and seasoning. Truss the birds and cover with a piece of bacon and rosemary. Roast for about thirty minutes or longer if necessary at Mk6, 375F, 190C, basting and checking for crispness as you go. Serve up on a piece of crisp fried bread and garnish with watercress and, perhaps, a touch of French dressing.

* *

Rabbit

10. Exmoor Rabbit Pie.

One of Ernest Bawden's great favourites. He would sit humming Flanagan and Allen's *"Run rabbit, run rabbit run, run, run"* while waiting!

Ingredients for 6 helpings.
2 rabbits.
12–160z of short crust pastry.
2 oz grated cheese.
A small onion
A stick of celery.
Seasoning.
3 or 4 tablespoons of milk.
Egg or milk for glazing.

Wash and joint the rabbits. Prepare stock from carcasses then stew the rabbit joints in their own stock until tender. Remove bones and cut meat into smaller pieces. Prepare a suitable pie dish with half the pastry then put in the rabbit, cheese, chopped celery and onion, adding seasoning. Cover with the other half of pastry, glaze with egg or milk and bake in a fairly hot oven of Mk5–6, 375–400K, 200C for about thirty minutes. Serve hot or cold – lovely for summer picnics.

⁂

Extras

1. Marinade.

Not too heavy or you will kill off the flavour of the meat. The aim is to enhance the flavour – not drown it! Try this:

Bottle and a half of red wine.
3 teaspoonfuls of brown sugar.
1 tablespoonful of black peppercorns.
1 tablespoon of vegetable oil.
5 cloves.
7–10 bay leaves.
A small spoonful of mild curry powder.
Some crushed sprigs of fresh rosemary, sage and thyme.
Mix everything together then pour over the meat making sure to cover.
Leave like this for two–three days
but stir from time to time.

⁂

2. Stock.

Simply the essence boiled out of whatever bones you want – venison, beef, chicken etc. Bake them hard first for thirty minutes or so then add 2 pints of water plus the crushed garlic, mixed herbs, plus a sprig or two of rosemary and seasoning and boil until you are happy with the flavour.

⁂

3. Queen Victoria's Sauce.

A small glass of port.
8 oz of redcurrant jelly.
A small stick of cinnamon.
Thinly pared rind of a lemon.
Simmer all the ingredients for about ten minutes,
stirring well before straining into a sauce boat.

* *

4. Red Wine Sauce.

A quarter pint of venison stock.
1 large glass of red wine.
1 table spoon of rowan jelly.
1 table spoon of continental mustard.
Juice from half a lemon.
A small glass of brandy.
Reduce the stock and wine to half then stir in the rowan jelly, mustard, lemon juice and brandy.
Season to taste.

* *

5. Boar's Head Sauce.

The rind of 2 large oranges.
1 shallot.
Half pound of redcurrant jelly.
Small glass of port.
1 oz sugar.
Small teaspoonful of mustard.
Dozen black peppercorns.
Juice of 1 orange.
Grate the rind (but no pith!), chop the shallot. Put into a pan with the jelly and port. Mix well then heat slowly to simmer for half an hour, stirring frequently. Add sugar, mustard, cayenne and orange juice. Stir well then strain and allow to cool. Can be used with all game but especially venison and hare.

* *

6. Sage and Onion Stuffing.

Approx 12 ozs.
4 oz of onions.
4 young sage leaves or half teaspoon of powdered sage.
3 oz breadcrumbs.
1½ oz butter.
Seasoning and half an egg.

Slice the onions thickly, part boil them for ten minutes in very little water. Scald the sage leaves then chop with the onions. Mash and work everything together then season to taste.

* *

7. Veal Stuffing or Forcemeat.

Approx 12 ozs.
4 oz breadcrumbs.
2 oz margarine.
1 tablespoon of chopped parsley.
Half teaspoon of chopped herbs.
Nutmeg and grated rind of half a lemon.
1 beaten egg.
Seasoning.

Mix everything together and season to taste.

Annex G

Obituary

(Taken in full from the archives of the *West Somerset Free Press*)

* *

Ernest Bawden's Death

Harvesting Accident Proves Fatal

Countryside's tribute to a great Huntsman

Three days after he was brought into the Minehead and West Somerset Hospital suffering from the injuries which he sustained on Tuesday of last week while helping with harvest work on Hynham Farm, near Dulverton, Mr Ernest Bawden, of Hynham Bungalow, for twenty years Huntsman to the Devon and Somerset Staghounds, and before that whipper-in, passed away. So severe were his injuries that his condition was very critical when he was admitted to hospital, and his death, which took place soon after mid-day last Friday, in circumstances so distressing, came as a real shock to all the countryside in which he was so well known, and evoked the deepest sympathy on every hand with his wife and son, Mr Percy Bawden. Scores of letters of condolence, which they have received, bore testimony to the admiration and esteem which followers of the Devon and Somerset Hunt had for Ernest Bawden's qualities as a huntsman and as a sportsman and to the measures of regard in which he was held in hall and farm and cottage throughout the Exmoor country.

Ernest Comer Bawden, to give him his full name, was sixty-five years old. Except for a couple of years in his youth, he had lived all his life on Exmoor. It is not surprising perhaps that he became one of the most famous of the Devon and Somerset Staghounds long line of huntsmen, for it might be said that he was born to staghunting. His father, the late Mr James Bawden, of Hollowcombe Farm, Hawkridge – Ernest was his fifth son – was a great staghunting enthusiast, and the story is still told of how Ernest, when only three years old, rode on horseback in front of his father and was in at the death. Certainly he had ridden to hounds ever since he could remember, and opportunities for doing so were plentiful during his boyhood at Hawkridge and later when he was helping his father at Hollowcombe.

A South African War Veteran

While yet in his 'teens he joined the Royal North Devon Hussars, of which Colonel R.A. Sanders (who became Lord Bayford) was the Commanding Officer in those days, and during the South African War against the Boers. When the call went out for volunteers, he with others of the Regiment went to South Africa and served in the 7th Battalion of The Imperial Yeomanry, who proved their worth in that campaign. He went out in 1900 and returned in 1902 *(1901)* with the rank of Corporal and the medals he received for the campaign included one commemorating "the magnificent response of Britain's sons to the Empire's call to arms." Subsequently, as Sergeant in the North Devon Hussars he was awarded the Long Service and Good Conduct medal of the Imperial Yeomanry. In 1902 he had the honour, with other NCO's of the regiment, of representing it among the troops that took part in the Coronation pageantry in London when King Edward VII was crowned.

A born rider and a fearless horseman, Ernest was, of course, perfectly at home in the Yeomanry, and trophies which had adorned his sideboard since those days included a silver cup for the best turned-out man and horse in the regiment (1899) and two cups which he won in Yeomanry races when they were in camp on Ashwick Hill *(Exmoor)* after the South African War. He rode, too, and won in other race meetings including the first Devon and Somerset point-to-point at Larkbarrow. He was also, in his youth, a good runner, more particularly in long distance and steeplechase events: on one occasion, at Exford, he beat a well-known professional runner.

He joins the Hunt Staff

For a couple of years after his return from South Africa, Ernest assisted his brother, Mr James Bawden, who then had the White Horse Hotel in Exford with the hunter side of the business. Then, in 1904, Col Sanders, Master of the Devon and Somerset Staghounds, induced him to join the Hunt staff as whipper-in. Fred Barber, who had for a short time occupied that position, had been unable to continue on account of his health. Sidney Tucker was huntsman at this time, and on his retirement, in 1917, in Mr Badco's Mastership, Ernest was appointed as his successor. His retirement at the end of the spring staghunting season of 1937, a few months after the death of Col W.W.Wiggin, terminated their twenty-five years association – a remarkable one in many ways – as Master and Huntsman, was the occasion of a presentation to Ernest, made privately, of a cheque for £1,300, subscribed by 1,100 followers and supporters of the Hunt. At the same time Mrs Bawden was presented with a silver lamp.

To Ernest Bawden's qualities as a huntsman many notable tributes have been paid. A writer in *The Times* some years ago averred that "as a possessor of an eye for a country Ernest was in a class by himself," and described him as "the greatest living artist" in his ability to "cover the country at a full gallop for hours together, without apparent effort, seldom or never taking the wrong line or turning, always in touch with his hounds, and usually in touch with the deer as well." Earl Fortescue, at the first Exford Horseshow luncheon after Ernest's retirement, declared that he had served the Hunt in a most exceptional way; "thanks to his great foresight and knowledge, and with Col Wiggin's help and keenness, he had bred a superb pack of hounds, and had hunted them in a most remarkable and uncanny fashion."

Earl Fortescue, writing to Mrs Bawden on behalf of the Hunt Committee, said "the committee can never be sufficiently grateful to Ernest for all he did for them in producing a first-rate pack of hounds and showing the splendid sport he did for so many years."

Puppy Show Judge

During his service as huntsman and since his retirement, Ernest Bawden had frequently acted as one of the judges at local puppy-shows. He invariably acted in that capacity at the Quantock Staghounds' puppy-judging, and his qualifications for such an office were such that puppy-walkers generally had the fullest confidence in his decisions.

Home Guard Service

When in 1940 the call went forth for volunteers for the L.D.V. (now the Home Guard) Ernest Bawden was among the first of many Exmoor men to answer it, and, as Section Commander, he was one of the most zealous and efficient figures in the mounted unit that patrolled the Exmoor hills. He left the Home Guard in 1941 but had been serving since in another arm of National Service organised against the possibility of invasion.

Mr Bawden was a member of the Exford branch of the British Legion and of the Old Comrades' Association of the Royal North Devon Hussars.

* *

Big attendance at funeral
Over one hundred floral tributes

At the highest point of the churchyard at Hawkridge, overlooking Anstey Common which, during the course of his active career, he had traversed so often, the mortal remains of Ernest Bawden were laid to rest on Wednesday afternoon, this sad duty falling to a bearer party representative of the whole countryside viz Messers M.Westcott (Draydon), T. Pugsley (Sanctuary), F. Webber (Bampton), Ned Lang (Miltons), Oliver Robbins (Lydcott) and J.H. Prideaux (Barnstaple). It took place in the presence of a very large number of friends and sympathisers, many of whom had walked miles to be there and not all of them, by any means, were able to gain admittance to the little parish church where, throughout the previous night, the body, enclosed in a coffin made entirely of English oak, had rested. In the vicinity of the entrance to the church numerous floral tributes carpeted the green. The service was conducted by the Rector of Hawkridge-with-Withypool, the Rev. F.M. Etherington, and it included the hymn "O God our help in ages past" and, as the cortege was leaving the church, the "Nunc Dimittis" was chanted. Miss Lock, who also played appropriate voluntaries, rendered the accompaniments. Internment was in a grave partly walled, the brickwork being crested with hill-moss studded with chrysanthemums.

* *

An Appreciation

Anonymous

The following appreciation from one who hunted with Ernest for very many years has been received:

It was the late Lord Bayford who persuaded Ernest Bawden to exchange farming for the chase. As a whipper-in he was superlative. A light-weight and fine horseman, he seemed able to do the work of two, and at one moment would be viewing the deer and the next throwing tail hounds in at the head. For an eye for the country *The Times* hunting correspondent described him as in a class by himself. The responsibilities of a huntsman provided more scope for his talents. Having studied the deer since boyhood, he seemed in moments of difficulty to know instinctively what his deer had done, and backed his intuition with a dogged perseverance that would not own defeat. He was a great hound man. After the last war the late Col Wiggin and he together built up what was admittedly one of finest packs in England. His hounds worshipped him. And his control of them in the field was a wonder of many hunting visitors. His kennel management was equally good, and it is in the kennel that deer, like foxes, are really killed. He would bring his hounds through August heat and winter storms and cold to the vagaries of April "on their toes" all the way. When he meets Tom Firr and Will Goodall and the other great huntsmen in the Elysian fields there will be much talk of hounds. *"Amen" to that!*

Glossary

Belling
The loud, guttural challenge of a stag during the mating season (the rut). The roar sounds like the gurgling bellow of a bullock.

Cap
The daily charge raised against those hunting for the day. The cheque or cash is often placed in the Secretary's cap, hence the term.

Company or Squadron
The standard fighting unit of around a hundred and twenty officers and men.

Country
The territory over which one hunt has the exclusive right to hunt in agreement with its neighbours. A neighbouring pack may come into the country in hot pursuit or by invitation.

D and S or D&S
The recognised abbreviations for the Devon and Somerset Staghounds.

Drafts
Hounds passed from one pack to another, either sold or as gifts.

Earth
The home of the fox. Usually a deep hole in a bank or hillside.

Field
Mounted followers of the hunt.

Flags
Flagstones with which the working areas of most kennels were floored and, in particular, an area outside, where hounds were shown.

Foil
A term to describe the scent of an animal which has blended with or been obliterated by others – ie his foil was lost amongst the ewes and lambs.

Forage
The act of gathering food or the food itself.

Forest
A term used loosely to describe the heights of Exmoor, most of which was once a Royal Forest upon which only Royalty hunted.

Frog
The leather or webbing holder for the metal sheath in which the bayonet was kept.

Front
The general line along which the leading elements of two armies faced one another. As the battle progressed so the line would move in relation to the position of the opposing forces.

Line
The route taken by the hunted deer or fox. The huntsman and field would have their own lines across the countryside.

N.C.O.
A junior commander who is a Non-Commissioned Officer (N.C.O.) ie a Corporal.

Meet
The location where mounted and foot followers meet the hunt staff and hounds.

Numnah
Padded protection between the saddle and the back of the horse placed there to prevent rubbing and saddle sores.

Picquets or piquets
Small groups of men put out on high ground to detect the approach of the enemy.

P.T.
Physical Training ie vigorous exercises.

Racks
Footprints left by deer crossing hedges or other obstacles when they move in single file and can create clearly identifiable tracks.

R.S.M.
Regimental Sergeant Major. The senior soldier in the Regiment (apart from the

officers). A very severe gentleman responsible for discipline and from whom all others keep well clear.

Sett
Home of the badger. A deep hole burrowed into a bank or the hillside.

Slot
Quite literally the cloven hoof of the deer, thus slot marks would be hoof prints.

Soil
The act of wallowing in water or liquid mud.

S.N.C.O.
A more senior man than the J.N.C.O such as Sergeant or Staff Sergeant.

Stags
Not deer in this instance (!) but the colloquial expression used by soldiers for a spell of guard duty.

Stern
The tail of a hound.

Tush
The eye teeth of deer. The plural is tushes.

Whipper-in or whip
The huntsman's assistant in both kennels and the field.

Venery
Hunting. Thus the art of venery is the art and lore of hunting.

BIBLIOGRAPHY

Aldin, Cecil. *Exmoor. The Riding Playground of England.* J. and J. Gray of Edinburgh. 1935.

Bailey's Hunting Directories. Various Dates. J.A.Allen. The Anchor Press and others.

Bourne, Hope.L. *Exmoor. A Little History.* M. Dent and Sons, London. 1968.

Browne, Colonel P.J. CB. *A Rough Diary (Kept on the Veldt).* Published privately.

Chappel, M. *British Cavalry Equipments 1800 – 1941.* Osprey Publishing. 2002.

Clayton, Michael. *Ronnie Wallace. A Manual of Foxhunting.* Swan Hill. 2002.

Collyns, C.P. *The Chase of the Wild Red Deer.* 1862.

Collyns, Lt Col G.G. *Exmoor Staghunting. From 1066 to 1914.* Wellington Printers, Wellington.

Dunbar Eva. *Famous Huntsmen of the 18th and 19th Centuries.* A selection of private essays.

Eardley-Wilmot, Hazel. *Yesterday's Exmoor.* Exmoor Books. 1990.

Farwell, Byron. *The Great Boer War.* Wordsworth Editions. 1996.

Freeman, Benson. *The Yeomanry of Devon.* W.H.Smith and Son. The Arden Press. 1927.

Goss, Fred. *Memories of a Stag Harbourer.* J. and J. Gray, Edinburgh. 1931.

Greaves, Ralph. *A Short History of The Devon and Somerset Staghounds.* Reid Hamilton Ltd.

Hendy, E.W. *Wild Exmoor Through the Year.* Eyre and Spottiswoode, London. 1946.

Heron, Roy. *Tom Firr of the Quorn.* Roy Heron and Learnex. Unwin Bros. 1970.

Hewett, H.P. *A Stag-Hunter's Diary.* Cox and Sons, Williton.

Hewett, H.P. *The Fairest Hunting.* Allen and Co.

Lloyd, E.R. *The Wild Red Deer of Exmoor.* The Exmoor Press. 1970.

MacDermot, E.T. *The Devon and Somerset Staghounds 1907–1936.* Collins 1936.

Marshall, H.J. *Exmoor. Sporting and Otherwise.* Eyre and Spottiswoode. 1948.

Munby, Lionel. *How Much is that Worth?* Phillimore. 1996.

Munnings, Sir Alfred. *Ballads and Poems.* London Museum Press Limited. 1957.

Nimrod. *Nimrod's Hunting Tours 1825.* Kegan Paul, Trench, Trubner and Co Ltd. 1903.

Pape, Archie. G. *Diary of a Hunt Follower.* Private diaries.

Peel, J.H.B. *A Portrait of Exmoor.* Robert Hale. 1970.

Rowe, John. *The North Devon Yeomanry 1794 – 1924.* North Devon District Council.
Scruton, Roger. *On Hunting.* Yellow Jersey Press. London. 1999.
Stapeldon, R. *Exmoor. Elegance and Rhythm.*
Summerhayes. *A Lifetime with Horses.* Nicholas Kaye Ltd. 1962.
Surtees, R.S. *The Analysis of the Hunting Field.* Kegan Paul, Trench, Trubner and Co Ltd. 1903.
Wallace, Captain R. E. *Private Hunting Diaries.*

General Index

For the sake of brevity the index has been compiled from the main body of the book only; even then the myriad of names in Chapter 13 have been omitted.

Abbot, Miss B.K. "Biddy," 152
Anstey, 97
Anstruther-Thompson, John, Huntsman, 15,16,17
Assheton-Smith, Thomas, Huntsman, 12,17,158

Badco, Mr William, Master, 87,99,100
Barber, Mr Fred, Whip, 67
Bawden,
Archie, 61.
Ernestine 'Dolly', 118.
Ernest, 11,12; born 18; leaves school 29; first hunt 30; running 32,92; racing 33, 65; joins R.N.D.H. 36,37; oath of Allegiance 43 et seq; homecoming 60; his rifle 61; back home 62; promotion and awards 63; marriage 69; resigns from Yeomanry 78; testing hunt horses 79; winning over the pack 80; family life 83; disability 85; volunteers for WW1 86; drawing the water 92; car followers 94; daily routine 107 et seq; injuries 110; boot money 111; diaries 112; the new order 146; Hinam 150; WW II 152; death 155
Francis, 27,65
Frederick, 27,69
Harold, 61
Harriet (Jessie), 27, 65
James (Snr), 25,25,26, 29,41
James (Jnr), 27,65,69
John, 27,65
Joseph, 61
Mary-Elizabeth, 28,61
Percy, 82, 106 et seq, 147, 149
Beaufort, The Duke of, 113,152
Bell, Mr Isaac, 115
Blackmore Gate, 64
Bisset, Mr Mordaunt Fenwick, 24
Boevey, Mr James, 21
Boers, The, 46,51,60,154
Bolitho, Capt. W. D.S.O., 49,54,60
Boyles, Dennis, Huntsman, D and S, 14
Brendon Two Gates, The Hunt, 125
British Army, Situation in 1894, 43
British Legion (now The R.B.L.), 83
Browne, Colonel, 52,54,55,57
Buccleuch, The Duke of, 113,152

Caratacus or Caractacus Stone, 66
Cavalry Week, Barnstaple, 44
Cloggs Farm, Hawkridge, 22
Cloutsham, 115
Collyns, Mr G.G., 119
Comer, Harriet (E.B.'s mother), her marriage to James (Jim), 24
Coronation procession of King Edward VIIth, 64
Cow Castle, 80
Cromwell, Oliver, and The Civil War, 21
Crown Hotel, The, Exford, 114
Cuzzicombe Post, 90,91,99,116, The Hunt 131

Danesbrook or Danes' Brook, 20, 156
Deakin, William, Huntsman, 157
Denmark, The Prince and Princess of, 112
Devon and Somerset Staghounds (D and S or D&S), 11, early days 24, new era 67, size of 71, Puppy Show 87, 114, visitors 104
Devonshire Regiment, The, 43
Devonshire Yeomanry, The, 43
Diamond Hill, Battle of, 53
Dulverton, 60,68, The Hunt 123, Town Hall 152, Home Guard 153
Dunbar, Eva, Hunting correspondent of The *Morning Post*, 12,13,16,17,41,76
Dunster, 99

Ebberley Lawn Barracks, Barnstaple, 48,62,64
Ebrington, Colonel The Lord, (later Lord Fortescue), 48,64,67
Edgehill School for Girls, Bideford, 69
Edwards, Mr Lionel, Artist, 119
Everard, The family, Philip, Guy and Christopher, 86,87
Exe Cleeve, 80
Exeter, 59
Exford, 20,99, Horse Show 102,150
Exmoor, As a Royal Forest 20; Forest Law 21; Parish of 24; in 1904 68; the red deer herd 72,103, the countryside 97,101; N.P.A. 98

Firr, Tom, Huntsman, 13,17,70,158
Fortescue, The Fourth Lord, 36,86,102,105,113,144,145,146
Fortescue, The Fifth Lord, 146,150
Fortescue, The Hon Grenville, 86
Fortescue, The Hon Lionel, 53
Freeman, Frank, Huntsman, 112
Fyldon Ridge, 121

George Hotel, The, South Molton, 86
Goodall, Will, Huntsman, 14,17
Goosey, Tom, Huntsman, 14,16,17,24,158
Goss, Mr Fred, Harbourer, 27,32,73,74,85,106
Great War, The, 85, casualties 87
Greig, Major Morland, Master, 35,36,85,86,87,147
Greig, Mr Philip, Secretary, 147,148
Griffith, Mr Walter, 108

Hancock, Mr Froude, 85,105,144,145,146
Hancock, Mr Tommy, Master, 147,148,152
s.s. *Hawarden Castle*, 57,59
Hawkcombe Head, The Hunt 126
Hawkridge, 19; the Bawdens settle 22; school 28; village characters 30 and life 31; the "wild streak" 31; night life 34; E.B.'s return 60; 115,116; The Hunt 135; St Giles' church 156
Heal, Arthur, Huntsman, 32
Heywood, Elizabeth-Ann, 33,49,65,66; marriage 69 (hereafter usually known as "Missus").
Heywood, Harris, 33; joins army 36; returns home 60,61
Heywood, Hector, Harbourer. 150,151
Heywood, Sidney, 33,150
Hill, Tom, Huntsman, 12,17
Hinam Farm (also Hinham or Hynham), 149, 150 et seq
Hussars, 11th, 112
Huxtable, Anthony, Huntsman, 32, 178

Imperial Yeomanry, The, 57
Indian or 'Sepoy' Army, The, 43

Jefferies, Judge, "Bloody Assizes" 22
Jenah, E.B.'s favourite hunter, 80
Jones, William, Huntsman, 13

Knight, Sir Frederic, Builds Simonsbath, 23
Knight, Mr John, Buys Exmoor, 23,97
Knutsford, The Lord, 113,152

Lamb Hotel, The, Dulverton, 26
Landacre Bridge, 80
Lang, Ned, Harbourer, 106
Larkbarrow, 99,121; The Hunt 129
Las Casas, Lieut, 54,112
Lee-Enfield rifle, 51,61,154
Lenthal, Alfie, Huntsman, 11,106,148,152
Lloyd, Capt. "Ned," 105,117,146,147
Lloyd, Capt. Dick, 93,117 and brother Pat
Local Defence Volunteers, (The Home Guard), 152
Lock family, The, Hawkridge 31
Lucas, Mr Stucley of Baronsdown, 24
Lynton, 68

Maggersfontein, 47
Maitland Camp, 50
s.s. *Manchester Merchant*, 49
Mauser rifle, 51
McKinney, Dr Stuart, 156
Meynell, Hugo, Master, 13,16,70
Minehead, 68; Hospital, 156
"Missus" (E.B.'s wife), 106 et seq
Molland Moor Gate, 78
Monmouth, Duke of, 21
Mounsey Hill Detachment (Home Guard), 153
Murphy, Col Michael, 71
Musters, Jack, Huntsman, 13,17,24,158
Mytton, John, Huntsman, 12,15,17,100

New Zealand Mounted Rifles, 57
Nimrod, 13,14,70,72,87
North Molton, 99,103, 115; The Hunt, 133

Oare, 121
Old Comrades (R.N.D.H.), 62,83
Olympic, HMT, 35

Packs of Hounds
  Atherstone, 17
  Belvoir, 14,17,24

Mr Billy Coke's, 13
Brocklesby, 115
Duke of Beaufort's, 14
Dulverton, 35,75.
Dulverton Farmers, 97
Exmoor, 35
Garth, 114
Garth and South Berks, 97
Hain's Beagles, 35
Haldon Harriers, 35
Heythrop, 114
Holderness, 157
King George IVth's, 13,24
Lord Poltimore's, 115
North Devon Staghounds, 24
Old Surrey and Burstow, 97
Pytchley, 13,15,112
Quantock Staghounds, 106
Quorn, 12,13,17,70
Shropshire and Shifnal, 12,100
South Devon, 35
South Notts, 13,24
Stevenstone, 35
Tailby, 15
Tetcott, 35
Tiverton Staghounds, 115
Warwickshire, 157
West Kent, 97
Woodland Pytchley, 78

Pape, Mr Archie, 95
Payne, Philip, Huntsman, 14
Pendry, Mr Barry, 38,63
Peterborough Hound Show, 102
Peterloo Massacre, 44
Porlock, 95,97,115
Pretoria, 53,54
Protesters, 98
Psychology, An analysis of E.B.'s character, 38 et seq

Quantock Hills, The, 103
Queen's Own Worcestershire Hussars, The, 100

de la Rey, General, 54
Royal 1st Devon Yeomanry, The, 44,59
Royal North Devon Hussars, The (R.N.D.H.), 36,44,48,119
Rugby Hound Sales, 102
Russell, Parson Jack, 24

Sanders, Sir Robert (later Lord Bayford), 36,66,67,78,95
Sandyway, 116; The Hunt, 137,146
Scoins, George, E.B.'s second horseman, 81,93,101,116
Sebright, Tom, Huntsman, 17
Sharpe, George, Huntsman, 13,24
Shelley, Colonel, 48
Sloley, Gilbert, Huntsman, 106
South Africa, 46 et seq
South Molton, 36,116
Staffordshire Volunteers, 100
Stanley, Mr E.A.V., Master, 78,114
Stapledon, Mr Richard, 119
Stockleigh Lodge, Exford, 100,106
Summersgill, Donald, Huntsman, 14,95
Surtees R.S., 70,72

Tarr Steps, 19,121
Times, The, 47,113
Tufters, how they operate, 74
Tucker, Sidney, Huntsman, 32,67,78,84,89,95,99,114

Wallace, Captain R.E., 70,81,91,113,158
West Somerset Imperial Yeomanry, 64
White Horse Hotel, The, Exford, 65
Wiggin, Captain Bob, 103
Wiggin, Christopher,
Wiggin, Mrs Edith, 100,102,149
Wiggin, Colonel Walter, Master, 71,74,100et seq; 105,121,144,146,149
Willingford Bridge, 145
Winsford, 20
Winsford Hill, 66,121; The Hunt, 128
Withypool, 20; The Royal Oak Inn, 34
World War, The Second, 97,152 et seq

Yeomanry, 35,86
Yarde Down, 99,121; The Great Staghunt, 139